COMMUNICATION, PEDAGOGY, AND THE GOSPEL OF MARK

RESOURCES FOR BIBLICAL STUDY

Editor
Tom Thatcher, New Testament

Number 83

COMMUNICATION, PEDAGOGY, AND THE GOSPEL OF MARK

Edited by
Elizabeth E. Shively and Geert Van Oyen

Atlanta

Copyright © 2016 by SBL Press

All rights reserved. No part of this work may be reproduced or transmitted in any form or by any means, electronic or mechanical, including photocopying and recording, or by means of any information storage or retrieval system, except as may be expressly permitted by the 1976 Copyright Act or in writing from the publisher. Requests for permission should be addressed in writing to the Rights and Permissions Office, SBL Press, 825 Houston Mill Road, Atlanta, GA 30329 USA.

Library of Congress Cataloging-in-Publication Data

Names: Shively, Elizabeth E., 1969– editor.
Title: Communication, pedagogy, and the gospel of Mark / edited by Elizabeth E. Shively and Geert Van Oyen.
Description: Atlanta : SBL Press, 2016. | Series: Resources for biblical study ; Number 83 | Includes bibliographical references and index.
Identifiers: LCCN 2015048410 (print) | LCCN 2015050112 (ebook) | ISBN 9780884141143 (pbk. : alk. paper) | ISBN 9780884141167 (hardback : alk. paper) | ISBN 9780884141150 (ebook)
Subjects: LCSH: Bible. Mark—Study and teaching.
Classification: LCC BS2586 .C66 2016 (print) | LCC BS2586 (ebook) | DDC 226.30071—dc23
LC record available at http://lccn.loc.gov/2015048410

Printed on acid-free paper.

For our teachers who wed their research with their teaching.

"There are two things on which all interpretation of scripture depends: the process of discovering what we need to learn, and the process of presenting what we have learnt."
Augustine, *On Christian Teaching* 1.1

Contents

Abbreviations ix

Introduction: Recovering the Relationship between Research
and Teaching
Elizabeth E. Shively 1

Part 1. Processes: Relationships between
Researching and Teaching Mark

Mark in the Frame of Ancient History Writing: The Quest
for Heuristics
Eve-Marie Becker 13

Teaching Mark's Narrative in a Markan Narrative Way
Elizabeth Struthers Malbon 29

Teaching Mark as Collective Memory
Sandra Huebenthal 45

Part 2. Test Cases: Orality and Performance in
Researching and Teaching Mark

Teaching Mark as Performance Literature: Early Literate
and Postliterate Pedagogies
Thomas E. Boomershine 73

How to Hear and Teach Textual and Contextual Echoes in Mark
10:42–45
Alberto de Mingo Kaminouchi 95

No Performance Criticism without Narrative Criticism:
Performance as a Test of Interpretation
Geert Van Oyen 107

Teaching the Most Difficult Text in the Gospel of Mark:
Mark 9:42–50
Francis J. Moloney, SDB, AM, FAHA 129

Hiding in Plain Sight: Performance, Pedagogy, and Mark 15
Richard W. Swanson 151

Part 3. Strategies: The Second Orality for
Researching and Teaching Mark

Mark in a Digital Age: The Internet and the Teaching of
Mark's Gospel
Mark Goodacre..175

Bibliography..193
Contributors..215

Index of Ancient Sources..219
Index of Modern Authors...222
Subject Index..225

Abbreviations

ASNU	Acta Seminarii Neotestamentici Upsaliensis
AYB	Anchor Yale Bible
BDAG	W. Bauer, F. W. Danker, W. F. Arndt, and F. W. Gingrich. *Greek-English Lexicon of the New Testament and Other Early Christian Literature*. 3rd ed. Chicago: University of Chicago Press, 2000.
BEH	Bibliothèque de l'Évolution de l'Humanité
BETL	Bibliotheca Ephermeridum Theologicarum Lovaniensium
BibSem	The Biblical Seminar
BNTC	Black's New Testament Commentaries
BPC	Biblical Performance Criticism Series
BSNA	Biblical Scholarship in North America
BSR	*Bulletin for the Study of Religion*
BTB	*Biblical Theology Bulletin*
BZNW	Beihefte zur Zeitschrift für die neutestamentliche Wissenschaft
CBQ	*Catholic Biblical Quarterly*
CGTC	Cambridge Greek Text Commentaries
EBib	*Etudes bibliques*
EKKNT	Evangelisch-katholischer Kommentar zum Neuen Testament
ETL	*Ephemerides Theologicae Lovanienses*
EvT	*Evangelische Theologie*
FRLANT	Forschungen zur Religion und Literatur des Alten und Neuen Testaments
GPBS	Global Perspectives on Biblical Scholarship
HNT	Handbuch zum Neuen Testament
ICC	International Critical Commentaries
JBL	*Journal of Biblical Literature*

JR	*Journal of Religion*
JSNTSup	Journal for the Study of the New Testament Supplement series
JTI	*Journal for Theological Interpretation*
NA²⁸	E. Nestle, K. Aland, et al. *Novum Testamentum Graece*. 28th ed. Stuttgart: Deutsche Bibelgesellschaft, 2013.
NICNT	New International Commentary on the New Testament
NIGTC	New International Greek Testament Commentary
NovT	*Novum Testamentum*
NRSV	New Revised Standard Version
NTL	New Testament Library
NTOA	Novum Testamentum et Orbis Antiquus
NTS	*New Testament Studies*
NV	*Nova et Vetera*
RBL	*Review of Biblical Literature*
RBS	Resources for Biblical Studies
RGG	*Religion in Geschichte und Gegenwart*. Edited by K. Galling. 3rd ed. 7 vols. Tübingen: Mohr Siebeck, 1957–1965.
RHR	*Revue de l'histoire de religions*
SBL	Society of Biblical Literature
ScrB	*Scripture Bulletin*
SemeiaSt	Semeia Studies
SNT	Studien zum Neuen Testament
SNTSU.A	Studien zum Neuen Testament und seiner Umwelt, Series A
SP	Sacra Pagina
STK	*Svensk teologisk kvartalskrift*
SUNT	Studien zur Umwelt des Neuen Testaments
TLZ	*Theologische Literaturzeitung*
TSAJ	Texte und Studien zum antiken Judentum
WBC	Word Biblical Commentary
WUNT	Wissenschaftliche Untersuchungen zum Neuen Testament

Introduction:
Recovering the Relationship
between Research and Teaching

Elizabeth E. Shively

The idea for this book grew out of a conversation at the meeting of the 2013 International Society of Biblical Literature in St. Andrews, Scotland. Geert Van Oyen and I had just launched a new Gospel of Mark unit at this meeting, and we were pleasantly surprised by the overwhelming attendance for the session we held on Mark and pedagogy. The connection between research on Mark and the teaching of it is important to us, and we planned an invited session for which we had asked a group of seasoned scholars to explain how they work out their approaches to the Markan text in their classrooms. The result was a master class that gave us a view into the intersection of research and teaching that we rarely have the opportunity to see at academic conferences. Afterward we started brainstorming over lunch about how we could expand this into a project by planning another session on pedagogy for the next year's international meeting, and that led to our contemplation about a book of essays based on these presentations.

It is not the first book on pedagogy and the biblical text in recent years, however, or even the first time that essays have been collected from Society of Biblical Literature meetings on the subject to form a volume. Two books come to mind. Both critique the dominance of historical criticism for its exclusionary stance toward non-Western and female interpreters, among others. First, Fernando Segovia and Mary Ann Tolbert edited a collection of essays, *Teaching the Bible: The Discourses and Politics of Biblical Pedagogy*,[1] which draw out the significance of a variety of

---

1. Fernando Segovia and Mary Ann Tolbert, eds., *Teaching the Bible: The Discourses and Politics of Biblical Pedagogy* (Maryknoll, NY: Orbis, 1998).

social locations for interpretation and their implications for pedagogy. As a point of departure, Segovia provides an introduction in which he examines the pedagogical implications of rhetorical criticism, literary criticism, and cultural criticism, respectively, and concludes that each of these methods promulgates a pedagogical model that is

> highly pyramidal, patriarchal, and authoritative; a model where the teacher/critic, as the voice of the informed, universal, and self-enlightened reader, captures the sociocultural mysteries of the text and mediates it to student/readers; a model where teacher/critics rise above social location and ideology through self-knowledge to arrive at the meaning of the text.[2]

Although I question whether these approaches must necessarily result in the kind of pedagogical model Segovia suggests, I accept his fundamental principle that hermeneutical approaches inform pedagogical models.

Second, Elisabeth Schüssler Fiorenza and Kent Harold Richards edited a collection of essays that emerged from seminars at Society of Biblical Literature national and international meetings from 2003 through 2007, *Transforming Graduate Biblical Education: Ethos and Discipline*.[3] The book is concerned specifically with the transformation of doctoral education in biblical studies from a Western into a global discipline.[4] Schüssler Fiorenza envisions this transformation particularly at the level of *research* that shifts away from a "scientist-positivist" approach to focus "on the constructive ideological functions of biblical and other ancient texts in their past and present historical and literary contexts, as well as on the ideological justifications presented by their ever more technically refined interpretations."[5] This volume is valuable for seating interpreters from various social locations and academic contexts around the disciplinary table who might not have been given a chair before now.

---

2. Ibid., 12.

3. Elisabeth Schüssler Fiorenza and Kent Harold Richards, eds., *Transforming Graduate Biblical Education: Ethos and Discipline*, GPBS 10 (Atlanta: Society of Biblical Literature, 2010).

4. Elisabeth Schüssler Fiorenza, "Introduction: Transforming Graduate Biblical Studies: Ethos and Discipline," in Schüssler Fiorenza and Richards, *Transforming Graduate Biblical Education*, 2, 16.

5. Ibid., 2; see also 15.

Both of these books expose issues and break barriers that have excluded groups of readers from biblical studies because of long-held assumptions and practices of hermeneutics, pedagogy, and research. In this introduction to the present collection of essays, I wish to touch on a different issue: a fracture between research and teaching. These essays look at what academic staff *actually do in the classroom* to integrate their research and methodologies with their teaching, giving a glimpse of how their approach to the biblical text informs their pedagogy.

The Need for Research-Led Teaching in Biblical Studies

Currently I find myself in a (UK) world in which universities are generally interested in research excellence that generates social or economic impact and secures funding and teaching excellence that generates student satisfaction; both are to increase the global standing of the universities. But the relationship between research and teaching tends not to be clearly spelled out on an institutional level.[6] I came from a (US) world in which adjunct teaching, on the one hand, or heavy teaching loads, on the other, often preclude meaningful, ongoing research that might inform teaching. There, also, the relationship between research and teaching faces institutional complexities. A fracture between research and teaching is not unique to biblical studies but is endemic in higher education.[7] This fracture is worth repairing, because a symbiotic relationship between research and teaching benefits both faculty and students. Such a relationship not only forces faculty to communicate their ongoing work and fosters new possibilities for their own learning as they engage with their students; but it also promotes the best kind of learning for the students themselves, that which is active, inquiry-based, involves critical thinking, and promotes investigation and discovery.[8]

---

6. On the institutional problems in the United Kingdom that perpetuate a rift between research and teaching, see Geoff Stoakes and Pauline Couper, "Visualizing the Research-Teaching Nexus," in *What Is Research-Led Teaching? Multi-disciplinary Perspectives*, ed. Alisa Miller, John Sharp, and Jeremy Strong (London: Crest, 2012), 11.

7. For example, the Consortium for Research Excellence Support and Training (CREST; see http://www.crest.ac.uk) published a writing that addresses pedagogy for research-led teaching in the United Kingdom across a number of disciplines: music, physiology, art, technology, history, health science, theater, and biological sciences; see Miller, Sharp, and Strong, *What Is Research-Led Teaching*.

8. Mick Healey discusses how inquiry-based learning builds on direct student

I remember getting a glimpse of it when I was in seminary. I took a Revelation course with Greg Beale while he was working on his New International Greek Testament commentary.[9] He would dash into class with barely legible, handwritten handouts for us to devour and would become so animated while discussing the text that he would nearly knock over the overhead projector (smart boards had not arrived quite yet). No one cared if he kept us late. It was exciting, and we felt like we were experiencing something at the cutting edge of his research, even as we learned from his modeling in class and assignments that replicated his method how to exegete the text for ourselves and to discover our own interpretive voices. Simultaneously, my husband was taking a Greek class with Beale, which he ended up referring to as "eschatological Greek" because all of the illustrations came from Revelation!

How then might we define "research-led teaching"? Although I have not found a common definition in the literature,[10] I think it happens when teachers apply and model their ongoing research in their teaching and allow student-led, research-based learning to occur (in groups, as individuals, in preparation for assessed work) so that students become learners and researchers in their own right ("first-handers" rather than "second-handers").[11] The contributors to this volume carefully reflect on the ways that their ongoing research and their approach to the Gospel of Mark shape

---

engagement with research in "Linking Research and Teaching: Exploring Disciplinary Spaces and the Role of Inquiry-Based Learning," in *Reshaping the University: New Relationships between Research, Scholarship and Teaching*, ed. Ronald Barnett, Society for Research into Higher Education (Berkshire, UK: Open University Press, 2005), 67–78.

9. Greg Beale, *The Book of Revelation*, NIGTC (Grand Rapids: Eerdmans, 2013).

10. It is important for each institution and/or department to determine for itself the relationship between research and teaching. The literature on the topic displays a range of terms, from "research-led" to "research-oriented" to "research-based" teaching, each with a different emphasis. See Healey, "Linking Research and Teaching," 3–4. In addition, one study of a number of universities in the United Kingdom found that academic staff and students surveyed had differing ideas about what was meant by the practice of "research-led teaching and learning." See Barbara Zamorski, "Research-Led Teaching and Learning in Higher Education: A Case," *Teaching in Higher Education* 7 (2002): 414–15.

11. See the definitions of research-led teaching in Stoakes and Couper, "Visualizing the Research-Teaching Nexus," 13; Di Drummond, "Research That Matters: Expanding Definitions of 'Research-Led Teaching' in History," in Miller, Sharp, and Strong, *What Is Research-Led Teaching*, 67.

the way they teach and specifically what they do with their students and how they involve them in the learning process. My hope is that this short collection of essays will show various ways that links between research and teaching may be developed, using the Gospel of Mark as a case study. Also, I am confident that these essays will provide readers with models and strategies for their own teaching of Mark and other biblical texts.

Research-Led Teaching Applied

The contributors to the volume write from different institutional contexts and different social locations and employ different methodologies. These differences inform their hermeneutics, which, in turn, informs their pedagogy. The volume is divided into three parts. The essays in part 1 ("Processes") address the symbiotic relationship between research and teaching by discussing the specific pedagogical approaches that grow directly out of the research and interpretive methods of the contributors. The essays in part 2 ("Test Cases") also discuss strategies and pedagogical approaches, but they focus specifically on the extent to which performance criticism— a relatively recent development in the trajectory of the study of oral tradition—may be integrated into interpretive and pedagogical approaches. That is, the contributors display their ongoing research in a particular area and then work it out pedagogically. When we originally invited the contributors to present papers at Society of Biblical Literature meetings on how their research or approach to Mark informs their pedagogy, we did not specify performance criticism; but this is what each of them chose as a current area of research that impinges upon their present research and teaching. Thus the essays in part 2 form a sort of conversation about an ongoing issue in Markan research and teaching. Mark Goodacre offers the single essay in part 3 ("Strategies") on the use of the Internet in research and teaching, an area that has become a particular research interest and pedagogical tool for him.

Eve-Marie Becker's essay (ch. 1) serves well as the first of part 1 and the introductory essay to the book, because she makes a clear argument for research-led teaching. She challenges those who teach in an academic context to provide "reflective insight in [their] concepts of and approaches to textual interpretation" and then to connect this with their teaching. She argues for a model of research-led teaching that necessitates heuristics. Using herself and her own approach of researching Mark in the frame of ancient history writing, Becker then suggests a model of autobiographical reflection for understanding how teaching and pedagogics contribute to the development of heuristics. All the other authors then take up her challenge in various ways, some more explicitly than others: they show how their respective pedagogical approaches emerge from and are in dialogue with their (past and present) research and methodologies, serving to demonstrate the necessity and effectiveness of research-led teaching. Although differing in their respective approaches, the essays take seriously that Mark's Gospel was composed and/or performed in a particular ancient historical, social, and/or oral context and bring this to bear on their pedagogy for today's classroom.

Elizabeth Struthers Malbon (ch. 2) illustrates the way that hermeneutics and pedagogy, and research and teaching, are, respectively, mutually informative. She describes a pedagogical approach that marries form and content, in which what is central to the text shapes strategies for teaching and learning. First, Malbon identifies what she sees as critical aspects of narrative criticism and of the Markan narrative and then what she considers a critical aspect of the narrative of Markan scholarship and the narrative of teaching and learning. By this, she indicates how her research, approach to Mark, and teaching intersect. Then she applies the categories of narrative analysis to her recent experience of teaching the Gospel of Mark.

Sandra Huebenthal (ch. 3) reads Mark through the hermeneutical lens of social memory theory and regards it as an artifact of collective memory. She argues that, on the one hand, Mark is about the (accurate) understanding of the character Jesus; on the other hand, the text is about the constitution and organization of an adequate community of followers. In the course of the discussion, Huebenthal demonstrates how she leads students through the Gospel according to the kind of social memory approach she has come to develop in her own research and gives specific examples of ways she constructs a syllabus and assignments she uses in class.

The essays in part 2 articulate and apply research on orality and performance criticism in various ways. Thomas E. Boomershine (ch. 4) argues that there is a direct correlation between presuppositions about ancient communication culture and contemporary pedagogies in the teaching of Mark. He observes that current pedagogical practices tend to assume that Mark was a text originally read silently by readers. He challenges this assumption with the claim that study of first-century communication culture has revealed that Mark was performance literature that was composed to be heard (rather than read in silence) and memorized.

Boomershine aims to teach Mark in light of its original historical context by developing pedagogical methods that invite students to hear the sounds of Mark's story and to perform it by heart. He discusses ancient and modern pedagogical practices for teaching Mark as performance literature using specific Markan texts as test cases for suggesting ways of employing these practices.

Alberto de Mingo Kaminouchi (ch. 5) brings together the Jesuit context in which he teaches with his research on orality studies to bear upon his pedagogy. He approaches the text of Mark with the assumption that Mark retains features of oral literature, among them the use of modulated repetitions that give coherence to the narrative. His goal, however, is to go beyond literary criticism of these "textual echoes" to study the "contextual echoes" that resonate with the reader's social experience. He brings his approach to the Markan text into the classroom by demonstrating how students can deepen their reading of Mark by "listening" to how a text resonates with other passages in Scripture and with tradition, using Mark 10:42–45 as a test case. His goal is for students to see that Mark's contextual echoes resonate with practices of the church as an alternative polis that challenges the powers of the world.

Geert Van Oyen (ch. 6) takes a different approach than Boomershine (and Kaminouchi), arguing that performance criticism is a helpful pedagogical tool for opening up pathways of communication and interpretive nuances but that it should be employed today on the basis of its current interpretive and pedagogical payoff, rather than on the basis of supposed oral practices of the first century. He argues that in order to perform Mark's Gospel well, one first has to perform narrative criticism of the text. This becomes especially apparent with regard to those passages where a "subtext" cannot be found at first glance or where the interpretation depends on the understanding of the whole Gospel. After discussing the relationship between narrative criticism and performance criticism, Van Oyen looks at a number of texts that may give rise to plural interpretation and shows how he has led students to examine the possibilities for performance and, on the flip side, to ask questions of the validity of different performances of the same texts and thereby put into practice "performance as a test of interpretation" (David Rhoads).

Francis J. Moloney (ch. 7) takes an eclectic approach to exegesis, arguing that no single approach can claim to communicate everything that needs to be known about a text. He sees performance criticism as an approach that must work together with historical and literary approaches and as a necessary way for bringing the past world of the narrative to the present of the audience. As a test case, he uses what he considers to be one of the most puzzling texts in Mark (9:42–50) and demonstrates how a teacher might lead students through an eclectic approach that begins with questions about the origins of the text and follows through to its contemporary appropriation and reception. The essay culminates with some suggestions concerning the features of a student oral performance shaped by prior historical and literary analyses of the text.

Richard W. Swanson (ch. 8) explores ways that embodied ensemble performance can function in teaching undergraduate students to interpret the Gospel of Mark, using Mark 15:40–42. He discusses the difference between an interpretation based on silent reading, which is generally not too surprised by the sudden appearance of women in this account, and one based on performance, which is more likely to surprise students when the storyteller points to women, many of them, who are standing nearby and watching. Swanson explains how embodied performance by an ensemble, because of its unique demands and difficulties, creates the most promising and productive situation for interpreters, teachers, and students: the women must be discovered and must be discovered to have been present all along, always and from the very beginning in Galilee. He demonstrates how this mode of analyzing the text draws students into the surprise that makes this story work.

Lastly, Mark Goodacre (ch. 9) considers the challenges and opportunities of teaching Mark's Gospel in the Internet age and discusses how his research on Mark intersects with his ongoing interest in and use of the Internet for research and teaching. He discusses ways that the Internet encourages instructors to rethink their approach to Mark and how the use of blog posts, podcasts, and websites can open up new avenues for both instructors and their students.

Finally, Geert and I want to thank those who have made this project possible. Our editor, Tom Thatcher, embraced the idea for the book immediately and eagerly and provided expert guidance for its shape. Also, Elizabeth Struthers Malbon and Steve Holmes gave helpful advice at different points about the conception of the book. Toward the end of the process, Kai Akagi provided crucial, meticulous editorial help. When we first embarked on this project, each of the presenters responded with enthusiasm to our invitation to expand their papers into contributions for a book. We are grateful for this outstanding group of international contributors who have persevered with commitment and professionalism through a long process until we could see it to completion. They have exhibited passion for the Gospel of Mark and its teaching and expertise in communicating their subject matter, making this an altogether satisfying project. We owe a debt of gratitude to our families for their love, support, and encouragement. Especially our spouses, Todd and Mia, have made countless sacrifices that have made it possible for us to follow a career in biblical studies in which it often seems like the work of teaching preparation, research, and writing never ends. Without their help and support, we would not have completed this project.

Part 1
Processes: Relationships between Researching and Teaching Mark

1
Mark in the Frame of Ancient History Writing: The Quest for Heuristics*

Eve-Marie Becker

The Need for Heuristics

When placing Mark in the frame of ancient history writing in our *academic research*, we are following a certain, more or less well-established trend in Synoptic studies of interpreting the Gospel narratives through the approach of a *literary-historical contextualization*. This is the case especially in relation to Luke and Luke-Acts but also in regard to other authors and pieces of historiographical literature in the early imperial period.[1] Mark fits well into this picture of first-century CE narrative literature.

When applying this paradigm to our *academic teaching*, however, we are forced to reflect upon and explain the heuristics in the background of our research. *Pedagogic contextualization* thus requires reflection on and explication of *heuristics*. Relevant questions to be discussed in class are: What is our particular interest when relating Mark to Hellenistic-Roman literature? How does this interest in interpretation fit into the history of

---

* I would like to thank Elizabeth Shively and Geert Van Oyen, the organizers of the ISBL session in St. Andrews from which this paper originates, for inviting me to participate, and especially Elizabeth Shively for her helpful comments on the manuscript and much help with language revision.

1. See, for example, David E. Aune, *The New Testament in Its Literary Environment* (Cambridge: Clarke, 1988); Detlev Dormeyer, *Das Neue Testament im Rahmen der antiken Literaturgeschichte: Eine Einführung* (Darmstadt: Wissenschaftliche Buchgesellschaft, 1993); Jörg Frey, Clare Rothschild, and Jens Schröter, eds., *Die Apostelgeschichte im Kontext antiker und frühchristlicher Historiographie*, BZNW 162 (Berlin: de Gruyter, 2009).

research in Markan and/or Synoptic studies? What does the academic context in which our research is located look like today (theology, humanities, cultural studies)? How does it influence our scholarly approach? Which methods do we use? In what sense does our approach help us to better understand the rise of Christian culture, literature, and theology? What is our contribution to Christian theology as well as to modern societies in the global world of the twenty-first century?

In my essay, I will not only present a current approach to Markan studies that at the same time is quite relevant for teaching Mark in class, but I will also try to reveal how teaching and pedagogics contribute to the development of and reflection on heuristics, indeed, in a very specific sense. Since a literary-historical approach to Markan studies will in many respects challenge our students, especially because of its *diachronic programmatic* analysis, teaching it in class leads even more to a critical reflection on our research. We have to discuss what it means that the Markan Gospel—though read with modern eyes—appears as a piece of ancient, more precisely, Hellenistic literature, and hereby matches various patterns of history-oriented prose narratives. Does Mark, in the end, remain an ancient writing only? To what extent does such a literary-historical contextualization help us to read Mark with fresh eyes? And, in more general terms, what is the outcome of the method of a *literary-historical contextualization*?

By raising these questions and dealing with them we move forward in the field of *heuristics*,[2] that is, the scientific questioning that leads to discovery. Most evidently, heuristics can profit from pedagogics: as we are permanently involved in a "scientific" discourse about questions, methods, and our individual as well as common aim(s) of interpreting Gospel narratives, we meet similar quests in a pedagogic setting. Vice versa, discourses about heuristics are proper places to inspire pedagogics also: when students demand accountability regarding research in Mark, heuristics opens up and steers the process of scholarly questioning. We may even say that heuristics offers a field of reasonable interaction between teacher and

---

2. See Eve-Marie Becker, "Heuristik," in *Lexikon der Bibelhermeneutik: Begriffe—Methoden—Theorien—Konzepte*, ed. Oda Wischmeyer (Berlin: de Gruyter, 2013), 255–56: "H[euristik] ist der noetische Ausgangspunkt und das leitende Frageinteresse der Forschung, die der Erkenntnis des Neuen verpflichtet ist, welche sich als Verstehen, also als hermeneutischer Akt, realisiert" (256). See also Frithjof Rodi, ed., *Urteilskraft und Heuristik in den Wissenschaften: Beiträge zur Entstehung des Neuen* (Weilerswist: Velbrück Wissenschaft, 2003).

student, research and teaching, which itself is developed during that interaction. At the same time, pedagogy itself resembles the basic idea of heuristics in that it takes its points of departure from raising and discussing questions and enforcing communicative interaction. In order to elaborate a bit more on the issue of "questioning," let me take the Markan Gospel itself as an example.

It is, for instance, typical for Markan "Streit- und Schulgespräche" (controversy stories) to begin dialogues by posing a question (e.g., Mark 2:18, 24). Teaching—either in a pedagogical, didactic, or even controversial setting—often results from raising questions within an interactive context. In the Markan narrative, the questioner is usually a disciple (e.g., 13:4) or an opponent (e.g., 11:28)—in any case, a person whom Jesus teaches, persuades, or even provokes.[3] In many situations, though, Jesus himself puts opening questions to his disciples (e.g., 8:27) or to his opponents (e.g., 3:4) that appear to be only partly rhetorical. Jesus as the teacher does so in order to reveal the hidden dispute, which is, indeed, not far from the Socratic method of maieutics.

Teaching, as we learn it from Mark, is based on the lively interaction of the questioner and the respondent. This insight can easily be unfolded and applied to the topic of this contribution. Consequently, the basis for reflecting pedagogics is to get involved, in principal, in a discourse about the methodology of questioning, that is, heuristics. Evidently, such a discourse presupposes the vital interest in how the interplay between research and teaching works: elaborating the field of academic questioning, indeed, traditionally has its *Sitz im Leben* where research and teaching meet.

---

3. See Eve-Marie Becker, "Die markinischen 'Streitgespräche' im Plan des Evangeliums: Eine kritische *relecture* der formgeschichtlichen Methode," in *Polemik in der frühchristlichen Literatur: Texte und Kontexte*, ed. Oda Wischmeyer and Lorenzo Scornaienchi, BZNW 170 (Berlin: de Gruyter, 2011), 433–63; Lorenzo Scornaienchi, "Jesus als Polemiker oder: Wie polemisch darf Jesus sein? Historische und normative Aspekte," in Wischmeyer and Scornaienchi, *Polemik in der frühchristlichen Literatur*, 381–413; Boris Repschinski, "Die literarische Form der Streitgespräche," in Wischmeyer and Scornaienchi, *Polemik in der frühchristlichen Literatur*, 415–32.

"Research and Teaching": A Paradigm under Political Discussion

In modern academic life, the classical paradigm of academic teaching, where research and teaching interact ("Humboldtsches Bildungsideal"), is widely under discussion.[4] Either research is privileged, so that researchers are more or less free of teaching obligations—as in certain institutes, which meanwhile are more or less independent of university organization[5]—or teaching is seen as the primary task of academic activities in humanities and theology, so that faculties of arts can legitimate themselves on campus widely by referring to the number of students graduating each term.

The increasing effort spent for hunting external funding for research activities (such as conferences, doctoral and postdoctoral students, and guest lectures), especially at European universities, points to the fact that the traditional role of a professor in the field of humanities or theology does not self-evidently lie in the interplay of teaching and research. In regard to research initiatives, one rather needs at least economic reassurance if not official legitimization from the administrative side. The growing need of legitimizing our academic tasks in theology and humanities, indeed, implies a decrease of the individual role of a teaching professor as a researcher, and consequently research and teaching are themselves divided. In this situation, it is imperative for the professor to take *individual responsibility* to claim and represent both the role of a researcher and the role of a teacher in order to guarantee the eminent interplay between both sorts of academic activities: research and teaching. Only then, on the basis of academic interaction, can heuristics develop toward future scholarly needs.

It seems as if by governmental wish the paradigm of connecting research and teaching is no longer stable as such, even if university management from time to time underlines the necessity of involving successful researchers in teaching activities.[6] Although I do see an increasing

---

4. In general, see Eve-Marie Becker, "The Place of Theology in the Contemporary Universities: Research and Resources," *STK* 88 (2012): 171–77.

5. See recently the establishment of AIAS (Aarhus Institute of Advanced Studies, June 2013), Aarhus University, Denmark.

6. See the interview of the former president of Princeton University, Shirley Tilghman, with the FAZ (*Frankfurter Allgemeine Zeitung* or Frankfurt General Newspaper) in June 2013. In this respect, however, I am curious because sentiments like this rather seem to have a different agenda. Read with a "hermeneutics of suspicion," they

trend of splitting research and teaching in various political, strategic, and administrative senses, I also observe the reverse: quite programmatic trends of linking both activities again.[7] Indeed, I will focus on a concrete issue in which the interplay of research and teaching at (continental) European state universities is indispensable: the scholarly aim of educating students in theology by preparing them for academic quests on the BA, MA, and PhD levels. A failure to conduct research-based teaching, on the contrary, would mean an ignorance and decrease of academic heuristics as defined earlier.

Despite all political trends, I consider it to be our task to argue in favor of a *research-based teaching* on *all* levels of education since such a rationale defines legitimate academic as well as societal expectations. First, as a university teacher, I am not only allowed but rather more expected to include research activities in my teaching plan. In other words, I am forced to share my knowledge without limit. Second, and eventually even more important: as a researcher, I could and should take my teaching as a fundamental point of departure as well as a certain guiding principle for what I consider to be fundamental projects for research in New Testament, or more particularly, in the Markan Gospel, indeed today and—as much as my students are concerned—in the long run. In other words, research is continuously informed and challenged by societal needs. In consequence, teaching is led by research as much as research is to a large extent designed by teaching. The discussion about "research-based teaching," that is, the interlinkage of research and teaching, thus enforces our reflection on heuristics. We will soon see that such a discussion goes much beyond strategic reasoning only, but rather moves into the center of our research activities as scholars in New Testament,[8] indeed in a global perspective.

---

somehow sound like an apology. The relevant university might wish to explain that there is not enough budget backing for dispensing talented researchers from teaching obligations as they might demand.

7. It seems to me as if the one dominant move—toward the divide of research and teaching—is continuously counteracted, however, with unclear results.

8. In this paper, I am limiting myself to the interplay between research and university teaching—not thinking of the quite important task of research communication here, which is as much as teaching a strategic issue of current university policy.

Discussing Pedagogics at the Society of Biblical Literature: Chances and Limits

From these more general observations on the contemporary situation of teaching New Testament (at European state universities), let me now move on to another kind of preliminary reflection. I clarify my approach by reflecting on the aim of the Society of Biblical Literature session on "Communication, Pedagogy, and the Gospel of Mark." What could be the possible intention behind it?

It seems to me that it is not only the above-mentioned political debate at contemporary universities on whether and how to relate research and teaching to each other that enforces our need for heuristics. Nor is it the pure interest in pedagogics that makes us think more particularly about the teaching of the Markan Gospel in class. Rather, in the history of (International) Society of Biblical Literature sessions a continuous attempt is visible to thematize education in biblical studies in regard to a variety of contemporary challenges, both academic and sociocultural, such as gender mainstreaming, globalization, postcolonial readings, interreligious communication, and so forth. But why does the issue of pedagogics in the field of New Testament studies come on stage? And why has it become increasingly important?

Most prominently, Elisabeth Schüssler Fiorenza and Kent H. Richards chaired several sessions on similar topics at Society of Biblical Literature and International Society of Biblical Literature meetings between 2003 and 2007. As a substantial part of this effort, they have edited a Society of Biblical Literature volume on this topic.[9] Here it becomes most evident that the challenges that we, as scholars in New Testament, have to face in regard to future academic education lead us fundamentally to quests of heuristics, pedagogics, and hermeneutics.[10]

Thus it seems to me that the discourse about teaching and pedagogy in biblical studies has become a more or less fixed part of the Society of Biblical Literature session "canon." But why is that? Here we move beyond the local university setting since we are dealing with an issue of global academic *recruitment*, in other words, strategy and academic

---

9. See Elisabeth Schüssler Fiorenza and Kent Harold Richards, eds., *Transforming Graduate Biblical Education: Ethos and Discipline*, GPBS 10 (Atlanta: Society of Biblical Literature, 2010).

10. See my review of this volume in *TLZ* 137 (2012): 917–19.

empowerment in a globalized world that is based on international networking—indeed, in a competitive sense. By reflecting on pedagogy we try to take into account if and how our research will be and can be applied and transformed to future scholarship in an international dimension as well as on a curriculum level. Pedagogics thus has finally become an issue of an international scholarship debate. How do we best enter and organize this debate?

My claim—again—is that we are confronted with a basic issue of heuristics here: It is a pattern of scientific work in humanities and theology to compete in research by providing a reflective insight into our concepts of and approaches to textual interpretation. Specifically, it may be the discussion about our pedagogy that forces us even more to make the premises of our exegesis and textual interpretation transparent to students as well as colleagues in scholarship. But how can we best reflect premises and hermeneutical concepts of textual interpretation?

In what follows, I will suggest the model of an "autobiographical reflection" in order to ask quite concretely: What is the theoretical and methodological concept behind my approach to Markan studies? How did I get to this particular field of research where the Markan Gospel is contextualized in the frame of ancient history writing? What is the relevant scientific heuristics that has led me there—a heuristics according to which Mark is read *comparatively* to ancient writings in historiography? What does it imply and mean to look at Mark as a comparable piece of ancient literature, placed in the setting of Hellenistic historiography of the early imperial period? And what is the heuristics of *comparative exegesis and interpretation* about?

By referring to "my own story" as an academic scholar working in the field of Markan studies, I will now try to point out how textual interpretation, in my case, implies heuristics. I will discuss how my story possibly can act as a case study in class: being told, it will evoke approval or disapproval; in any case it will contribute to the interaction of research and teaching. In a particular sense, pedagogics thus can profit from research that is being told, since research is part of a lifelong communicative learning process that is in dialogue with research history as well as with current scholars and students.

Such an autobiographical narrative is based on the conviction that, on the one hand, the individual scholar's biography is not at all contingent; it rather reflects how research history develops and changes in a certain constellation when seen through the prism of a scholar's biography. On the other hand, telling about the individual case might help to build up a series of mirrors through which a student of today envisages his or her interest in the Markan Gospel and questions it as well as communicates it back to his or her teacher. Autobiographical reflection can help to inform heuristics.

Telling and Reflecting "My Own Story"

There is always a "story" behind a scholar's work, independent from the scientific approach she or he will specifically choose (for example, historical-critical, narrative). In a globalized and transcultural world, the diversity of research quests will increase so that we are even more forced to reveal our particular "stories"[11] in order to shape a shared platform of heuristic knowledge.

Such a story behind specific research aims and projects has most appropriately to be depicted in a biographical and in a narrative sense.[12] I would hope that a reflection like this will most clearly and transparently reveal how methodology interferes with a scholar's individual "epistemological interest" and why this is the case. Since scholars might consider themselves as forerunners for the academic generation to come, autobiographical reflections do have a crucial pedagogical as well as didactic value at the same time. First, in autobiography, research and teaching meet, and heuristics thus becomes most lively. Second, since academic teachers and researchers of today may serve more or less as exemplars or paradigms for scholars to come, the autobiographical account visualizes the "type" of a researcher and teacher. Third, by asking and discussing how I got to where I am, I will try to open up how the individual scholar continuously lives at the intersection of research and teaching—as long as he or she as researcher considers himself or herself to be part of a lifelong process of learning and teaching.

To sum up: to reveal and discuss the intersection of research and teaching in an autobiographical manner in and beyond class will de facto mean to reflect upon heuristics in a pedagogic and a scientific sense. So, how did research and learning meet in my case? How did I get to my research

---

11. See Vincent L. Wimbush, "Signifying the Fetish II: Outlines for a New Critical Orientation," *TLZ* 138 (2013): 909–22.

12. See Eve-Marie Becker, ed., *Neutestamentliche Wissenschaft: Autobiographische Essays aus der Evangelischen Theologie*, UTB 2475 (Tübingen: Francke, 2003).

project, which was and to some extent still is: contextualizing Mark in the frame of ancient history writing?

The Curiosity about Mark and/in History

When I started my *Habilitationsprojekt* on the Markan Gospel in 2001/2002[13] after having completed my doctoral dissertation on 2 Corinthians (2001), I was—from the very beginning—most strongly interested in the literary genesis of the oldest Gospel narrative. The Markan Gospel is, as we all know, in many respects a special case among New Testament Gospel writings. According to the two-source theory, we could have a certain idea about how Luke and Matthew composed their Gospel narratives, which sources they relied on, and which literary as well as theological agenda stood in the background of each of their compositions. In contrast, the "prehistory" of the Markan Gospel is comparably dark. It belongs to the very last meters of what Carl R. Holladay once called the "tunnel period" of transmission history between about 30 and 70 CE.[14] So I was interested in knowing how we get light to shine in here.

It was and still is important to me to reconstruct crucial data of, for instance, Jesus's or Paul's life and biography in order to better organize the past, that is, to get a clearer picture of what happened around 30 CE in Palestine and between about 33 and 62 CE around the Mediterranean. Thus I wished to reconstruct how the Markan Gospel came into being as a literary concept, when and why—eventually in competition with Q—it was written, and to what extent the events of the Jewish-Roman War (66–70/73 CE) had an impact on processes of literarization as well as interpretation of the past in earliest Christian times, and so forth.[15]

---

13. Eve-Marie Becker, *Das Markus-Evangelium im Rahmen antiker Historiographie*, WUNT 194 (Tübingen: Mohr Siebeck, 2006). In the following notes, I will refer to some publications that are to be seen in connection and/or continuation to my *Habilitationsschrift*.

14. See Carl R. Holladay, *A Critical Introduction to the New Testament: Interpreting the Message and Meaning of Jesus Christ* (Nashville: Abingdon, 2005), 69.

15. See in general Eve-Marie Becker, ed., *Die antike Historiographie und die Anfänge der christlichen Geschichtsschreibung*, BZNW 129 (Berlin: de Gruyter, 2005); Becker, "Dating Mark and Matthew as Ancient Literature," in *Mark and Matthew*, vol. 1: *Comparative Readings: Understanding the Earliest Gospels in Their First-Century Settings*, ed. Eve-Marie Becker and Anders Runesson, WUNT 271 (Tübingen: Mohr Siebeck, 2011), 123–43.

Chiefly, my *intention* behind this attempt to reconstruct early Christian writings was mainly to get a clear picture of the beginnings of early Christianity and its developing literary culture. My *presumption* behind this set of questions certainly was that the transition from orality to literacy and literaricity in earliest Christian times as such is significant and calls for a comprehensive reflection.[16] This transition, indeed, partly responds to biological needs (for example, shift of generations), partly is an effect of contemporary history (especially events ca. 70 CE), and partly is a characteristic of how the groupings of Christ believers organize their "memory" in sociocultural terms.[17] We may suppose that it is specifically *literary activity* in various surroundings—which we could in principle call either an epistolary or a narrative culture[18]—that finally also encourages the articulation of "Christ-believing identity." Moreover, we must not forget how literacy and literarization early on affect the later process of canonization and subsequently influence the formation of religious and cultural identity once again.[19]

---

16. See Werner H. Kelber, *The Oral and the Written Gospel: The Hermeneutics of Speaking and Writing in the Synoptic Tradition, Mark, Paul, and Q* (Philadelphia: Fortress, 1983); see also, for example, Richard A. Horsley, Jonathan A. Draper, and John Miles Foley, eds., *Performing the Gospel: Orality, Memory, and Mark: Essays Dedicated to Werner Kelber* (Minneapolis: Fortress, 2006).

17. Compare various contributions in Alan Kirk and Tom Thatcher, eds., *Memory, Tradition, and Text: Uses of the Past in Early Christianity*, SemeiaSt 52 (Atlanta: Society of Biblical Literature, 2005).

18. See Eve-Marie Becker, "Earliest Christian Literary Activity: Investigating Authors, Genres and Audiences in Paul and Mark," in *Mark and Paul: Comparative Essays*, vol. 2: *For and against Pauline Influence on Mark*, ed. Eve-Marie Becker, Troels Engberg-Pedersen, and Mogens Mueller, BZNW 199 (Berlin: de Gruyter, 2014), 87–105. A similar case of articulating identity via literary culture might be observed in the Greek culture of the first century BCE; see Thomas A. Schmitz and Nicolas Wiater, "Introduction: Approaching Greek Identity," in *The Struggle for Identity: Greeks and Their Past in the First Century BCE*, ed. Thomas A. Schmitz and Nicolas Wiater (Stuttgart: Steiner, 2011), 15–45.

19. See Eve-Marie Becker, "Literarisierung und Kanonisierung im frühen Christentum: Einführende Überlegungen zur Entstehung und Bedeutung des neutestamentlichen Kanons," in *Kanon in Konstruktion und Dekonstruktion: Kanonisierungsprozesse religiöser Texte von der Antike bis zur Gegenwart; Ein Handbuch*, ed. Eve-Marie Becker and Stefan Scholz (Berlin: de Gruyter, 2012), 389–97. For general reflections on canonization and identity building, see Simone Winko, "Kanon/Kanonizität VII: Literaturwissenschaftlich," in Wischmeyer, *Lexikon der Bibelhermeneutik*, 316–17.

I became convinced that the quest for the genesis of Mark cannot on any account be solved by means of a traditional diachronic analysis only, based on exegetical methods, such as *Formgeschichte, Quellenkritik,* or *Redaktionskritik*. In order to value the comprehensiveness that lies behind the construct of a "written Gospel narrative" in the last third of the first century CE, we rather have to take into account how the Gospel writings can best be placed in the sociocultural and sociohistorical as well as the religious and literary environment of their time.

Finally, I saw that the Markan Gospel does not stand alone. In order to be read, transmitted, and imitated (especially by Matthew and Luke), it must have had a decisive place in early Christian groupings and their commencing literary activities. Reflections like these make it indispensable, in the long run, to apply genre criticism as well as social history and literary history to Markan exegesis.[20]

The Aim of Comparative Readings

Since the Markan Gospel is not at all a unique writing but is rather contextualized in Hellenistic literary culture (LXX writings) of the early imperial period, framed by a variety of Hellenistic-Jewish and Roman literature (e.g., Josephus, Tacitus, Suetonius), preceded by Pauline epistolography, and succeeded by a series of later Gospel narratives, which are partly moving forward on the track of history writing (Luke-Acts), we have to work on a *comparative* level when reading and interpreting "Mark." This is true with regard to New Testament writings[21] as well as contemporary Hellenistic-Roman and early Jewish literature.

For me, it was initially the quest for sources in Mark that led me to a comparative analysis of Mark with contemporary historiographical authors. This approach was based on the insight that the usage of sources

---

20. See Eve-Marie Becker, "The Reception of 'Mark' in the 1st and 2nd Centuries C.E. and Its Significance for Genre Studies," in *Mark and Matthew,* vol. 2: *Comparative Readings: Reception History, Cultural Hermeneutics, and Theology,* ed. Eve-Marie Becker and Anders Runesson, WUNT 304 (Tübingen: Mohr Siebeck, 2013), 15–36.

21. See the Mark and Matthew project: Becker and Runesson, *Mark and Matthew,* vol. 1; Becker and Runesson, *Mark and Matthew,* vol. 2. See also the Mark and Paul project: Oda Wischmeyer, David C. Sim, and Ian J. Elmer, eds., *Paul and Mark: Comparative Essays,* vol. 1: *Two Authors at the Beginning of Christianity,* BZNW 198 (Berlin: de Gruyter, 2014); Becker, Engberg-Pedersen, and Mueller, *Mark and Paul: Comparative Essays,* vol. 2.

is to be seen as an elementary part of the ancient historian's methods as well as his narrative strategy. It is by far not only the use of sources and traditions, however, that raises the question of the relationship between how the Gospel writers work and write and how Hellenistic-Roman historians work and write.[22] Also, seeing Mark from the point of view of reception history supports or even imposes a consideration of the Gospel as a prehistoriographical writing. The Markan incipit (Mark 1:1)—even though it always remains a polyvalent proposition regarding its temporal aspect (ἀρχὴ τοῦ εὐαγγελίου)[23]—might indeed imply its author's awareness of shaping a narrative that is thought to reach back to the actual *temporal origins* of the gospel proclamation by defining them explicitly (Mark 1:2–3 as reference to Isa 40:3 LXX). Thus in a certain sense Mark, in his incipit, lays open his narrative strategy from the outset. By doing so, the author offers an original construct of how the "gospel story's beginning" can be best put in a narrative, that is, in a chronological setting as well as in a logical order. Accordingly, the Markan Gospel leaves behind the various Pauline attempts (see, e.g., 1 Cor 15:1–5) of reciting and memorizing the kerygmatic content of the oral gospel proclamation in that it, both in a literary (narration) as well as in an interpretive (see Mark 1:14–15) sense, transforms kerygma to a narrative.

To sum up: the quest for Mark's composition history soon led me further—beyond source criticism—to a set of questions that needed to be raised as long as I did not take the Markan Gospel out of its first-century literary setting. Even though the author of Mark is to some extent the founder of a new type of prose narrative ("gospel story") that in reception history soon found imitators[24] as much as it appears as a genre sui generis, his work has to be seen in the broad field of Hellenistic prose

---

22. As I have pointed out (see above nn. 13 and 15) and will point out elsewhere (see below n. 26), there are various points of similarity between the New Testament narrators and Hellenistic historians: it is not only their way of relying on sources and traditions, but also their choice and styling of diverse narrative forms (e.g., miracles, legends) as well as some attempts of interpreting the "history of events" on a metahistorical level that indeed make Mark and Luke-Acts fit various demands of Hellenistic history writing.

23. See Eve-Marie Becker, "Mk 1:1 and the Debate on a 'Markan Prologue,'" *Filologia Neotestamentaria* 22 (2009): 91–106.

24. See lately J. Andrew Doole, *What Was Mark for Matthew? An Examination of Matthew's Relationship and Attitude to His Primary Source*, WUNT 2/344 (Tübingen: Mohr Siebeck, 2013).

literature—early Jewish as well as Greco-Roman. The quest for the genesis of the Markan Gospel thus goes hand in hand with an overall literary-historical contextualization of narrative literature. It was and still is most plausible for me to combine the diachronic analysis with a literary-historical approach that is based on a comparative literary method.

It is part of an autobiographical reflection, then, finally to comment on the hermeneutical implications and consequences of such a literary-historical contextualization. Putting it in the frame of ancient history writing does not make the Markan Gospel to be a more proper "historical account" of Jesus's life and mission. The interpretation of Mark in proximity to history writing does not serve any approval of historicity either; however, we need to take the "narrative turn" as well as the debate on constructivism in history seriously here:[25] the *tertium comparationis* for contextualizing Mark in the world of ancient history writing lies in the prose narrative that is directed toward a narrative account of an event-based story that already presupposes a wide range of interpretation at work when construing "events." Thus it is the interpretive dimension behind the narrative construct of "events," as well as the logical display of these "events" within a story, that is of specific significance, rather than the historical valuation of events as "historical facts."

So, where have we come? The contextualization of the Markan Gospel in the frame of ancient history writing has huge implications for textual interpretation. It leads us to a comprehensive view of Mark's literary concept as well as its theological outline. Seen against the broader frame of ancient history writing, the Markan Gospel appears to be a piece of literature in which past time is depicted as a narrative construct of "history," while the display of "time" becomes a matter of temporal orientation. By transforming the memory of the past into a cohesive narrative account for contemporary readers as well as for posterity, the Markan Gospel largely contributes to the shape of a narrative identity in early Christian times. To be sure, it hardly claims to be historiography *stricto sensu*, but it does certainly prepare the way for historiographical access (Luke-Acts; Eusebius) to the beginnings of the gospel proclamation and its memorization among Christ-believing groups.[26]

---

25. On the general problem from the point of view of historians, see, for instance, Thomas Nipperdey, "Kann Geschichte objektiv sein?" in *Kann Geschichte objektiv sein? Historische Essays*, ed. Paul Nolte (Munich: Beck, 2013), 62–83.

26. Fortunately, in a current monograph project on history writing in New Testa-

Applying "My Own Story" to Class

How will I tell my story in class? How will it influence my teaching then? And how will the reflection of heuristics that is narrated and stimulated by class discussion continue to influence my further research?

In general, I do not know the extent to which my approach to the Markan Gospel is convincing to present and future students. I have to try it out continually—and I have tried it out already, more or less explicitly, in various courses on all levels of education.[27] For instance, I have discussed with my students the very method of literary-historical contextualization as such; or we have read ancient historiographical authors (e.g., Josephus, Tacitus) as textual materials as well as contemporaries to Mark and Luke-Acts; or I have taught the implications and aims of a comparative reading; or I have encouraged my students to work with literary hypotheses, such as the quest for possible sources or literary *Vorlage* of Gospel narratives—hypotheses that have to be verified or falsified regarding their plausibility during the process of textual interpretation.

In other words, it is specifically the methodological insights gained by research that can be of further use for students who have to be trained in their reading competencies. The outcome of the discourse in class about heuristics thus may in the end primarily lie on a *methodological level*. And indeed, this goal behind a debate on heuristics seems to be much more important to me than to insist on a particular approach to the Markan Gospel as such. Rather, by reflecting on *how* we read texts and how we might best understand each other during this process of textual interpretation, we finally build up ways of *academic understanding*.

As I see it, such an understanding develops in two steps. First, by telling why I got where I got, I try (and hope) to offer my story as a helpful paradigm for how to study Mark, indeed, in order to look at the earli-

---

ment times, I can work out more in detail how the Markan Gospel and rather more Luke-Acts in various ways match the conditions of history writing in the early Imperial period: see Eve-Marie Becker, *Writing History in New Testament Times* (New Haven: Yale University Press, forthcoming).

27. However, I need to confess that such an autobiographical narrative has not been explicated so far. I have rather tried to take up the subject "objectively." Nevertheless, as argued in this paper, I am convinced that an autobiographical account could be a fruitful instrument of teaching since it could bring individual readers—teacher and student—into the interaction of questioning, that is, a discourse about heuristics.

est Gospel narrative beyond its canonical setting; to consider Mark as a crucial part of Christian religion and literature as well as world literature; and to reach a fruitful glimpse of Mark's composition, its outline and its contemporary setting(s).

Second, by reflecting and discussing the heuristics that is implied in literary history, teacher and class will experience the value of methodology. We will better understand the text, as well as our dealing with it, by reflecting and developing the instruments of a shared reading. And it is precisely here, at the horizon of better understanding the text *through* its interpreter(s) and their methods, that my "own story" can lose its particular meaning and vanish again. As I will get back to my research with fresh impressions after class, my students may have succeeded in learning *how* to read Mark in a shared attempt.

In the end, it is thus my hope, as a researcher and a teacher, that students will come to share the endeavor of exegesis and interpretation as well. Like New Testament exegesis in general, Markan studies is a field of learning how we best start out our work where our forerunners have delivered it to us: we start as exegetes and interpreters, being curious about textual interpretation and the appropriate methods that can shed light on relatively dark sides of earliest Christianity. In the long run, we may become readers of New Testament texts who, by using and developing various tools of interpretation, learn to see the Markan Gospel and its imitators as bright products of early Christian literary culture and theology.

2

Teaching Mark's Narrative
in a Markan Narrative Way

Elizabeth Struthers Malbon

The theme of "Communication, Pedagogy, and the Gospel of Mark" has been much on my mind in recent years, but, obviously, I have not been alone in thinking about this topic. My own interest has come from both my research and my teaching. I have long been interested in *how* the Markan story unfolds, from an initial interest in the settings of Mark as they contribute to the overall meaning of the narrative[1] to a subsequent interest in how the various characters in the story are portrayed and interact— including their effect on the audience, both ancient and contemporary.[2]

In my thirty-five years of teaching undergraduates at Virginia Polytechnic Institute and State University (the largest comprehensive state university in Virginia; Virginia Tech for short), I have had the opportunity to teach an undergraduate seminar on the Gospel of Mark seven times, with small enrollments ranging from two to fourteen participants. The prerequisite for this upper-level class on Mark has been the successful completion of an introductory-level class on the New Testament, a class that stresses the historical context of the New Testament books and the implications of their genres. My most recent experience with the seminar on Mark, and a truly exciting and satisfying one, was in the fall of 2011, with nine undergraduates, two graduate students (one in Educational

---

1. Elizabeth Struthers Malbon, *Narrative Space and Mythic Meaning in Mark* (San Francisco: Harper & Row, 1986; republished as volume 13 in the series Biblical Seminar (Sheffield: Sheffield Academic Press, 1991).
2. Elizabeth Struthers Malbon, *In the Company of Jesus: Characters in Mark's Gospel* (Louisville: Westminster John Knox, 2000); Malbon, *Mark's Jesus: Characterization as Narrative Christology* (Waco, TX: Baylor University Press, 2009).

Leadership and Policy Studies and one in ASPECT, the Alliance for Social, Political, Ethical, and Cultural Thought), and three senior citizens. This juxtaposition of my Markan research and my Markan teaching provides the background for these reflections.

Critical Aspects and Goals

Before I can suggest how I teach Mark's narrative in a Markan narrative way, I must identify what I think are critical aspects of narrative criticism and of the Markan narrative and also what I consider a critical aspect of the narrative of Markan scholarship and the narrative of teaching and learning.

First, what do I mean by narrative criticism? I mean, as the title of my essay on the subject in *Mark and Method* makes clear, a focus on *how* the story means by exploring the narrative aspects of "implied author" and "implied audience," setting, characters, plot, and rhetoric.[3] That essay, and my usual technique with students, first explains the concept of an "implied author," who communicates with an "implied audience" analogously to the way a real author communicates with a real audience. While historical critics may hope to learn about the real author and the real audience, for ancient narratives at least, certainty is not attainable. Narrative critics focus on the implied author and the implied audience as they may be reconstructed from clues in the narrative. Then I assist students in isolating four elements of this communication between the implied author and the implied audience: setting, characters, plot, and rhetoric. Finally, my essay on narrative criticism as *how* the story means integrates these four elements in an explication of sample material from Mark in its narrative sequence.

Students usually find it easy to attend to setting, characters, and plot by starting with the analysis of one pericope. Rhetoric takes a bit more working up to. When I was given the task of introducing the Gospel of Mark in fifteen hundred words for the handbook *Sundays and Seasons 2009*, I organized my compact discussion around the idea of Mark's rhetoric of juxtaposition, which involves juxtapositions in setting, characters, and plot but also the rhetorical devices of intercalation, chiasm, repetition,

---

3. Elizabeth Struthers Malbon, "Narrative Criticism: How Does the Story Mean?" in *Mark and Method: New Approaches in Biblical Studies*, ed. Janice Capel Anderson and Stephen D. Moore, 2nd ed. (Minneapolis: Fortress, 2008), 29–57. The essay in its 1st ed. (1992) version is republished as the first chapter in Malbon, *In the Company of Jesus*, 1–40.

parallelism, framing, and irony.[4] All of these techniques involve audience participation—anticipating what is foreshadowed, hearing echoes, connecting events, and so on.[5] Thus, for me, teaching Mark in a Markan narrative way involves honoring these two critical aspects of the narrative of Mark's Gospel, as revealed by narrative criticism: (1) the sequence of the Gospel as we attend to setting, characters, plot, and rhetoric; and (2) the Markan rhetoric of juxtaposition and the implied author's high expectations of audience involvement.

Second, what do I mean by the narrative of Markan (and New Testament) scholarship? I mean the dialogic nature of this scholarship and the interaction of a range of critical approaches. In my own experience as a student, both undergraduate and graduate, it was still redaction criticism that was providing the excitement in research and pedagogy. What was being communicated and explored was how comparing the Synoptic Gospels helped clarify the particular interests of each. However, since Mark was nearly universally agreed upon as the first Gospel to be written, in the case of Mark redaction criticism quickly moved to composition criticism and to literary criticism in general and narrative criticism as it developed in Gospel studies. As literary criticism was challenging the historical paradigm of biblical studies, I was in graduate school, and I became an original and continuous member of the Literary Aspects of the Gospels and Acts Group of the Society of Biblical Literature from 1981 through 1999. During those eighteen years, narrative criticism not only developed its own methodological identity but also interacted with a variety of emerging critical approaches—structuralist, reader-response, feminist, deconstructivist, ideological, and orality and performance studies.[6] So today when I think of narrative criticism, I conceive of it in relation to these many discussion partners, and when I teach the Gospel of Mark from my standpoint as primarily a narrative critic, I provide opportunities for my students to be involved in these conversations as well.

---

4. Elizabeth Struthers Malbon, "The Year of Mark," in *Sundays and Seasons 2009* (Minneapolis: Augsburg Fortress, 2008), 13–14.

5. See also Elizabeth Struthers Malbon, "Echoes and Foreshadowings in Mark 4–8: Reading and Rereading," *JBL* 112 (1993): 213–32.

6. See the entries on these and related approaches in Stephen L. McKenzie et al., eds., *Oxford Encyclopedia of Biblical Interpretation*, 2 vols. (Oxford: Oxford University Press, 2013). I served as one of five area editors, focusing on varieties and outgrowths of a "literary" approach.

For me, after the initial feeling of the "great divide" between historical criticism and literary criticism (still to be seen in some of my first published essays), narrative criticism has always been one approach among many—to be sure, the one I have found most interesting and in which I have invested my time, but never the only meaningful approach to the text or its context or its meaning. I have found that students more fully appreciate one scholarly approach when comparing and contrasting it with another one. At their initial encounter with academic study of the New Testament, many undergraduates are struggling with the differences between this scholarly approach and their own faith-based appropriations. Being able to appreciate the differences among a range of scholarly approaches represents a second step. Thus, for me, teaching Mark in a Markan narrative way involves honoring this critical aspect of the narrative of Markan scholarship: its dynamic participation in ongoing conversations with a range of scholarly approaches.

Third, what do I mean by the narrative of teaching and learning, the narrative of communication and pedagogy? I mean that there is a narrative to each class; there is a story of teaching and learning together. It is the teacher's role to start telling this story and to invite students into it. This is especially the case in an undergraduate seminar in a large state university with a fair number of large classes; however, in a small class it is easy to encourage and build up this story together.[7] My 2011 class story included a significant spatial change due to an accidental plot event: because I broke my foot on a cobblestone in Copenhagen after the first class, we moved from our third-floor classroom with individual desks pulled into a circle to a first-floor seminar room where we crowded around a large table. This spatial shift solidified our sense as characters in a shared story, as peers in a common endeavor. Our common plot motif was simple: we are learning how to interpret Mark responsibly and for ourselves. We also enjoyed certain side stories together—including shared tender accounts by two students, one female, one male, of their engagements to be married.

The interaction of autobiography and pedagogy was highlighted for me in 1997 when I chaired a Society of Biblical Literature session of pre-

---

7. For my reflections on teaching a large (over one hundred students) New Testament survey class, see Elizabeth Struthers Malbon, "The SBL in the Classroom: Pedagogical Reflections," in *Foster Biblical Scholarship: Essays in Honor of Kent Harold Richards*, ed. Frank Ritchel Ames and Charles William Miller, BSNA 24 (Atlanta: Society of Biblical Literature, 2010), 169–88.

sentations that were incorporated into *Semeia* 72 (1995), *Taking it Personally: Autobiographical Biblical Criticism*. I wrote this poem for those contributors; it is entitled "Teaching It Personally":

> I once read a student's comment
> on a faculty colleague's teaching:
> "How can I learn anything from him?
> I don't know anything about him."
> I don't even know
> what he thinks he knows
> about
> what he thinks
> he's teaching me.
> The distance he maintains
> between
> the truth he would proclaim
> and his proclaiming it
> is vast
> and void
> and empty.
> I am underwhelmed by nothingness.
> There is no he,
> no we,
> no me.

In a class I taught on "Jesus and the Gospels" in the fall of 2012, also a small class in a seminar room, I noticed that students kept arriving earlier and earlier—a bit surprising for a 9:30 a.m. class—just to talk with one another, usually about the Gospels! Indeed, one student said, "I don't think of this as a class; I think of it as my book group." When the class itself develops such a narrative, with students talking with one another, learning is increased, because everyone participates in teaching as well; and, as teachers know, the best way to learn is to teach. Thus, for me, teaching Mark in a Markan narrative way involves honoring this critical aspect of the narrative of teaching and learning: the dynamic participation of diverse individuals in a common endeavor.

Specific Teaching Strategies

To illustrate more concretely these three goals—honoring the narrative of Mark's Gospel, the narrative of Markan scholarship, and the narrative of teaching and learning—I wish to share some of my specific strategies in teaching Mark's narrative in a Markan narrative way.

(1) Start by viewing as a class an oral presentation of the entire Gospel of Mark. For this purpose, I have used both David Rhoads's presentation and that by Philip Ruge-Jones.[8] Sometimes we view the presentation in its entirety outside class; sometimes we view it in two class sessions. Always I provide opportunities for students to reflect on—both in writing and orally—the differences between their experiences of reading the Gospel of Mark silently and listening to and viewing an oral presentation of it. Inevitably this is an eye-opening experience for students, helping them to appreciate Mark's Gospel as a story—with recurring characters and a developing plot—and also laying the groundwork for later discussions of the contributions of orality and performance studies in Markan scholarship. When students are confronted with an oral presentation, and thus an interpretation, of Mark's Gospel, they begin to realize that they too have an interpretation. This realization is an important step in becoming a self-aware and critical interpreter.

(2) Organize the syllabus according to the narrative of Mark, from 1:1 to 16:8 (with a parenthetical comment on 16:9–20). While this may seem obvious, there are many resources on Mark that are arranged in topical order, with sections on provenance and authorship, Christology, discipleship, parables, eschatology, and so on. Clearly such topics come up in a course that moves through Mark's Gospel in narrative order, but they come up, as they do in Mark, over and over again and are revealed in that ongoing process. I also follow narrative sequence when teaching a course on Jesus and the Gospels. We read Mark all the way through, then Matthew, then Luke, then John. So when my students read *Gospel Parallels*, they must learn to read both vertically, following one Gospel at a time, and horizontally, making side glances to what is distinctive about the Gospel in focus and how that Gospel may have used its sources.[9]

---

8. David Rhoads, *A Dramatic Presentation of the Gospel of Mark* (DVD, Select Learning, 1992), and Philip Ruge-Jones, *The Beginning of the Good News* (DVD, Select Learning, 2009). The latter DVD is available for purchase from Select Learning, http://www.se.ectlearning.org/, but the former DVD is no longer available.

9. Interestingly enough, when Mark Goodacre and I reviewed Zeba A. Crook's *Parallel Gospels: A Synopsis of Early Christian Writing* (Oxford: Oxford University Press, 2011) at a session at the Society of Biblical Literature Annual Meeting in Chicago in November 2012, we both critiqued the book because (among other reasons) of

(3) Have students read different Markan commentaries and report on their readings to the class. This is a strategy I have employed in my two most recent Markan seminars, and I have been quite excited and pleased by the results. At first, my undergraduate students were taken aback that everyone would not be reading exactly the same assignments. How would they be tested? However, after the first week or so, they were completely immersed in "their" commentaries. There were constraints: I chose four commentaries that were approximately equal in length and readability (to avoid having the majority of students choose the shortest or easiest one!); the four commentaries were by M. Eugene Boring, John R. Donahue and Daniel J. Harrington, Morna Hooker, and Francis J. Moloney.[10] With graduate students, one would likely include a broader range of commentaries. Before classes began, I made information about each commentary available to students and solicited their top two choices; from their replies I assigned commentaries, with two or three students reading each one. In addition, this strategy made it easy to assign the occasional student to a commentary specific to her needs. One year, an undergraduate classics major read about half of Adela Yarbro Collins's commentary,[11] and when she needed a change, I switched her to Sharyn Dowd's commentary.[12] Another year, a graduate student moving toward a dissertation on a social justice issue read Ched Myers's commentary.[13] Twice in the term, each student offered an oral (and written) report on what his or her commentary had to say on the portion of Mark up for discussion that day. Then other students were invited to contribute comments from their commentaries, and I filled in from there. Discussions were amazingly lively. Students soon began to feel the responsibility of being spokespersons for "their" commentators, although they

---

the difficulty of reading it "vertically," which is not an option Crook (and several other reviewers) had even imagined.

10. M. Eugene Boring, *Mark: A Commentary*, NTL (Louisville: Westminster John Knox, 2006); John R. Donahue and Daniel J. Harrington, *The Gospel of Mark*, SP 2 (Collegeville, MN: Liturgical Press, 2002); Morna Hooker, *The Gospel according to Saint Mark*, BNTC (London: Black; Peabody, MA: Hendrickson, 1991); Francis J. Moloney, *The Gospel of Mark: A Commentary* (Peabody, MA: Hendrickson, 2002).

11. Adele Yarbro Collins, *Mark: A Commentary*, Hermeneia (Minneapolis: Fortress, 2007).

12. Sharyn E. Dowd, *Reading Mark: A Literary and Theological Commentary on the Second Gospel*, Reading the New Testament 2 (Macon, GA: Smith & Helwys, 2000).

13. Ched Myers, *Binding the Strong Man: A Political Reading of Mark's Story of Jesus*, 2nd ed. (Maryknoll, NY: Orbis, 2008).

also gained a sense of what other commentators could add. We occasionally referred to students by the name of "their" commentators, as in, "What would you say about that, Moloney?" while looking at Auriel or William. Students learned that the goal of the course (and what they would be tested on) was to become better interpreters of the Gospel of Mark, and all the commentaries were simply means toward that end.

(4) Work in readings exemplifying a variety of scholarly approaches to Mark. Since the publication of *Mark and Method* in 1992, I have found this collection of essays the most convenient way to meet this goal.[14] The original five approaches (narrative, reader-response, deconstructive, feminist, and social criticism) were supplemented by postcolonial criticism and cultural studies in the 2008 revision.[15] I have noticed recently, when clearing out some older course records, that I frequently asked students to explicate one similarity and one difference between various approaches as we worked our way through this book. I remember vividly a student in the 2009 class saying, "How do you expect us to keep these approaches separate? You are all over each others' footnotes!" And so we were, because we were reading some of the same books, as well as reading and critiquing one another's writing and entering into vigorous face-to-face conversations with one another at the annual Society of Biblical Literature meetings. I tell my students these stories of Markan scholars; by personalizing scholarship for my students, I bring it closer to them. I let them know that, when I think of the effect of reader-response criticism on my work, I think of the times when I was writing something and wondered, what would Bob Fowler say about that sentence? For me the abstractions of deconstructive criticism were personalized by wondering, how would Stephen Moore deconstruct what I just wrote? It was my long association with folks in the Bible in Ancient and Modern Media Section of the Society of Biblical Literature, Tom Boomershine, Joanna Dewey, and David Rhoads, and later Phil Ruge-Jones, that resulted in my moving from writing and speaking about Mark's "readers" to Mark's "audience." I realized how far this had gone when my students also started consistently using the term *audience*, indicating that my free speech in the classroom had also become consistent. My classroom is a small window on the dialogic world of Markan scholarship.[16]

---

14. See n. 3 above.

15. The 2008 revision had hoped to include a chapter on orality, but arrangements with an author could not be worked out at that time.

16. Boomershine, Dewey, Rhoads, and Ruge-Jones, as well as Holly Hearon,

I hope you have begun to see that I adopt and adapt the Markan rhetoric of juxtaposition as my own strategy of communication and pedagogy. Students are both forced and enabled to juxtapose one commentator's insights with another's and the limits and possibilities of one scholarly approach with another. They are also engaged in exploring Mark's rhetoric of juxtaposition directly.

(5) Carry out a series of classroom activities that involves students in both experiencing and analyzing the details of the story. When studying Mark 2:1–3:6, students are led to discover both the chiastic structure and the forward plot movement in these controversy stories in Galilee by dividing into five groups to analyze each of the five pericopes separately, then reporting back to the class by completing a matrix on the board (event, controversy), which serves as the basis for a discussion of *how* the implied author is communicating *what* to the implied audience. To explore the significant (and symbolic) geography of Mark 4–8, I have used a variety of strategies: in a room with a large table, we construct a map of Galilee on the table, with a roll of blue crepe paper for water and signs for the place names, and trace the movement of the Markan Jesus through the narrative. Without the table, we construct the map on the floor and have students take turns walking across the map to the next destination. Without a large table or room on the floor, I project a map of Galilee on the white board, and students take turns marking the journey with colored markers on the white board. In a good-size church, I once envisioned the main aisle as the River Jordan and the chancel area as the Sea of Galilee and marked the journeys with my own movement in those spaces. In a Sunday school classroom, I once used a child's wading pool for the Sea of Galilee, and we made paper boats to blow across the sea. While Mark's geographi-

---

Whitney Shiner, and Richard Swanson, are among those scholars who focus more specifically on orality in both their scholarship and their teaching. A good preview of their work is Holly E. Hearon and Philip Ruge-Jones, eds., *The Bible in Ancient and Modern Media: Story and Performance*, BPC 1 (Eugene, OR: Cascade, 2009). I do not think it is coincidental that most of these scholars have been or are teaching in seminaries, theological schools, or religiously affiliated colleges, where proclamation of the gospel is not only permitted but is also an important pedagogical task. Like Whitney Shiner, I teach in a state university, and I have found that undergraduate students have a harder time maintaining a scholarly point of view when orally interpreting New Testament passages. I think this observation speaks to the power of the spoken word in both forming and communicating one's interpretation of a text, whether narrative or expository, and one's religious beliefs more broadly.

cal knowledge has been denigrated in twenty-first-century terms, I am convinced that the Markan author intended the audience to understand, in first-century terms, the ethnography indicated by the geographical references;[17] this is a story about Jesus interacting with Jews and Gentiles. I knew I had communicated to students a connection between the parabolic teaching of Mark's Jesus and Mark's overall parabolic rhetoric when I concluded a discussion with, "So, Mark's Jesus teaches in parables, and Mark's Gospel teaches in parables," and one student added, "And *you* teach in parables," and we all laughed.

(6) Have students discover, research, and write about an issue in Markan interpretation that interests them. In this fairly traditional assignment, students are able to integrate what they have learned about the Markan narrative and about the narrative of Markan scholarship by becoming beginning participants in that scholarship. The graduate student in education, herself interested in communication and pedagogy, prepared a paper on "The Use of Rhetorical Questions in the Gospel of Mark." An undergraduate student double majoring in religion and classics wrote a paper exploring Greek words for "fear" in Mark. One student's narrative critical and reception historical study of the Gethsemane passage was selected for presentation at a regional Society of Biblical Literature meeting.

(7) Put students in direct e-mail communication with other Markan scholars. My students, of course, come to realize that I am a Markan scholar. They are at first surprised to see my name in others' footnotes; there was a class joke about notes that said, "see Malbon," with students writing in the margin, "I will, tomorrow." But putting students into direct e-mail contact with other Markan scholars has done even more to help them see how scholarship works. This exercise, naturally, depends on the fantastic cooperation I have received from Markan scholars, most recently the commentary authors mentioned above, who toward the end of the semester exchanged at least one and sometimes two rather full e-mail responses with the pair or triplet of "their" readers who sent questions to "their" commentators.[18] In a Markan seminar in 1999, I employed a more elaborate system that included the Markan scholar we were reading each

---

17. See Eric C. Stewart, *Gathered around Jesus: An Alternative Spatial Practice in the Gospel of Mark* (Cambridge: Clarke, 2009); and my review in *RBL* (March 2011), http://www.bookreviews.org/bookdetail.asp?TitleId=7638.

18. I extend my personal thanks to Gene Boring, John Donahue and Dan Har-

week in a class e-mail listserve for that week, with the handful of students asking a question each and the scholar replying to them either individually or as a group.[19]

There is great excitement and satisfaction in joining form and content in teaching Mark's narrative in a Markan narrative way. As a Markan scholar, I have argued that Mark's Gospel presents the character "Jesus" with a certain tension—creative tension—between the Markan Jesus's point of view and the point of view of the Markan narrator and other characters.[20] This narrative rhetoric of juxtaposition that demands audience engagement serves for me as a model of communication and pedagogy. Thus the Gospel of Mark is teaching me how to teach the Gospel of Mark.

Beyond the Gospel of Mark

Of course, these pedagogical strategies are easily applicable to the other biblical narratives: in my own teaching, the other Gospels and the Acts of the Apostles. I have already noted that, when using *Gospel Parallels* in a course on the Gospels, I have students read each Gospel in order—vertically through *Gospel Parallels*—with sideways horizontal looks rather than reading through *Gospel Parallels* just horizontally, that is, all the parallel passages on one page, followed by all the parallel passages on the next page, and so on. I encourage students to notice the differences within each pericope by a system of color marking, underlining with colored pencils, based on the primary and secondary colors on the color wheel (think paints, not computer technology). The primary colors are for material unique to each Synoptic: red for Mark, yellow for Matthew, blue for Luke. The secondary colors are for overlapping material: orange for Mark and Matthew, purple for Mark and Luke, green for Matthew and Luke. The tertiary color brown (made by mixing red, yellow, and blue)

---

rington, Morna Hooker, Frank Moloney, and Ched Myers for their generosity to my students in December 2011.

19. I am pleased to be able to thank in a more official way the twelve scholars who gave generously of their time—and their patience—as we worked out the listserve procedure of contact with my undergraduate students in the fall of 1999: Janice Capel Anderson, Brian Blount, Christopher Bryan, Joanna Dewey, John Donahue, Bob Fowler, Werner Kelber, Hisaka Kinukawa, Stephen Moore, Ched Myers, David Rhoads, and Mary Ann Tolbert.

20. Malbon, *Mark's Jesus*.

indicates identical material in all three Synoptics. But I also encourage students to notice larger ways in which the Gospels seem to have influenced one another. Color marking and reading vertically with horizontal glances are good ways to test the Q hypothesis (which asserts that Matthew and Luke utilize a hypothetical sayings source, *Quelle*, German for "source," in addition to Mark) over against the Farrer hypothesis (which asserts that Matthew relies on Mark, and Luke relies on Mark and Matthew). Asking students to write in the first-person voice of "Matthew" or "Luke" to explain their editing of their "sources" in particular passages (after color marking) has been a fun way to engage them in learning not only to detect differences but to question their possible significance and to construct and test hypotheses.

The letters of Paul, while not narratives themselves, also lend themselves to narrative thinking as students are led to construct the story behind each letter. As my students learn, the most important question to ask of a Pauline letter is, what's the occasion? That is, what occasioned the letter? Why was it written to this community at this time? I do have students do some writing in the imagined first-century voice of Paul, for example, explaining Paul's advice to the Corinthians on marriage. However, even more appropriate is their writing a letter in Paul's style to a community of which they (each student individually) are a part. Then we exchange these letters, and each student must write the letter *from* that community (the community of another student's letter) to which the letter they received in the exchange is "Paul's" reply. They find that they *can* understand how to read between the lines to construct the community situation, as scholars do when reading and interpreting Paul's letters. When I read some sample letters in class in the opposite order in which they were actually written but in their imagined chronological order, the fit is impressive. And, of course, the occasional misreadings, corrected by the "original" author in ways not possible with Paul's letters, are also constructive warnings of the difficulty of the interpretive task.

In-class activities reinforce the occasional nature of Paul's letters and their various dominant themes. In a class of fifteen to twenty-five students, we rearrange our desks in a circle; and, rather than lecturing, I often ask students questions individually, moving around the circle. I pass a "marker" to keep track of whose turn it is to answer a question (and also to reduce pressure; a student may simply pass the marker on if he or she is unable or unwilling to answer). But the marker changes for each letter, and the marker is symbolic or metaphorical. I never query students about the nature of the marker until the end of a session, but they start "getting it" early on. Here are some examples the biblical scholars reading this essay will easily "get": a small scroll for Galatians (in which midrash of scriptural texts is crucial), a small clay pot for 2 Corinthians (see 2 Cor 4:7), a small chain for Philippians (a "prison" letter). Some markers need—and elicit—more discussion: a rock for 1 Thessalonians (Paul is encouraged by the Thessalonians' rock-solid faithfulness, and he encourages them to be rock solid in their conviction about the inclusion of the entire community at the coming parousia, even those who may die beforehand); a mirror for 1 Corinthians (Paul is helping the Corinthians to look at themselves as others see them and to act not on the basis of superior "knowledge" but out of love for all in the community). Discussion of these markers, my metaphors, blends with discussion of Paul's metaphors and when and why people use metaphors.

So concepts central to a literary approach to the Bible (metaphor, point of view, redaction, setting/plot/characterization/rhetoric, juxtaposition, genre, and context) are central to my teaching of the Bible. In introducing students to the New Testament in an initial survey course, I focus on context and genre. Early in the semester, I show the Coke bottle scene from the film *The Gods Must Be Crazy* (easily available on YouTube). It takes little prompting to solicit the realization that the humor of the scene, and of the movie, rests on the contrast between the way the "natives" look at the Coke bottle (as a gift from the gods, who must be crazy because the gift causes envy, jealously, and strife) and the way the movie audience views the Coke bottle (as litter thrown out by the bush pilot). The most direct answer I have ever received when asking, "Why do you think I showed this movie clip?" is "Because the Bible is a Coke bottle!" The analogy is easy to push: Do people ever beat each other over the head with the Bible? (Laughter.) Who are the "natives" in this analogy? (We are—if we read the Bible without reference to its originating context.)

Role-play is often an effective strategy to give students practice in inhabiting a first-century context. Early on in a small class on the Gospels, I have given each student a label (known only to each student): Sadducee, Pharisee, Essene, or Zealot, then instructed them to find the other members of their group without using any of those four label names. Having done some reading on the four groups, they ask each other questions such as, "Do you believe in the oral Torah?" "Do you work in the temple?" "Do you live in the desert?" Then, when the four groups are formed, I ask each group to discuss among themselves and then present to the class their attitude to the Roman government, their reasons for that attitude, and what happened to their group during the Roman-Jewish War of 66–70 CE. Toward the end the semester in a small class on the Gospels, I stage a First Gospel Writers Workshop. A panel of several students represents each canonical Gospel (and sometimes the Gospel of Thomas) in answering these questions I ask as the moderator: When did you write? Why did you write and for whom? What were your sources? How did you structure your material? What were the main ideas you were trying to communicate? What could you have titled your work? Do you think your readers have understood you? Would you do it differently if you could do it again?[21] The chart we fill in on the board (and which students fill in individually on paper) becomes part of a study guide for the final exam.

Frequent use of small groups (two to five students) working together and then reporting back to the whole involves all the students, even the more quiet ones who are hesitant to jump into the discussion quickly. More importantly, this procedure can lead students to *experience* literary features of a text as well as basic content and context. For example, I have one-third of the class prepare a pantomime of 1 Cor 12 (the body metaphor as a guide to the use of spiritual gifts), one-third prepare a choral reading of 1 Cor 13 (on love), and one-third prepare a skit on proper and improper worship according to 1 Cor 14 (problems with glossolalia). When the presentations are made in order, without additional commentary by me, they make the point of the linkage of these three chapters more strongly than I ever could by simply lecturing.

Generally I use teams not only to liven up the classroom and "cover" material but also to make a point experientially. When I divide the class into teams in order to ask questions about the opening chapters of 1 Corinthians, I have each team choose a name, and I keep score on the board. The competition develops easily. At the end, I ask, "Why do you suppose I organized teams today?" The best answer ever was, "Oh, no. You made us into bickering Corinthians!" When I organized teams recently for our

---

21. If my memory serves me, I think I have adapted this idea (and the initial questions in the list) from David Barr, applied in a seminar on the Synoptic Gospels taught many years ago at Florida State University by Dr. Robert A. Spivey, who asked each graduate student to come up with a way to help others review the material. My contribution was a list of short quotations chosen from the Gospels on the basis of dominant themes and unique stories; that list is still the core of a section of my tests for students today.

discussion of Rom 12–16, I named the two teams "Jews" and "Greeks" (although both teams also choose additional names, "David Stars" and "Turbulent Togas"!). When I asked, "Who goes first?" they answered almost in unison, "the Jews first and also the Greeks." I had to finagle things a bit to get the scores to tie at the end of the discussion. It did not take much prompting for them to see what I had done and why (we had just finished reading Krister Stendahl's *Paul among Jews and Gentiles*[22]), but one student asked, "So, are you God?" We all laughed, and I said, "No. Like Paul, I am clear about not being God or knowing the mind of God. But I am trying to represent the hope of Paul as expressed in Romans, especially chapters 9–11."

Thus, not only in my teaching of Mark, but in all my teaching of New Testament materials (and those of you who teach Hebrew Bible/Old Testament will have your own parallel and unique strategies to share), I experience joy in joining form and content, in devising strategies for teaching and learning that help us experience, rather than just hear about, what is central to the text, whether that text is a narrative or a letter or a sermon or an apocalypse. Paul's letters entice me to teach them in a Pauline dialogic and metaphorical way. Mark's narrative encourages me to teach it in a Markan narrative way, with its contrasting settings and characters, its developing plot, and its rhetoric of juxtaposition that demands audience engagement and thus serves as a model of communication and of pedagogy.

---

22. Krister Stendahl, *Paul among Jews and Gentiles and Other Essays* (Philadelphia: Fortress, 1976).

3
Teaching Mark as Collective Memory

Sandra Huebenthal

In the course of the recent changes of paradigm in New Testament scholarship, there has been a remarkable shift of attention from atomistic to synthetic readings of the Bible—or, in other words, from pericopes to unabridged biblical books. After *Redaktionskritik* rightly rehabilitated the evangelists as theologians, the Gospel texts themselves—considered as narrative theology and interpreted experience—consequently gained more and more attention in the exegetical guild. Though this development might have been unexpected for some, it is not in the least surprising. As has often been the case in the history of research, the pendulum swings back in the opposite direction.

This latest paradigm shift in research is deeply connected with the *cultural turn* and has been especially welcomed by teachers and pastoral ministers. They frequently experienced great difficulties when faced with the task of developing and structuring lessons, catecheses, or sermons on the basis of the insights and outcomes of historical-critical research. The renewed scholarly interest in biblical books and their theologies, which replaces the concentration on particular texts, traditions, and possible origins, is most helpful in their working fields. Having myself been a secondary school teacher for a couple of years, and beyond that involved in a curriculum in confirmation catechesis, I am quite sensitive to the difficulties that a predominantly origin-focused approach to the Bible entails.

As the tide has turned, my German context currently experiences a larger emphasis on *Ganzschriftlektüre*, that is, the reading of unabridged biblical books. Already customary for Old Testament books when I attended secondary school twenty years ago, this approach has only lately been applied to New Testament books. Given that almost every new method in New Testament studies is put to the test on Mark,[1] it is not surprising at the moment that the Gospel of Mark has gained the undivided attention of religious education teachers and pastoral ministers and is a recent topic of both advanced training in religious instruction and scholarly publications in this area.[2]

This renewed interest, of course, raises methodological questions. How can one fruitfully read the entire and unabridged Gospel of Mark? As strange as this question might sound to an unbiased reader, it actually poses difficulties for the exegetically trained one. A thorough look into the average New Testament scholar's methodological toolbox almost instantly reveals a hermeneutical gap: neither a *literarkritisch*-genetic approach alone, as widely dominant in historical-critical research, nor a pure narrative analysis, which ignores the text's history of origin, will be a satisfactory approach for this enterprise.[3] This explains not only the enthusiasm of the readers from nonacademic contexts, but also the rise of the *canonical approach*, the renewed interest in *biblical theology*, and, most recently, *theological interpretation* as attempts to close the gap.[4]

A fruitful and theologically sound reading of an entire and unabridged biblical book requires an approach that is able to combine both a hermeneutic that takes seriously the origin and history of the text, including its oral prehistory and the different tangible written forms, as well as its rootedness in a particular sociohistorical situation, *and* one that is able to unlock the experiences and theological reflections that are expressed in a narration. Of course, since this hermeneutic should be as unbiased

---

1. Janice C. Anderson and Stephen D. Moore, *Mark and Method: New Approaches in Biblical Studies*, 2nd ed. (Minneapolis: Fortress, 2008), ix.

2. Gudrun Guttenberger, "Das Markusevangelium in religionspädagogischer Perspektive," in *Religionspädagogischer Kommentar zur Bibel*, ed. Bernhard Dressler and Harald Schroeter-Wittke (Leipzig: Evangelische Verlagsanstalt, 2012), 433–51; Peter Müller, *Mit Markus erzählen: Das Markusevangelium im Religionsunterricht* (Stuttgart: Calwer, 1999); and Ricarda Sohns, *Das Markusevangelium: Das biblische Buch als Ganzschrift*, Religion betrifft uns 2013.1 (Aachen: Bergmoser & Höller, 2013).

3. Pontifical Biblical Commission, *The Interpretation of the Bible in the Church* (Rome: Libreria Editrice Vaticana, 1993), I.A.4.

4. Ibid., I.C.1; for theological interpretation, see Richard Hays, "Reading the Bible with Eyes of Faith: The Practice of Theological Exegesis," *JTI* 1 (2007): 5–21; Walter Moberly, "'Interpret the Bible Like Any Other Book'? Requiem for an Axiom," *JTI* 4 (2010): 91–110; and quite critically, Marcus Bockmuehl, "Bible versus Theology: Is 'Theological Interpretation' the Answer?" *NV* 9 (2011): 27–47.

as possible by later theological and ecclesiastical developments, it also requires a self-critical or at least metareflective attitude on the part of the reader.

I have dealt with these questions in a recently completed research project, *Das Markusevangelium als kollektives Gedächtnis*. The project resulted in the development of a reading model for the New Testament on the basis of *social memory theory* that aims to do justice to the history of the text as well as to provide a set of fresh reading glasses.[5]

Once the scholarly work is done, the question arises about how it can be introduced to those who will apply it to their own practice fields and spheres of activity. In this contribution, I will thus address the question of how the new hermeneutical approach can be brought fruitfully to an average lecture room. Thus my remarks will focus more on didactical considerations and how this approach can be taught and less on the impact for Markan scholarship or exegesis in general. The contribution consists of three sections. The first section will provide a very brief summary of the intention and the outcomes of my research project. The second and more extended section will introduce the course "Mark as Collective Memory" in order to deal with the question of how the approach can be brought to the lecture room. Finally, concluding reflections will shed some light on the question of the wider methodological and didactic impact of the project, including the question of how the ideas can contribute to the teaching of the Bible on a more general level.

Reading Mark as Collective Memory

The initial point of my research on *Mark as Collective Memory* was the question of how social memory theory can bear fruit for the understanding and interpretation of New Testament texts. What made the project a challenging enterprise was not so much the application of the findings and insights of social memory theory to biblical exegesis but the implicit change of perspective when biblical texts are read as cultural texts.

---

5. Sandra Hübenthal, *Das Markusevangelium als kollektives Gedächtnis*, FRLANT 253 (Göttingen: Vandenhoeck & Ruprecht, 2014); Hübenthal, "Reading Mark as Collective Memory," in *Social Memory and Social Identity in the Study of Early Judaism and Early Christianity*, ed. Samuel Byrskog, Raimo Hakola, and Jutta Jokiranta, NTOA/SUNT (Göttingen: Vandenhoeck & Ruprecht, forthcoming).

Historical-critical scholarship has provided the exegetical guild with the paradigm of the Gospels as writings drafted by authors who depended heavily on tradition and wrote for a particular audience ("community") in a particular sociohistorical context and thus with particular aims and pragmatics. This model not only sees the evangelists or redactors as carriers of (memory) traditions, but usually also focuses on Jesus as the *object* of memory. It is this Jesus—not only his life and death, but also his impact—that the texts give information about. A certain type of *Gattungsdiskussion*, using terms such as *vita*, *bios*, or *biography* bears witness to this model. The question of referentiality, that is, how a text relates to the extratextual and extralinguistic reality, plays an important role in this discussion. Since, on the one hand, narrative texts are generally suspected to be more fictional than historiographical and, on the other hand, historical research and especially (historical) Jesus research asks for factual texts, it is obvious that the Gospels, read as literary compositions, are not fully satisfactory. The Gospels, which have been composed out of small and discernible units, are much better read as tradition literature, especially if the units can be separated and questioned independently about their peculiarity and their historical usability.

Even though many members of the exegetical guild claim to have largely left behind historical-critical methodology, the depicted historical-critical model of the origin and growth of the texts is quite vivid and frequently still forms the basis of their research. On the other end of the spectrum, some scholars have thrown out the baby with the bath water and analyze the biblical text exclusively as a literary composition, disregarding its value as a historical source.

Thus applying social memory theory to the study of the Gospels first of all means developing a model for the text and its genesis that takes seriously both its literary and its historical character. Reading the Gospel of Mark as collective memory, or, to be more precise, as the *excarnation* of a collective memory,[6] thus entails the necessity of distinguishing and defending this approach over against two other concepts: on the one hand, against a misconceived objectification and historiography of eyewitness testimonies, a view that does not take seriously the constructional character of recollection and memory; and, on the other hand, against the view

---

6. Aleida Assmann, "Exkarnation: Gedanken zur Grenze zwischen Körper und Schrift," in *Raum und Verfahren*, ed. Jörg Huber and Alois Martin Müller (Basel: Stroemfeld/Roter Stern, 1993), 133–55.

that sees the author, redactor, or evangelist as the authority who can evaluate the accuracy, significance, and (theological) adequacy of traditions and their future tradition.[7] Having said this, I should also mention that the keyword *tradition* invokes particular concepts of community, church, and organizational structure that very often—and mostly implicitly—structure the exegetical discourse. Indeed, one's own perception of church is crucial when it comes to picturing the processes of tradition, as can be gathered, for example, from the recent discussion of orality.

Often, the reality might be quite different from what common sense and ecclesiastical tradition teaches us. The broad interdisciplinary research in the field of recollection and memory reveals, for example, that individual and social memory are not only processes whose structures are largely analogous and follow similar patterns, but also that their forms of expression, that is, socially accepted memory stories, originate as individual episodes and are developed only later into larger narratives. Taking this character of memory seriously, one can understand and read New Testament texts as texts of collective recollection. The research of Maurice Halbwachs[8] and its continuation both by Jan Assmann[9] and Aleida Assmann[10] can be applied fruitfully to exegetical discourses. Connecting their insights with recent research on intergenerational recollection and identity construction,[11] sociology,[12] and historical psychology[13]

---

7. Hübenthal, *Markusevangelium*, 52–60.

8. Maurice Halbwachs, *Les cadres sociaux de la mémoire*, 2nd ed., BEH 8 (Paris: Michel, 1994); Halbwachs, *La mémoire collective*, 2nd ed., BEH 28 (Paris: Michel, 1997).

9. Jan Assmann, *Das kulturelle Gedächtnis: Schrift, Erinnerung und politische Identität in frühen Hochkulturen* (Munich: Beck, 1992); Assmann, *Religion und kulturelles Gedächtnis: Zehn Studien* (Munich: Beck, 2000).

10. Aleida Assmann, "Wie wahr sind Erinnerungen?" in *Das soziale Gedächtnis: Geschichte, Erinnerung, Tradierung*, ed. Harald Welzer (Hamburg: Hamburger Edition, 2001), 103–22.

11. Harald Welzer, "Das gemeinsame Verfertigen von Vergangenheit im Gespräch," in Welzer, *Soziale Gedächtnis*, 160–78; Welzer, *Das kommunikative Gedächtnis: Eine Theorie der Erinnerung* (Munich: Beck, 2002); Welzer, *Grandpa Wasn't a Nazi: National Socialism and the Holocaust in German Memory Culture* (New York: American Jewish Committee, 2005).

12. Bernhard Giesen, *Kollektive Identität*, Die Intellektuellen und die Nation 2 (Frankfurt: Suhrkamp, 1999).

13. Jürgen Straub, "Geschichten erzählen, Geschichte bilden: Grundzüge einer narrativen Psychologie historischer Sinnbildung," in *Erzählung, Identität, und historisches Bewusstsein: Die psychologische Konstruktion von Zeit und Geschichte*, ed.

allows the development of a matrix that classifies processes of collective recollection or social memory as *social memory, collective memory,* and *cultural memory.* This taxonomy is a powerful tool not only to describe and analyze processes of recollection and memory more precisely, but also to connect them to the interdisciplinary scholarly discourse on memory.[14] Memory might be a highly theologized category, but it is not a genuinely theological concept, and there is thus no reason to seal off the exegetical and theological reflections on recollection and memory from the lively transdisciplinary scholarly discourses.

This approach offers new possibilities: one major advantage is that memory texts can (again) be accessed as historical sources; another is that they can also be placed beyond their historical contexts—according to the categories of social memory theory. The latter means, first of all, that the specifics and character of collective memory texts can be illustrated. For this illustration, the distinction between social memory and collective memory is crucial. Following Halbwachs's distinction, *social memory* can be understood as the development of memories (and, as a result, identities) within given social frames, while *collective memory* describes the fabrication of novel social frames for future memory and identity construction processes. Applied to the Gospel of Mark, this means that Mark, read as collective memory, is such a frame. It invites readers to locate themselves within this mnemonic framework and thus allows identity construction on the basis of Jesus memories.

The theoretical and hermeneutical foundation might be evident; nevertheless, it proves to be quite difficult to provide a reading model that allows the unveiling of these characteristics for particular biblical texts. I have carved out the following definition with the aim of bridging the gap between the theoretical foundation and the study of a particular text—a bridge that does justice to both of the needs mentioned above. It runs as

---

Jürgen Straub, Erinnerung, Geschichte, Identität 1 (Frankfurt: Suhrkamp, 1998), 81–169; Straub, "Psychology, Narrative, and Cultural Memory: Past and Present," in *Cultural Memory Studies: An International and Interdisciplinary Handbook,* ed. Astrid Erll and Ansgar Nünning (Berlin: de Gruyter, 2008), 215–28; Kenneth Gergen, "Erzählung, moralische Identität und historisches Bewusstsein," in Straub, *Erzählung, Identität, und historisches Bewusstsein,* 170–202; Donald E. Polkinghorne, "Narrative Psychologie und Geschichtsbewußtsein: Beziehungen und Perspektiven," in Straub, *Erzählung, Identität, und historisches Bewusstsein,* 12–45.

14. Hübenthal, *Markusevangelium,* 142–50.

follows: *The Gospel of Mark is an episodically structured, perspectival narration, which is oriented to forms and patterns available in its context(s). Due to its guiding perspective and its narrative gaps, the narration is transparent for its narrating community and invites the recipients to familiarize themselves with the Gospel.*

One of the crucial points when it comes to reading Mark as collective memory is to avoid the category mistake of blending the textual and the extratextual worlds or, in other words, of extending the text into reality. The challenge is to read and understand the biblical text as a historical source without taking it as a meticulous report of what actually happened while still taking seriously the experience verbalized in the text. This can be achieved only by working with a clear model of the text as a narrative and with a distinct conception of the different levels of communication in the text.

For the Gospel of Mark, the results of such a reading are indeed stunning. It becomes evident, for example, that the narrator and the character Jesus do not speak with the same voice: the narrator aims to proclaim Jesus, while Jesus himself wants to proclaim God and his βασιλεία, which is at hand.[15] Jesus invites the other characters and the readers to actualize the βασιλεία and thus become part of this possible world. Taking a thorough look at the whole Gospel, it is quickly apparent that, despite their differences, in the end the narrator follows Jesus's perspective and makes him the norm of his/her/their own world. Apparently this does not go without additional interpretation: "classical" themes of Markan theology, like the *messianic secret* and the *disciples' lack of comprehension*, are not dimensions of the narrated world (i.e., the world of the characters) but become visible only on a higher level of textual communication. The same holds true for the discussion of different Jesus images. In addition, the answer to the question of what an adequate perception of Jesus looks like provides an insight into the configuration and organization of the remembering community (*Erinnerungsgemeinschaft*) that stands behind the text, and it invites Jews and Gentiles alike to familiarize with the text and thus join the group.

---

15. Elizabeth Struthers Malbon, *Mark's Jesus: Characterization as Narrative Christology* (Waco, TX: Baylor University Press, 2009), 191.

Teaching Mark as Collective Memory

The experience we all share when it comes to teaching is that doing research is quite a different kettle of fish from bringing its outcomes to the lecture room—or at least putting some of the ideas to the test. It is, of course, always possible to present outcomes of current research in a lecture and teach them as knowledge that students have to be able to present in an exam. That much is easy. But bringing students to understand a particular hermeneutical or methodological approach and enabling them to work with it independently is more of a challenge. In this case, it is no longer sufficient just to lecture students about what an appropriate application would look like and then present some examples. If I expect them to demonstrate the approach in the exam—and thus prove that they have understood the principle—I need to go beyond theoretical introduction and colorful examples and allow them time to work with this approach themselves. If the goal is that the students are able to compare different approaches (including the one that springs from my latest research), criticize them, and evaluate them, then the course design must again be different, for the critical examination of a hermeneutic or a methodology entails more than just a user's competence. Fulfilling that task requires a whole theoretical framework, field knowledge, and criteria.

Two different points can be gathered from this: (1) a course on the same subjects can have different goals or outcomes, and (2) these goals determine the structure of the course. When we take these insights seriously, it becomes clear that a course is best planned backward instead of forward, and that the starting point of the course planning should be the intended goal, or the *learning outcome*. The learning outcome describes *what the students are expected to know, understand, and/or be able to demonstrate after the completion of a process of learning*.[16] This definition is rather open and, as demonstrated above, allows for different kinds and

---

16. Declan Kennedy, Áine Hyland, and Norma Ryan, "Writing and Using Learning Outcomes: A Practical Guide," in *Neues Handbuch Hochschullehre*, ed. Brigitte Berendt et al. (Berlin: Raabe, 2009), Griffmarke C 3.4-1; Margret Schermutzky, "Learning Outcomes— Lernergebnisse: Begriffe, Zusammenhänge, Umsetzung und Erfolgsermittlung Lernergebnisse und Kompetenzvermittlung als elementare Orientierungen des Bologna-Prozesses," in Berendt et al., *Neues Handbuch Hochschullehre*, Griffmarke E 3.3.

types of learning goals.[17] Writing learning outcomes has almost become a skill itself in the last decade, and a very helpful one, for the learning outcome is the core of the course, and everything else builds on it.[18]

Defining this core is the first step when planning a course according to the principles of *constructive alignment*. Constructive alignment is best understood as synchronizing what the teacher wants the students to learn with what the students themselves plan to do by designing an assessment that connects both goals. Both parties, however, plan the course backward: when the teacher models the assessment along the lines of the intended learning outcome, the ordinary student, who organizes his or her learning process according to the exam questions, will follow the intended learning steps exactly because only these will prepare him or her to pass the exam.[19] The fringe benefit of designing a course according to these principles is that it is very hard for the students to get away with *surface learning*—if the course is modeled correctly, a *deep-level approach* is almost inevitable, and learning will be much more sustainable.[20]

The learning outcome sets the goal for the course. The second step is to model a matching assessment, that is, a setting in which the teacher can measure whether the students have reached the learning goal. This again allows for a variety of forms and methods. The crucial question is what exactly the students should know or be able to demonstrate in the assessment, for this expectation will be the key to the course design. Generally speaking, one has to make sure that the course leads to the ability to pass

---

17. Benjamin S. Bloom, ed., *Taxonomy of Educational Objectives, Handbook 1: Cognitive Domain,* 2nd ed. (White Plains, NY: Longman, 1984); and David R. Krathwohl, Benjamin S. Bloom, and Bertram B. Masia, eds., *Taxonomy of Eductional Objectives, Handbook 2: Affective Domain*, 2nd ed. (White Plains, NY: Longman, 1999).

18. Dagmar Schulte, "Veranstaltungsplanung: Probleme und Methoden," in Berendt et al., *Neues Handbuch Hochschullehre*, Griffmarke B 1; Johannes Wildt and Beatrix Wildt, "Lernprozessorientiertes Prüfen im 'Constructive Alignment,'" in Berendt et al., *Neues Handbuch Hochschullehre,* Griffmarke H 6.1.

19. Wildt and Wildt, "Lernprozessorientiertes Prüfen," 2011.

20. Claus Brabrand and Jacob Andersen, "Teaching Teaching and Understanding Understanding" (Aarhus: Aarhus University Press, 2006), *Daimi.au.dk*, http://www.daimi.au.dk/~brabrand/short-film/ (a 19-minute film about constructive alignment). For the terms see John Biggs, *Teaching for Quality Learning at University* (Buckingham: SHRE and Open University Press, 1999); Noel J. Entwistle, *Styles of Learning and Teaching* (London: David Fulton, 1988); Paul Ramsden, *Learning to Teach in Higher Education* (London: Routledge, 1992).

the exam: one can only expect students to be familiar with the models, forms, and approaches one has introduced in class. This excludes settings in which the lecturer presents facts in class and expects the undergraduate students to come up with a critical discussion and evaluation.[21]

When the learning outcome and the assessment are clear, the third step is to reflect upon the learning steps that the students must take in order to be well prepared for the exam. This involves a change in perspective, a *shift from teaching to learning*.[22] The focus clearly lies on the students' learning process. The crucial questions are, *Which steps do they have to take to reach the goal set for the course?* and *What impulses and/or didactic interventions are necessary to get them on their way?*

Application, or Designing a Course

Thus, when it comes to planning my course on "Mark as Collective Memory," the first concrete step is to formulate a clear and manageable learning outcome: what should the students know, understand, and/or be able to demonstrate after the completion of the course? For this course, the learning outcome will be: *Students will be able to explain what it means to read the Gospel of Mark as collective memory and to demonstrate this hermeneutical approach with exemplary readings.*

Step two is to come up with an assessment that matches the learning outcome. The assessment for the course on Mark as Collective Memory can be either a written or an oral exam or an essay. The form of the assessment is, however, flexible according to the needs of the program in which it will be implemented. The task I am asking my students to deal with remains the same in each case: *Describe what it means to read the Gospel of*

---

21. Rolf Dubs, "Besser schriftlich prüfen: Prüfungen valide und zuverlässig durchführen," in Berendt et al., *Neues Handbuch Hochschullehre*, Griffmarke H 5.1; Oliver Reis and Sylvia Ruschin, "Kompetenzorientiert Prüfen: Bausteine eines gelungenen Paradigmenwechsels," in *Prüfungen auf die Agenda! Hochschuldidaktische Perspektiven auf Reformen im Prüfungswesen*, ed. Sigrid Dany, Birgit Szczybra, and Johannes Wildt, Blickpunkt Hochschuldidaktik 118 (Bielefeld: Bertelsmann, 2008), 45–57.

22. Johannes Wildt, "Vom Lehren zum Lernen," in Berendt et al., *Neues Handbuch Hochschullehre*, Griffmarke A 3.1; Oliver Reis, "Kompetenzorientierung als hochschuldidaktische Chance für die Theologie," in *Vom Lehren zum Lernen: Didaktische Wende in der Theologie?*, ed. Monika Scheidler and Oliver Reis, Theologie und Hochschuldidaktik 3 (Münster: LIT, 2011), 19–38.

Mark as collective memory and pick two or three examples to illustrate this hermeneutical approach.

If the assessment is a written or an oral exam, I let the students know the exam question at least two weeks in advance. The first part of the assessment might seem to be more of a knowledge question, but as the hermeneutics is quite complicated, it can be helpful to have some time to think about how this is best addressed and presented. The second part of the assessment requires a more thorough reflection. The students have to come up with their own examples and think them through before they are able to present them in a conclusive way. I also encourage the students to form working groups in order to discuss their ideas while preparing for the exam and to consider this phase an important part of their learning process.

After having formulated the learning outcome and developed a matching assessment, I can finally take step three and start to plan the learning process. Just like the ordinary student, I plan the learning steps backward from the exam. The leadings questions for this third step are: *Which learning steps do the students have to take to reach the learning goal?* and *What impulses will I have to give to stimulate their learning process?*

This third step involves another change in perspective. Modeling the learning process is not about how I reached my conclusions and obtained the knowledge but about how the students can reach that goal. The course is not about explaining to the students how I have obtained the tools necessary to answer the exam question (i.e., how I read Mark as collective memory) and then expecting them to pursue the same path, but about enabling them to find and pursue their own ways. This entails a lot more reflection than just giving a lecture on how I got there or on what they need to know. The benefit of this way of going about it is that it prevents the omnipresent problem of the lecturer planning the course from him- or herself, as we usually tend to. Forcing ourselves to take the perspective of our students proves to be an excellent tool to avert that danger and keep focused on the students and their learning process.

This third step tends to be the trickiest part, for, on the one hand, putting theory into practice is always a challenge, and, on the other, this is the moment in the process of designing a course when one is most likely to realize that what one has planned so far will not work. This might be due to a lack of time, resources, overly optimistic expectations, or sometimes even external factors. Although frustrating, this insight is helpful and spares the students a lot of trouble. For the lecturer, however, it might even mean going back to square one and reviewing the learning outcome.

In the case of my course, planning the learning steps proved to be an echo of the questions I was already struggling with in my research project. Though the overall hermeneutic is quite comprehensible, the methodological steps, that is, actually applying the hermeneutic to a specific text, are a bit more complicated. Reading Mark as collective memory means reading and analyzing a mnemonic narrative with a certain perspective and a certain pragmatics. For this task, the historical-critical toolkit is not particularly helpful, as historical-critical methods are aimed at revealing the history and constitution of a biblical text rather than its perspective or pragmatics. To get a better grasp of what a text aims to achieve, a more synchronic approach, using the tools of narrative analysis, proves helpful, as long as one keeps in mind that it is not a piece of literature one is dealing with but a text that springs from a particular experience and a particular sociohistorical context.

To be sensitive to both needs and to introduce the students to the methodological and hermeneutical questions in a practical and hands-on way without burdening them with my own preparatory reflections, I have decided to work with the sandwich technique. The course begins with a phase of practical work with both biblical and nonbiblical texts, turns to a phase of theoretical input and reflection, and then returns to working with the biblical text:

Learning Steps

- Grasping different kinds of hermeneutical lenses: *What is written, and how do you read?* There is no such thing as objectivity—we always read a text with certain reading glasses (classes 1–3).

- Getting to know a lens: *How do the memory theory-informed reading glasses work?* Introduction of social memory theory and social memory-informed reading model for the Gospel of Mark (classes 4–5).

- Using the reading glasses: *How does wearing them alter my readings of Mark?* Exemplary readings of Mark as collective memory (classes 6–14).

Transition to the Classroom

What does the course look like for the students? In order to get them directly involved, I do without lengthy theoretical introductions but bring examples from daily life that the learning group can relate to. My experience proves that this kind of introduction is a much better starting point for hermeneutical questions, since the students can take their own experience as a basis for more advanced reflections. Usually the students already have an intuitive idea of what is at stake, and it does not take much of an effort to make that prior knowledge visible. Working with an example from daily life in class also has the benefit of allowing the learning group to start with a joint experience we can come back to at any stage in the learning process.

In the first class, I would thus simply bring two recent texts that treat the same event, for example, an eyewitness account and a press release. The topic is not too important, as long as the two texts treat the same topic. It could be about an event that happened recently in town or something that moved people around the globe, like an accident, a natural disaster, or, less thrilling, a conference of politicians or a get-together of nobilities or celebrities—whatever seems appropriate. In order to preserve the down-to-earth and everyday character, I would not use an example from the area of religion or churches (and, of course, not a biblical text), and I would stick to something that could be understood as an event, not a larger topic like climate change or the financial crisis. In class, the students and I would explore together what both texts reveal about the event itself and about those who describe it.

During the discussion, it usually becomes obvious quite soon that we will need certain tools or criteria to get beyond gut reactions and contributions along the lines of "well, I think that …" or "for me it feels like…." Very often, students do not know how to objectify their impressions and make them accessible for discussion. This is the moment when I introduce a set of questions from the narratology toolkit to enable students to phrase their observations in a way that we can discuss them. Although developed for and usually applied to narrative texts, these questions can also be used for other factual and fictional texts. Press releases, newspaper articles, speeches, homilies, letters, and even song texts or poems can also be understood as telling a particular story and thus can be examined with these questions.

Question Sets

Set 1: Questions for narrative texts (both factual and fictional):

- What is being told? (story, plot)

- What is not being told? (gaps)

- How is the narration organized? (elements, connections, *Gattungen*)

- What type of a narration is it? (progressive, regressive, stabilizing)

- Which pragmatics or message does the text have?

With the help of these tools we soon are engaged in analyzing and comparing the two texts; even freshmen who have no training in the theory of literature or have never studied the Bible get an idea of how texts can be analyzed and of how two texts—even from different genres—can be compared by working with these questions. For students, this preparatory step is important for two reasons. First, they learn to ask questions about texts and their structure on the basis of objective and disputable criteria instead of using personal feelings or ideas as the point of origin. Second, this experience helps them drop reservations and anxieties about biblical texts. They come to realize that the Bible is a collection of texts and that, in order to read and understand these texts, common sense and confidence in one's ability to understand them are required in the first place.

For many students, the important step is to realize that understanding a biblical text does not require a special "spiritual" or "religious" hermeneutic but common sense and clear thinking. It continues to amaze me to see how relieved most students are when they realize that, when they read Bible in a lecture room, I will ask them neither for a confessional statement nor for insight into how it deepens their faith, but only for general curiosity. The quality of discussions about biblical texts improves almost instantly when students have learned that lesson and begin to put all sorts of ideas and questions to biblical texts without having to fear that the answers might not be orthodox or may differ from what the lecturer wants to hear.

The homework after the first class is rather simple. The students are asked to apply the questions we have used to discuss the first two texts to the accounts of the beheading of John the Baptist, narrated by Mark (6:17–29) and Josephus (*Ant.* 18.116–119). It is usually not difficult to apply the questions to narrative texts from the first century. When we then share impressions and observations in the second class, the students are already able to talk about the texts in a much more reflective and objective way.

After the second class, it will have become obvious that there is no such thing as objectivity and that everything is told from a certain point of view. At this point, the students have taken the first learning step: they have realized that *there are different kinds of hermeneutical reading glasses*. By comparing the narrations of Mark and Josephus, the students will have also realized that the way an event is remembered and passed on might tell a lot more about those who remember it and about their needs than about what actually happened.

The homework for the third class will bring us to the actual subject of the course: the Gospel of Mark. The students are asked to read the entire Gospel of Mark in preparation for the discussion in class. In order to generate more and different kinds of reading impressions, and thus more data to work with, I add a second set of questions:

Question Sets

Set 2: Additional Questions for the Gospel of Mark:

- Which images of Jesus are introduced in the text, and how are they evaluated?

- How does the βασιλεία τοῦ θεοῦ that Jesus proclaims to be at hand take shape, and what is proper conduct in this context?

- Which crises are narrated, and which strategies are introduced to deal with them?

- Which experiences and events narrated in the text match with your own experiences?

A thorough reading with these questions in mind provides more than enough material to describe and analyze what it means to read the Gospel of Mark with regard to *memory*. The third class will be dedicated to gathering the students' impressions and observations and to structuring and establishing them for future work with the text. The last question of each set will require special attention, since this is an area not usually considered in academic settings. This process might require more than one class, which is fine. The teacher will only make sure that the discussion does not get out of hand, that all questions are discussed, and that the insights and outcomes are recorded and made accessible to every student.

After the three (or four) introductory classes, we will turn to social memory theory. In the following two classes, the teacher unfolds a reading model that understands the Gospel of Mark as an *artifact* or an *excarnation* of collective memory. This involves both a basic grasp of social memory theory and insights into how the findings of cultural studies can be made fruitful for the reading of biblical texts. We will read and discuss secondary literature to aid the second learning step, *getting to know the reading glasses*.

The third step, *reading with the spectacles*, will keep the learning group occupied for the rest of the course. If time allows, we will dedicate one class for each of the questions from the questionnaires and reexamine our findings in the light of the new reading glasses.

It is amazing how switching to memory-theory-informed reading glasses can alter the perception and evaluation of certain parts of the text. When they have successfully taken the third learning step, students will, for example, no longer analyze individual pericopes in order to find out *what actually happened* but look at parts in perspective. Stepping back from a microscopically close reading helps students recognize structures and patterns in the overall narration and make sense of them. Read this way, the Gospel of Mark reveals less about Jesus than about the impact he had on those who remember him. *The beginning of the Gospel of Jesus Christ, the Son of God,* tells this story with an open end—indeed, one that opens right into the lives of the recipients.

Exemplary Readings with Memory-Theory-Informed Reading Glasses

The range of possible observations and exemplary readings is huge, and it is impossible to present all or even most of them in the remainder of this contribution. The lecturer should thus be prepared for students to come up with readings and insights he or she has not been dreaming of. If the lecturer is armed for that, reading together can be a very rewarding and fruitful process, and the whole learning group can be once more surprised by Scripture. In order to give a brief insight into the large variety of observations students could make when they train to *read with these spectacles*—and, of course, to raise the reader's curiosity about trying the new spectacles him- or herself—I will briefly present some examples from my own readings.[23]

In the Gospel of Mark, the theme εὐαγγελίου Ἰησοῦ Χριστοῦ υἱοῦ θεοῦ is closely linked to the character Jesus and to its message that βασιλεία τοῦ θεοῦ is at hand. From the very beginning (1:15), μετάνοια and πίστις are introduced as adequate conduct in this situation. This programmatic summary is narratively unfolded along two questions: *How does the βασιλεία at hand take shape?* and *What is the proper attitude to this situation?* The handling of these questions is also closely connected to the character Jesus. Contrary to the other characters, his life shows that he has an answer to both questions. In the course of the narration, it becomes clear that the βασιλεία at hand is realized paradigmatically in Jesus's words and deeds and that he thus introduces a pattern that the other characters can relate to.

Two different strands navigate these ideas through the narration. On the one hand, Mark is about the (accurate) understanding of the character Jesus. On the other hand, the text is about the constitution and organization of an adequate community of followers. Thereby the weight of the first part of the Gospel (1:16–8:26) lies more strongly on the question of how the community of followers is *constituted*, while the weight of the second part (8:27–11:10) lies on the question of how they are *organized*. The third part (11:11–15:37) deepens both topics. It seems logical that the first part, dealing with the *constitution* of the community, also addresses the issues of *who* belongs and *how* admission can be achieved.

---

23. Hübenthal, *Markusevangelium*; Hübenthal, "Reading Mark as Collective Memory."

A closer look shows that in the narrative introduction (1:1–15) Jesus is at first announced to be a special character— Ἰησοῦ Χριστοῦ υἱοῦ θεοῦ— and then introduced as your average contemporary Galilean (1:9) who joins his fellows from Judea and Jerusalem (1:5) lining up at the banks of Jordan for the baptism of repentance. The turning point is narrated in connection with the baptism itself: the character experiences something very special that only the readers are invited to witness. The change of perspective from the author's to the inside view of the character Jesus might point out the preferred perspective for familiarization. This fits very well with the narrative gap in 1:8, "he will baptize you with the Holy Spirit," which in the following verses is fulfilled for the character Jesus. The offer to familiarize can hardly be overlooked, for baptism is a crucial turning point for everyone on the ὁδός of following Jesus.

After the baptism, the character Jesus is thrown into an ἔρημος, a desert or solitude. Recipients might also be able to identify with this experience, even without directly psychologizing the scene as showing the social isolation of the newly baptized. The narrative structure baptism/experience of vocation—desert/latency—onset of proclamation/onset of the ὁδός of following is much more interesting to note and relate to. The character Jesus, unlike many of those whom he has healed, does not take his personal turning point as the starting point for his "mission" but begins to pass on his experience only after latency.

To me, this is crucial. Before the actual story begins, the frame (1:1–15) narrates Jesus's baptism and his "vocation" by the voice from heaven. This part is antecedent to the narration in the same way as what is actually narrated is antecedent to membership in the community of followers. Confrontation with the εὐαγγέλιον takes place prior to the *constitution of the community of followers*. That this confrontation is also narrated for the main character Jesus and that it is even narrated as an experience connected with baptism is hardly a coincidence. Similar things happen again within the story. The confrontation with the εὐαγγέλιον marks the beginning of the community of followers. It is exemplified first with Peter, Andrew, James, and John (1:16–18, 19–20) and then repeated later with Levi (2:14) and the calling of the Twelve (3:13–19). Other than Jesus and the recipients, they are not baptized—a tiny detail that might well strengthen the emotional bond between Jesus and the recipient.

The emotional bond is made even stronger when one realizes that in the whole Gospel of Mark it is only Jesus himself who proclaims the βασιλεία and that the decision of how to respond to Jesus is completely left to the reader. This also means that the character Jesus is allowed to proclaim God and the *possible world* of the coming βασιλεία without the narrator forcing the reader to adopt a certain perspective. That also leaves a gap for the recipients to bridge. Because it is Jesus who addresses them through the Gospel, it is easier for them to recognize themselves and their experiences in the experiences narrated in the Gospel, which experiences also rest upon direct encounter with Jesus.

If one reads the narrative this way, it is not surprising that the narrative presents Jesus as the role model, although one may have expected the disciples to be the role model for the *founding story* of a remembering community of followers. Nevertheless, those who achieve πίστις, the adequate perception of Jesus, and become members of the community experience the beginning of their way with Jesus in much the same way that Jesus himself got started. Like him, they are baptized and experience not only closeness to God or even being God's child and community, but also incomprehension, hostility, and the necessity for withdrawal. The coming βασιλεία as the *possible world* Jesus has proclaimed is the new reality they seek to realize in their lives. In this process, they take over Jesus's perspective, not the perspective of the disciples.

The community of commemoration might well recognize itself in the fears, miseries, and doubts of the disciples. Nevertheless, they are invited to outgrow them and follow Jesus more consistently. Chronologically, they are standing in the succession of the disciples and are invited to accept their inheritance. Thereby the members of the community are called to set off with the disciples but not to repeat their mistakes. The disciples serve as a model from which they can learn both how to do it and how not to do it, while the real role model is Jesus himself.

A particular way of life that indicates how the remembering community is constituted as a community of followers is also part of this new reality. The model character cannot be easily overlooked. The community as narrated in the Gospel is structured both according to family ties and beyond family. Among the disciples there are two pairs of brothers, but, besides these relationships, new family ties form quickly when people who do God's will and follow God's ways become brothers and sisters (3:35; 10:30). The immediate family is not excluded from this tendency. Toward the end of the Gospel, Mary is depicted not as a family member of Jesus but as one of the women already following him in Galilee. This does not necessarily mean that the "old" family ties are overcome but that they are regarded in the context of the new reality of the βασιλεία at hand.

The community thus constructs itself beyond the usual and familiar frame without disrupting it. Boundaries such as clean/unclean, Jewish/gentile, rich/poor, sick/healthy, or inside/outside are overcome in and by Jesus or are no longer relevant. This can be seen nicely as Jewish and gentile characters have the same experiences with Jesus but do not constitute one single community. Over and over again, Jesus turns toward people who, for a variety of reasons, find themselves excluded. He exercises commensality with sinners and tax collectors, touches the sick and the unclean, actively addresses gentiles, and even eats with them. Resistances, distinctions, purity requirements, and socioreligious boundaries of all sorts are overcome in and by Jesus. They are obviously not a part of the *possible world* of the βασιλεία.

The remembering community constitutes finally, if not first and foremost, a commensality or communion that has the potential to transcend socioreligious ties and include those who are actually outsiders. The "others" are not "the Jews" or "the gentiles," but those who do not follow on the way. The symbol for this is the βασιλεία understood as an eschatological and messianic concept expressing itself especially in commensality—the multiplication of the loaves becoming the counter image of Herod's banquet—and healings. The remembering community or the "Mark people" are directed toward Jesus and share his vision of the βασιλεία. Their agreement is to live in the βασιλεία and thus to realize the *possible world* Jesus has proclaimed. The remembering community thus understands itself to be following Jesus's path. Their memory of Jesus, his proclamation, and his deeds is the binding factor. It proves again that *collective memory* is less about the events themselves than about their significance for the remembering community.

Conclusions

For the students, the learning process of the course closes here. If I have done my job properly, they have not only understood how the *memory-theory-informed reading glasses* work but have also had some significant insights into the Gospel of Mark. They might want to put these new reading glasses to the test with other texts of Mark. In the final class when we share our learning experiences, they might even ask whether they have become "Mark people" themselves in the course of the learning process and whether the academic approach to the biblical text actually contributed something to their own faith. This is an additional fruit of the learning process, not a learning outcome that can be planned and assessed. Nevertheless, it is not completely unlikely to happen and is a very satisfying fringe benefit of the course.

On a more theoretical level, this reveals two things. On the one hand, the learning process can be controlled only to a certain point and depends rather on the student him- or herself, what he or she actually takes home from class. The learning process remains largely inaccessible.[24] This knowledge emphasizes the importance of learning outcomes and of designing a course according to the principles of *constructive alignment* in order to guarantee a certain measurable outcome of the course. But it makes a case for the theory that only *cognitive* and *metacognitive learning goals* can be directly accessed, while *affective learning goals*, as desirable as they might be, are a surplus.[25]

It almost goes without saying that *constructive alignment* is not bound to a particular discipline or lesson format. In other words, any course can be planned according to these principles. In this process the crucial point usually is a consistent *shift from teaching to learning* and thus a student-centred outlook on teaching. Initially this change of perspective seems to be quite difficult, but it is nevertheless necessary. If the course design is to be successful, the focus must lie on the learning steps that the individual student has to take in order to reach the learning goals set for the course.[26] Planning the course thus involves a clear conception of the different actions the student will take. The teacher is less important; or, to make a bold statement, the key to successful and satisfactory learning is not what the teacher does in class, but what the student does. In many cases this implies that the teacher is less active and in charge than usual or than would feel normal. The challenge for most lecturers is to have faith in their students and trust that they will learn even without constant surveillance. My experience in this particular area is that students are generally

---

24. Elke Wild and Klaus-Peter Wild, "Jeder lernt auf seine Weise…. Individuelle Lernstrategien und Hochschullehre," in Berendt et al., *Neues Handbuch Hochschullehre*, Griffmarke A 2.1.

25. Bloom, *Taxonomy of Educational Objectives*; Krathwohl, Bloom, and Masia, *Taxonomy of Educational Objectives*.

26. Birgit Szczyrba and Matthias Wiemer, "Lehrinnovation durch doppelten Perspektivenwechsel: Fachkulturell tradierte Lehrpraktiken und Hochschuldidaktik im Kontakt," in *Fachbezogene und fächerübergreifende Hochschuldidaktik*, ed. Isa Jahnke and Johannes Wildt (Bielefeld: Bertelsmann, 2011), 101–10; Schulte, "Veranstaltungsplanung," Griffmarke B 1.

eager to learn once their intrinsic motivation has been roused. Thus I usually spend more time crafting an introduction to a course that will activate the students' intrinsic motivation than on putting together the facts they should take home from the first class.

Apart from the didactical insight, what else can be learned from this course for the study of the New Testament? A first insight refers to the hermeneutic I have developed during my research and have only briefly introduced here. According to the hermeneutical insights and the first attempts to bring them to the classroom, I would make the case that the whole New Testament can be read as *artifacts of collective memory* or as *snapshots of early Christian identity construction*.[27] This approach implies, however, another change of perspective: it means to ask different questions, to apply different methods, and to read synthetically instead of atomically, that is, to focus on whole books instead of individual pericopes. This last suggestion to read unabridged books instead of unconnected components seems to be only a minor alteration, but it can have a huge impact nevertheless. Reading only particular pericopes bereaves the text of important layers of meaning that become visible only when the book is read as a whole. Recognizing the βασιλεία as the *possible world* of Jesus or recognizing the messianic secret and the disciples' lack of comprehension as parts of the narrator's world are two examples of such an approach.

Moreover, reading New Testament texts as testimonies of particular moments of early Christian identity construction is not necessarily limited to the body of narrative texts. It is worth a try examining the epistolary literature—the authentic Pauline letters as well as the disputed and the Catholic Epistles—under the aspect of identity construction. One does not have to start with Romans; the letters to Philemon and Titus or the letters of James and Jude can be real eye-openers once one gets beyond questions of ecclesiastical structures, the quests for opponents, or the question of authenticity.

Reading New Testament letters as *artifacts of collective memory* and thus as telling the story of identity construction at a particular point in history, of course, needs slightly modified sets of questions. The first question set works well for narrative texts but does not capture all the aspects of a letter. It is nevertheless possible to ask which *story* a letter tells and

---

27. Sandra Hübenthal, "Social and Cultural Memory in Biblical Exegesis," in *Cultural Memory in Biblical Exegesis*, ed. Pernille Carstens et al. (Piscataway, NJ: Gorgias, 2012), 175–99.

how this story changes when the person claiming to be the sender is actually someone else, the alleged addressees are no longer existent, and the situation referred to is equally constructed. Or as I sometimes ask my students concerning the letter to the Colossians: why would someone who is no longer alive send a letter to a community that no longer exists in order to deal with problems that apply to different addressees? Approaching disputed letters from this perspective provides unexpected and intriguing insights. Read this way, by using the (real or alleged) Colossian correspondence, the unknown author exemplarily depicts one of the issues of new converts who have not yet fully made themselves at home in their novel Christian identity and run the risk of reverting to their old habits since the gospel has not yet sustainably taken root in their life and daily practice.[28]

It is finally evident that a narrative approach by itself will not be sufficient to understand a biblical book—just as a purely historical-critical approach will not grasp a text's full meaning. A model that takes seriously the history and growth requires both synchronic and diachronic observations. To phrase it differently: narratology without a model of textual origin (*Textentstehung*) will soon end up in a similar cul-de-sac as a purely diachronic approach. Social memory theory can provide this missing link and introduce a general model of textual origin without forcing the individual text into a particular social context, pattern, or literary genre. The theory is broad enough to cover many different textual expressions yet still precise enough to handle the interpretation of a particular text. Reading *Mark as Collective Memory* proved to be a good test case for this approach and will—both in scholarly debates and in lecture rooms—prepare the way for further exegetical, theological, and personal insights.

---

28. Sandra Hübenthal, "Erfahrung, die sich lesbar macht. Kol und 2 Thess als fiktionale Texte," in *Wie Geschichten Geschichte schreiben: Frühchristliche Literatur zwischen Faktualität und Fiktionalität*, ed. Susanne Luther et al., WUNT 2/395 (Tübingen: Mohr Siebeck, 2015), 295–336; Hübenthal, "Pseudepigraphie als Strategie in frühchristlichen Identitätsdiskursen? Überlegungen am Beispiel des Kolosserbriefs," SNTSU.A 36 (2011): 63–94.

Course Design for Mark as Collective Memory

A. Learning Outcome

What should students know, understand, and/or be able to demonstrate after completing the learning process?

- Students will be able to explain what it means to read the Gospel of Mark as collective memory and demonstrate this hermeneutical approach by exemplary readings.

B. Assessment

What will students do to demonstrate that they have reached the learning goal of the course?

- Students will describe what it means to read the Gospel of Mark as collective memory and pick two or three examples to illustrate this hermeneutical approach.

C. Learning Steps

What learning steps do the students have to take to reach the learning goal?

- Grasping different kinds of hermeneutical lenses: *What is written, and how do you read?* There is no such thing as objectivity—we always read a text with certain reading glasses (classes 1–3).

- Getting to know a lens: *How do the memory-theory-informed reading glasses work?* Introduction of social memory theory and social memory–informed reading model for the Gospel of Mark (classes 4–5).

- Using the reading glasses: *How does wearing them alter my readings of Mark?* Exemplary readings of Mark as Collective Memory (classes 6–14).

D. Question Sets

Set 1: Questions for narrative texts (both factual and fictional)

- What is being told?

- What is not being told?

- How is the narration organized?

- What type of a narration is it?

- Which pragmatics or message does the text have?

Set 2: Additional Questions for the Gospel of Mark

- Which images of Jesus are introduced in the text, and how are they evaluated?

- How does the βασιλεία τοῦ θεοῦ that Jesus proclaims to be at hand take shape, and what sort of conduct is proper in this context?

- Which crises are narrated, and which strategies are introduced to deal with them?

- Which experiences and events narrated in the text match with your own experiences?

Part 2
Test Cases: Orality and Performance in Researching and Teaching Mark

4
Teaching Mark as Performance Literature: Early Literate and Postliterate Pedagogies

Thomas E. Boomershine

A Reassessment of Pedagogical Methods

The pedagogical methods for teaching biblical literature have been shaped by two underlying factors: the dominant communication culture of each successive period and the conception of the original character of the Bible. In effect, biblical professors have reconceived and taught the Bible in ways that are congruent with the dominant communication culture of their period in history and with their conception of the Bible in its original historical context.

A correlation between the changes in the dominant communication culture in the history of Western civilization and changes in the practice of biblical interpretation and pedagogy can be identified.[1] In oral culture, the stories of Israel and of Jesus were interpreted by being retold and performed by heart. The stories were taught to new generations by oral transmission and memorized recital. In the manuscript culture of the medieval periods, the Bible was taught as a book that was read aloud

---

1. The most comprehensive overview of the relationship between communication technology and cultural and psychological formation is developed in the works of Walter Ong; see, for example, *The Presence of the Word* (New Haven: Yale University Press, 1967); and *Interfaces of the Word: Studies in the Evolution of Consciousness and Culture* (Ithaca, NY: Cornell University Press, 1977). Werner Kelber's essay on Ong paints a highly detailed picture of the implications of Ong's work for biblical scholarship: "The Work of Walter J. Ong and Biblical Scholarship," in *Imprints, Voiceprints, and Footprints of Memory: Collected Essays of Werner H. Kelber*, RBS 74 (Atlanta: Society of Biblical Literature, 2013), 441–64.

from a manuscript. The oral recital of the text served as a source for the exegesis of the four levels of meaning: literal, allegorical, moral, and anagogical. Memorization remained a central pedagogical practice because of the relative unavailability of manuscripts. In early print culture, the availability of printed copies of the Bible made it possible for students to engage in detailed study of the Hebrew and Greek texts (in Protestant universities) and the Latin Vulgate (in Catholic universities and seminaries) as well as vernacular translations. Both oral recital and memorization continued to play a significant but gradually declining role in the teaching of biblical literature.

In the document culture of the Enlightenment, the dominant pedagogy of the Bible has been the silent study of the texts in the original languages and in translation along with a series of reference works such as dictionaries, concordances, and commentaries. Lectures have traditionally been written out beforehand and then read aloud. The primary assignments for students have been written examinations and the writing of papers that are both written and read in silence. With the ready availability of texts, memorization has largely disappeared from the pedagogical landscape. Thus, biblical teaching has changed when new communication cultures have emerged, often in association with new communication technologies.

Another factor in the shaping of contemporary pedagogical approaches to the teaching of biblical literature in general and Mark in particular is the picture of the original communication culture of the biblical world. Historical-critical study of the Bible has assumed that ancient communication culture was analogous to the text-based communication culture of the eighteenth-nineteenth centuries. The biblical tradition has been conceived and studied as texts that were read by readers, usually alone and in silence. Signs of this assumption are the ubiquitous references in commentaries to "the reader" and to "the text."

The hermeneutical systems of what Hans Frei has called "meaning as reference" were formed in this period and were the foundation for "historical criticism."[2] The dominant methods for biblical pedagogy made the Bible credible and meaningful in the culture of the Enlightenment, which

---

2. Hans Frei's description of the emergence of "meaning as reference" as the dominant biblical hermeneutic of the eighteenth and early nineteenth centuries is also a helpful account of the communication culture in which modern historical criticism and its characteristic pedagogy was formed. See Hans Frei, *The Eclipse of Biblical Nar-*

was in turn the primary cultural context of the modern period. At the heart of this system was the scientific study of biblical documents in order to determine their meaningfulness as sources of reliable historical data ("ostensive reference") and theological doctrine ("ideal reference").

The teaching of Mark and of the Bible in contemporary education has utilized a text-based pedagogy that is congruent with the presupposed character of Mark's original historical context and with the communication culture of the Enlightenment. This conception and teaching of Mark has worked well in the text-based pedagogy of contemporary educational institutions with their libraries, papers, and degrees in the mastery of literary research and communication. Lectures have focused on the text of Mark and on the various documentary processes for exploring the meaning of the text in its original historical context such as source, form, and redaction criticism. Students are taught how to analyze the text by reading it objectively with their eyes and with constant critical awareness of the difference between contemporary and ancient culture. Student projects are papers researched and written in silence and read in silence by the professors.

The need to reexamine pedagogical approaches is implicit in the recognition that these two underlying factors in the shaping of biblical pedagogy have changed. First, recent historical investigation of ancient communication culture and of Mark within that culture has led to different conclusions about that culture and Mark within it.[3] Ancient communication culture at the time of the composition of the Gospel of Mark was an early literate culture in which literacy had great cultural power but in which the great majority of people were unable to read. Current estimates are that literacy in the first century ranged from a maximum of 15 percent

---

rative: A Study in Eighteenth and Nineteenth Century Hermeneutics (New Haven: Yale University Press, 1974), 86–104.

3. For documentation of the media culture of the biblical world, see Paul Achtemeier, "*Omni Verbum Sonat*: The New Testament and the Environment of Late Western Antiquity," *JBL* 109 (1990): 3–27; Pieter J. J. Botha, *Orality and Literacy in Early Christianity*, PBC 5 (Eugene, OR: Cascade, 2012); David M. Carr, *Writing on the Tablet of the Heart: Origins of Scripture and Literature* (New York: Oxford University Press, 2005); Moses Hadas, *Ancilla to Classical Reading* (New York: Columbia University Press, 1954); William Harris, *Ancient Literacy* (Cambridge: Harvard University Press, 1989); Ong, *Presence of the Word*; Ong, *Orality and Literacy: The Technologizing of the Word* (London: Methuen, 1982); Whitney Shiner, *Proclaiming the Gospel: First-Century Performance of Mark* (Harrisburg, PA: Trinity Press International, 2003).

in urban communities to as little as 2–3 percent in rural areas. Documents were copied by hand, were relatively expensive, and were owned primarily by communities and wealthy individuals. There was no mass distribution of documents, minimal evidence of private reading, and even less of silent reading.[4] Publication of documents was by performance for audiences. The grammatical literature of Greek rhetoricians and grammarians shows that ancient literature was composed as sounds with careful attention to cola and periods as breath units of sound.[5] When Mark is heard in the context of this communication culture, it is a skillful composition of sound structured for performance to audiences.

An additional characteristic of ancient communication culture was the centrality of memory. A trained memory was the goal of ancient education. A daily activity for children in Jewish and Greco-Roman schools was the memorization of a text, often a part of the Scriptures in Jewish schools and of rhetorical speeches in Greco-Roman schools. Written compositions were structured to facilitate memory, and performances of written compositions were often done from memory. Indeed, since ancient manuscripts were a string of undifferentiated letters, it was necessary virtually to memorize a composition in order to perform it, even with a manuscript in hand. Furthermore, mnemonic structures can be identified throughout Mark's composition.[6]

This reassessment of the character of Mark raises the question of appropriate contemporary pedagogy. In as far as historical-critical methods of scholarly study and pedagogy are based on the assumption that the Bible was a library of texts read by individual readers, those methods are an historical anachronism, a reading back into the ancient world of a later communication culture and its systems of interpretation. The first dimension of pedagogical reassessment is, therefore, the development of teaching methods that will give students an experience of Mark in its original context as an epic story that was performed for audiences.[7]

---

4. An exposition of exceptions to the general practice of reading aloud in antiquity is noted in Michael Slusser, "Reading Silently in Antiquity," *JBL* 111 (1992): 499.

5. Bernard Brandon Scott and Margaret Ellen Lee, *Sound Mapping the New Testament* (Salem, OR: Polebridge, 2009).

6. For a detailed exegesis of the mnemonic structures of Mark's composition, see Thomas E. Boomershine, *The Messiah of Peace: A Performance-Criticism Commentary on Mark's Passion-Resurrection Narrative*, BPC 12 (Eugene, OR: Cascade, 2015).

7. For an excellent description of a highly successful university course with this

Furthermore, twenty-first-century students of the performance literature of the Bible live in a postliterate world in which digital communication technology rather than mass printing is the dominant means of mass communication. In this culture, the pedagogical methods of the eighteenth-twentieth centuries are increasingly archaic and, frankly, boring. The underlying cultural hermeneutic of digital culture is the dynamic engagement with vivid experience rather than concepts. In the context of contemporary media culture, a vital experience of Mark as a performance event is more interesting than an exposition of the theological doctrine implicit in the document. Therefore, a combination of the pedagogical approaches of early literate culture and the pedagogies of postliterate, digital culture open new possibilities for the teaching of Mark and of biblical literature.

The purpose here is to outline pedagogical methods that have been effective in teaching Mark as performance literature in the context of digital culture. I have explored these approaches to teaching the Bible for the forty-plus years of my teaching career. While I will outline a wide range of possible approaches, the hope here is to generate thinking about some initial steps that could be tried in your teaching. Future discussion about educational theory and the relationship between these methods and traditional pedagogy will be additional steps in this exploration. A first step is to outline the new possibilities that have emerged from teaching Mark as a story told by storytellers.

Teaching Mark as Performance Literature

The major shift involved in the teaching of Mark as performance literature is to reorient the experience of Mark from silent reading of the text to embodied performance. When seen from a pedagogical perspective, our present practices would be analogous to a professor of piano who teaches students to study the manuscripts of the piano compositions of Bach, Beethoven, and Brahms and never plays the music or teaches the students to perform it. At every stage of the course work, experience of Mark as sound and as stories told to audiences is foundational. The possibilities range from weekly assignments and classroom experience to individual

---

structure, see Philip Ruge-Jones, "The Word Heard: How Hearing a Text Differs from Reading One," in *The Bible in Ancient and Modern Media: Story and Performance*, ed. Holly E. Hearon and Philip Ruge-Jones, BPC 1 (Eugene, OR: Cascade, 2009), 101–13.

and communal research projects. The more the pedagogical approaches of the course pursue a multifaceted exploration of Mark as stories told by heart to audiences, the better will be the overall course experience. The presupposition of teaching Mark in this manner is that students will learn more about the character and meaning of Mark by being actively engaged in learning and telling the composition.

An Introductory Performance of Mark by the Professor

Early in the course of study, preferably no later than the second class following the introduction to the course, a performance of some major section of Mark by the professor is the best introduction to the story.[8] Telling it live for the students is better than any recording, because the interaction between the storyteller and the audience is more immediate. Until students have experienced the Gospel as a story, the talk about it as a performed story remains abstract. Once they have experienced it, they have a much clearer idea about the subject of the course.

A further positive dimension of the experience is that the students have a model for their own work on the story and the development of their skills as tellers of Mark's story. The professorial model encourages students to arrive inductively at their own interpretations on the basis of their study of the manuscripts and independent exploration of how they might tell the stories. Many students do not know how to learn and tell a biblical story, because they have had no previous experience with the performance of literature. Generally the students who have been involved in drama earlier in their educational careers have the confidence and abilities to develop as storytellers more easily. But storytelling is significantly different than acting and requires different approaches to engagement with an audience. The most important difference is that storytellers have to be themselves rather than playing someone else.

Of course, the challenge for the teachers of Mark is that most have had no training or experience in performing Mark themselves, because doctoral programs have not included performance in their curricula. There

---

8. A full performance of Mark by Phil Ruge-Jones can be ordered at *Select Learning*, http://www.selectlearning.org/. For online resources, see "Biblical Performances and Performers," *Biblical Performance Criticism*, directed by Rhoads, Lutheran School of Theology at Chicago, http://www.biblicalperformancecriticism.org/index.php/performers-mainmenu-46.

are now resources of videotapes and organizations such as the Network of Biblical Storytellers in which there is the possibility of experiencing high quality performances of Mark.[9] But the most energizing step for the students is to experience the stories told "live" by their professor.

A Storytelling Workshop: Mark 10:46–52 as a Case Study

The foundational introduction enabling the students to begin performing Mark is a storytelling workshop in which each student is enabled to learn and tell a story. For the purposes of this essay, I will outline the basic stages of a storytelling workshop using the story of Bartimaeus as a case study.[10]

The essential preparations for the teaching of the Bartimaeus story are: (1) to learn the story by heart in the breath units of the story so that the instructor can both tell the story and introduce it, colon by colon, for the students; (2) to prepare a sound map of the story in cola, periods, and episodes;[11] (3) to identify the key features of the performance of the story; and (4) to formulate a connection question to lead the students in the exploration of their personal connections with the story.

The sound map of the story that follows is a translation for performance rather than for silent reading. The story is arranged in the breath units of cola and periods that were the basic forms of composition for first-century Greek composers of rhetoric and oral composition. It is also arranged in episodes in order to make visible the larger units of the story and the parallelisms that are a dimension of the mnemonic structures built

---

9. See n. 8 for resources.

10. For a more extensive description of a storytelling workshop, see Thomas E. Boomershine, *Story Journey: An Introduction to the Gospel as Storytelling* (Nashville: Abingdon, 1988), 23–59.

11. For the most comprehensive introduction to the composition practices of ancient Greek composers and sound maps of a range of New Testament works, see Scott and Lee, *Sound Mapping the New Testament*. For a fully integrated study of Mark's passion and resurrection narratives with sound maps, a performance criticism exegesis of each story, and video recordings in both English and Greek, see Boomershine, *The Messiah of Peace: A Performance-Criticism Commentary on Mark's Passion-Resurrection Narrative*, http://www.messiahofpeace.com. For sound maps of many of Mark's stories (also Matthew, Luke, and John), see Tom Boomershine, *GoTell Communications*, 2016, http://www.gotell.org, and choose "by stories" on the menu bar. The sound maps are titled "Stories in Episodes," under the entry for individual entries for each Gospel.

into the story ("the way" at the end of the first and last episode; the ABAC parallelism in episodes 2 and 3).

Sound Map (Mark 10:46–52)

And they came to Jericho.
And as he was leaving Jericho with his disciples and a large crowd,
    Bartimaeus, son of Timaeus, a blind beggar, was sitting by the way.

When he heard that it was Jesus of Nazareth, he began to cry out and to say,
    "Jesus, Son of David, have mercy on me!"
And many rebuked him to be quiet.

But he cried out even more loudly, "Son of David, have mercy on me!"
And Jesus stood still and said, "Call him."

And they called the blind man, saying to him, "Take heart;
    get up, he is calling you."
So throwing off his cloak and leaping up, he came to Jesus.

And answering him, Jesus said, "What do you want me to do for you?"
And the blind man said to him, "My teacher, I want to see again."

And Jesus said to him, "Go; your faith has made you well."
And immediately he regained his sight and followed him on the way.

Learning the Story

The first step in learning the performance of a Markan story is to master the words of the story. Good stories for an initial workshop are: the healing of the paralytic, the stilling of the storm, and Bartimaeus. My experience is that the best pedagogical approach is to dive in with no theory or introduction by utilizing the methodology of the teachers of antiquity: repeat after me. The process is simply to tell the story phrase by phrase with gestures and have the students say it back with energy and gestures. I have sometimes found it helpful for a class to have an outline of the episodes of the story available, preferably on a screen. The identification of the structure of the story can also be done on a flip chart or blackboard as the second step in learning the story. The structure of the Bartimaeus story is:

Setting: Jericho and Bartimaeus, son of Timaeus
First cry: rebuke
Second cry: call him
Calling and coming to Jesus
Jesus's question (what do you want?) and Bartimaeus's answer (I want to see)
Bartimaeus receives sight and follows

An initial process is for the students to say the story back to the teacher, then the teacher tell it after a brief description of the story's structure, the students say it back again, and finally they tell it to each other in groups of two. Sometimes it is helpful to give the students a copy of the story arranged as a sound map in case neither one of them is able to remember what comes next. But it is also possible for them to rely on their memories and to see how much they can remember together, with the distribution of the sound map to follow.[12] After sufficient time for the students to tell the story to their partners, a brief discussion about the process of learning the story is helpful, including an exposition of the performance cues in the sound map. Probably most of them have never learned and told a biblical story before. To probe the experience of learning and telling the story at this initial stage encourages their exploration of a native ability they did not know they had.

A next step in learning the story is to outline the structure of human memory. Memory training has been almost wholly eliminated from modern education. An introduction to the structures of human memory is helpful, especially for those who are convinced they cannot memorize. As Paul Nowak states in his online course on memory: "There is no such thing as a bad memory. There are only trained and untrained memories."[13] A brief outline of the structures of the brain that enable us to remember

---

12. This is the shortest and most basic process for story learning. For a range of story-learning processes, see Amelia Cooper Boomershine, "Biblical Storytelling in Christian Ed," *GoTell Communications*, 2016, http://gotell.org/learn/education/.

13. Paul Nowak, "Improving Your Memory," *Lynda.com*, http://www.lynda.com/Business-Skills-tutorials/Improving-Your-Memory/172858-2.html.

and that are activated by the mnemonic structures built into biblical stories is empowering for students.[14]

There are three structures of the brain that facilitate memory: sensory registers, short-term memory, and long-term memory. The sensory registers of the brain record and sort the five sense data—sound, sight, smell, taste, touch—that are constantly being processed in our brains. You can notice the sensory data of these five senses at any moment by simply focusing your attention on each. The process of attention sorts the data from the sensory registers and determines what is sent to short-term memory. Attention is sometimes conscious and intentional and sometimes unconscious and involuntary, as in a sudden trauma. The more data that one can identify from the sensory registers the better; that is, a combination of visual, sound, and movement data is more effectively remembered than data from only one sense, such as sound. The data that receives attention is moved from the sensory registers to short-term memory.

The second stage of human memory is short-term memory, which is best conceived as a workbench. The workbench of short memory can hold up to seven items easily and up to ten items as the outer limit; thus a local phone number in the United States is seven numbers and with an area code is ten. After ten, items simply fall off the workbench of short-term memory. A basic technique of memory processing is chunking in which several items are linked together and are thought of as one item. For example, a phone number can readily be thought of as the three numbers of the area code (visualized in parentheses), the first three numbers (separated by a dash), and the final four numbers—thus three chunks rather than ten single digits. The chunking of items of various sizes such as a set of notes in music, phrases and episodes in stories, and moves in a dance are helpful in facilitating easier and quicker learning of stories since chucking makes it possible to hold more items on the workbench of short-term memory.

---

14. For a summary lecture on the structure of human memory explicating this outline in greater detail, see Tom Boomershine, "Memory and Story," *GoTell Communications*, 2016, http://gotell.org/learn/workshops/. Click on the diagonal arrows at the right side of the directions at the bottom for full screen. Also see Boomershine, *Story Journey*, 28–31, 44–47, 53–59. For full expositions of the findings of psychological research on human memory, see Roberta Klatzky, *Human Memory: Structures and Processes* (San Francisco: Freeman, 1980); also Peter C. Brown, Henry L. Roediger III, and Mark A. McDaniel, *Make It Stick: The Science of Successful Learning* (Cambridge: Harvard University Press, 2014).

Repetition holds the items on the workbench of short-term memory and provides more opportunities for the data to be stored in long-term memory.

The third stage of memory is storing the items from short-term memory in the ordered shelves of long-term memory where they can be retrieved into consciousness. The two primary retrieval systems from the shelves of long-term memory are "episodic" storage and "syntactical or conceptual" storage. "Episodic" retrieval recalls items in the sequences of events or episodes such as the events of life from birth to now or the episodes of a story. "Syntactical" retrieval recalls items according to ideas or concepts: for example, "darkness," "soteriology," "infinity," and "blindness." There are no limits to the storage capacity of long-term memory. Vast amounts of data are stored in our long-term memories. We recognize this when a fragrance, a sight, a sound, or a feeling suddenly triggers a flood of memories that we did not even know were present in our memories. The issue for storytelling is to identify consciously the retrieval link to the data stored in long-term memory. When students understand the way their memory works, they are able to learn stories more easily and become more consciously aware of a process that they use constantly. Nevertheless, the absence of memory training is a major lacuna in contemporary education.

After outlining the structure of memory, it is often helpful to identify the mnemonic structures of cola/periods, episodes, verbal threads/sonic echoes ("have mercy"), gestures (eyes closed/open), and reversals of expectation built into the story they have just learned. The students can then tell the story to each other again using the analysis as a resource for remembering and telling the story.

The goal of this first stage of the workshop is that each student will be able to get through the story from beginning to end without omitting or adding anything of major importance. That is, the goal is significant interpretive resemblance between the story transmitted to us in a competent translation and the story we actually tell. At this stage in the work on a story, a workable guideline for the question that will often arise about "word-for-word accuracy" is "95 percent content accuracy and 75 percent verbal accuracy."

A related incentive for both students and faculty is that forming a trained memory is an asset that has benefit in many areas. Given that memory training is absent from most educational programs, it is a distinctive potential dimension of biblical study in a performance mode.

Listening to the Story

A second stage in a storytelling workshop is listening to the story in its original historical context. This segment of a storytelling workshop can vary in length depending on the goals of the session. This is the context in which all of the data from an exegesis of a biblical composition can be summarized. All of the resources of historical-critical study of Mark can be utilized in this stage of a workshop: word study, Jewish and Greco-Roman background, the history and politics of the first century, archaeological discoveries, tradition history, and so on. This can also include an introduction to the performance traditions of the ancient world as outlined in several recent books such as Moses Hadas's *Ancilla to Classical Reading*, Whitney Shiner's *Proclaiming the Gospel*, and David Rhoads's articles on performance criticism.[15]

A consistent theme of this literature is that the practices of contemporary performance of biblical literature are far less emotionally expressive, dramatic, and physically active than ancient performances. The monotone style of reading Scripture in worship is a pervasive performance tradition that has shaped what many now advocate as appropriate performance. In fact, the compositions of the Bible are more widely performed than any other literature. But there is great distance between the styles of ancient and modern biblical performance. Ancient performance was highly expressive; modern performance is often characterized by little or no variation in tempo, volume, or emotion. For this reason, an important dimension of a performance criticism exegesis is to identify the variations in tempo, volume, and pauses that are implicit in the story; for example, long periods are fast while short periods are slow; loud places are really loud and soft

---

15. See Shiner, *Proclaiming the Gospel*; also see David Rhoads, "Performance Criticism: An Emerging Methodology in Second Testament Studies," *BTB* 36 (2006): 118–33, 164–83. See Hadas, *Ancilla to Classical Reading*, 50–77, for a series of citations from ancient literature showing that performance of written works was the primary mode of publication. Even historical works were published by oral recitation, as is evident in Lucian's opening of his book, *Herodotus*, in which he tells the story of Herodotus taking the opportunity of the Olympic Games to read his work: "He seized the moment when the gathering was at its fullest, and every city had sent the flower of its citizens; then he appeared in the temple hall, bent not on sightseeing but on bidding for an Olympic victory of his own; he recited his Histories and bewitched his hearers" (Hadas, *Ancilla to Classical Reading*, 60).

places are really soft; pauses are intentionally marked, but generally a fast pace with limited pauses is needed for a long story such as Mark.

An explication of some of the performance features of the Bartimaeus story may be helpful. The first period of the story ("And they came to Jericho") is one short colon and is therefore slow. This creates emphasis on "Jericho" and evokes memories of the legendary Israelite victory. The repetition of Jericho in the two periods of this first episode ("he came to Jericho/leaving Jericho") makes it easy to remember. The shame associated with Bartimaeus's status as a blind beggar establishes the setting for the whole story. The unusual repetition and explanation of his name after its initial introduction, literally translated "the son of honor," heightens the poignant irony of his position.

The two cries of Bartimaeus are loud and louder. And Mark explicitly directs the volume level of the second cry. The combination of the emphasis on his name and his crying out for Jesus's help creates a highly sympathetic characterization of Bartimaeus. The contrast between the crowd's first rebuke and both Jesus's command to call him and the crowd's encouragement is another mnemonic link. Bartimaeus's first cry is introduced by an "inside view" of Bartimaeus's hearing that it was Jesus of Nazareth who was passing by.

The two episodes of the conversation between Jesus and Bartimaeus are slow and intensely intimate. The wonder of Bartimaeus's healing is embodied in the gesture of eyes closed when he asks to see again (with its implication that he once could see) and eyes opened when he receives his sight. The final period is an expression of joy followed by his immediately becoming a follower of Jesus "on the way."

The conclusion of this stage of the workshop is for the students to tell the story again. This time, however, the goal is that they will seek to tell the story in a manner that is congruent with the way it would have been told in its original historical context. Here the students can be encouraged to be as "big" as possible in their way of telling the story. This segment of the workshop can also be an introduction to the exegetical work of the course including the "performance criticism" papers the students will write.

Connecting with the Story

A third stage of a storytelling workshop is to explore the connections between the experiences of each person and the biblical story. The identification and telling of these stories will help each storyteller to discover the distinctive ways in which she or he would tell the story. The telling of personal stories also enables all students to tell the stories they know best.

The primary role of the professor in this stage of a workshop is to model personal storytelling and then to encourage the students to tell their own stories. The hermeneutical theory underlying this process of connecting the stories from Mark and personal stories is that Mark's stories address the deep structures of human experience. The identification of these deep structures is relatively easy. In the three stories I have suggested for an initial workshop, the deep structure of the story of the paralytic is the experience of being immobilized and reduced to a position of shame and dependence that is often instinctively felt to be the consequence of having done something wrong. The calming of the storm is about the experience of being overwhelmed with terror and fear at the prospect of being destroyed by the powers of chaos. The story of Bartimaeus connects with the experience of blindness and begging for help and then answering the question, "What do you want me to do for you?"

I have found that the best context for the exploration of personal connections with the story is a one-on-one conversation. I ask the students to find a partner and a place in the room that will be comfortable for an extended conversation. The stated covenant of this conversation between two persons is complete confidentiality. I will often ask at the end of this segment of a workshop whether there is anything that someone would like to share with the group. And often there are discoveries that people want to share. But there is neither the requirement nor even the expectation that this will be the case.

The range of questions that are the focus for personal sharing can be multiple. In the Bartimaeus story, possible questions are: When have you felt like a beggar sitting in the dust crying out for help? When have you been told to shut up and deal with your own problems? If Jesus were to ask you today, "What do you want me to do for you?," how would you respond?

In the workshop process, students often find it initially difficult or overwhelming to identify these dimensions of their own experience. I have found that sharing my own experience of these dynamics helps them to identify what the story is addressing. My stories of being hit by a car, being overcome with fear of paralysis and death, and asking for help have enabled students to identify their own stories and given them permission to be vulnerable in this way. I initially invite students to share with only one other person.

There are two possible dimensions of connecting with the story. The first is simply to identify and tell a partner the story of your experience:

for example, "When have you felt paralyzed and dependent on others?" "When have you experienced being afraid?" "When have you felt blind and unable to see any way forward?" or "What would be your answer now if Jesus asked you, 'What do you want me to do for you?'" The other possible dimension is to tell and hear the biblical story as an immediate response to the story of a felt need. Thus a partner might say, "Right now I feel paralyzed in relation to the paper I need to write" or "I feel ashamed about..." or "If Jesus asked me, 'What do you want me to do for you?' I would say, 'I want....'" The partner can then tell Mark's story, no counsel or advice, just the story. And the partner can then share what, if anything, the story meant as it was told. It is often the case that the story has more impact than the student expected.

When the group as a whole comes back together, it is appropriate to invite them to share their experience with the whole group: "Is there anything that someone would like to share with the group that you discovered as you listened or told the story?" Students are generally glad to share their experiences in telling these stories.

The purpose of this storytelling process is to make it possible for persons to explore the personal connections that these ancient stories invite. It has been surprisingly meaningful to most people who have done this, although this is not always the case. There have been instances in which persons have not discovered any significant connection, but that is the exception rather than the norm. And in my experience there have always been persons who have found that the stories connected deeply with their lives and enabled them to see their present life situation from a new perspective. The minimal result of this process is that students can better understand the transformative impact of these stories in their original historical context. The process may also help students to appropriate the stories as elements of their own existential belief system.

Telling the Story

The conclusion of the workshop is for the professor to gather the experience of the group in a concluding recital of the story that is informed by the accents, emphases, and experience of the group. Rather than talking about the story and its meaning as a source of referential information about history or theology, the telling of the story itself focuses the attention of the group on the meaning of the story as a story. It is also possible for a student to do this final retelling of the story. But my experience has been that on occasion a volunteer does not do it well because of her or his limited experience. For this purpose and at this moment in a workshop, the professor is best.

The storytelling workshop experience is highly generative and its value is not limited to the initial stages of introduction to storytelling processes. It can also be adapted to the needs of the curriculum at later stages in the course experience. I have often made a storytelling workshop a recurring element in classroom work throughout a term, leading up to a final sharing in the group of the stories they remember, both biblical and personal. As a term progresses, there are numerous variations in the use of performance that can be introduced, for example, trying out different interpretations of a story, exploring different attitudes in telling episodes of a story, or developing varied accents and characterizations of the characters of the story.[16]

The better the performance-criticism exegesis of a story, the better the performance will be. Furthermore, performing a story is an excellent test of the viability of a particular exegesis or interpretation of the story. There is a reciprocal and mutually revealing relationship between exegesis and performance that generates energy and, sometimes, the experience of a kind of revelation about the story, about oneself, and about God.

This process is both appropriate and generative at all levels of educational endeavor. The introduction of oral storytelling processes into the experience of students increases their sympathetic understanding of the compositions in their original context and their perception of the revelatory impact of telling and hearing the stories in the contexts of their life experiences.

Regular Performance of Markan Stories in Translation and in Greek

During every class, both the students and the professor have the opportunity to tell the stories from Mark that are either the subject or the background of the class session. It is possible to make this a required element of every class session. The students can tell the story of the day to each

---

16. Richard Swanson has initiated an innovative educational project based on a range of performances of biblical stories in *Provoking the Gospel Project*, http://www.provokingthegospel.com. The overall project has included an oratorio, highly developed student performances, and courses/seminars in which student "players" are encouraged to experiment with different dramatic interpretations of biblical stories. A basic pedagogical approach is to test different interpretations by acting them out in dramatic space.

other in pairs and then a student can be called on at random to recite the story to the whole group. People can sign up to be the storyteller of the day beforehand and the schedule distributed to the group. The possibility of random selection is a good motivation for the students to learn the stories on a weekly basis before class. It is also an opportunity for each student to have the experience of performing a story for the whole class in preparation for the concluding communal performance of Mark.

For a graduate school course in which everyone has studied Greek, there is surprising value in learning and telling the stories in Greek as well as in translation. The Greek tells well and is in fact better than any translation for those who understand some Greek.[17] Even those who have learned Greek will often be able to understand only some words in the story. But if they have learned the story in translation before doing it in Greek, they will be able to discern most of the story from the combination of words, gestures, and overall dynamics. Telling the story in Greek is an excellent opportunity for students who are studying Greek to utilize their new knowledge of the language.

This is also an opportunity for the professor to give the students a firsthand experience of the story in its original language. If the students know the story in translation, they will be surprised at how much they can understand from an expressive and well-gestured telling of the story in Greek. It is also an advertisement for studying Greek that recruits more students for the Greek classes in the curriculum. My suggestion is that the story be told regularly in Greek as an element of the class session. This is a significant additional preparation for the professor and may not always be possible. But it has great pedagogical value as the students become more familiar with the sounds of Mark in its original language.

Performance-Criticism Exegesis Papers

A foundational pedagogy for teaching Mark as performance literature is lectures and required papers on performance-criticism exegesis. I have found this to be the most difficult change in reorienting the teaching of Mark to the original character of Mark as stories composed for performance to audiences. The exegetical methods that have been the basis of

---

17. Performances of Mark's passion and resurrection narrative in English and in Greek are available at Boomershine, *Messiah of Peace*.

academic biblical pedagogy need major reformation because of the degree to which traditional exegesis is tied to the study of Mark as a text. For the purpose of this paper, I will outline the distinctive elements of a performance-criticism exegesis.[18] And I would also acknowledge that this is a work in progress rather than a finished product.

Many elements of textual exegesis are an integral dimension of a performance criticism exegesis of Mark such as word studies, Jewish and Greco-Roman background, comparison with other forms of the story in the other Gospels, and the context of the story in Mark. These elements are, however, refocused on the experience of the stories for ancient audiences. Word studies are refocused on the sounds of the words and their connotative as well as denotative associations from previous usage in the storytelling tradition. The Jewish and Greco-Roman background of the stories needs to identify the stories and experiences that would have been known by the ancient audiences. In the case of Mark, the experience of the Judean-Roman War and its consequences were a major factor in the meaning of the Bartimaeus story for Mark's original audiences. Everyone in the Judean community was feeling blind and unable to identify the way forward both individually and for the community of Israel as a whole. When heard against this background, Mark's stories were both allusions and contrasts to the stories floating around in the ancient communal memory. The comparison with other forms of the stories in the Gospel tradition in the context of performance also calls attention to the development of the sounds, structure, and overall impact of the stories in the Jesus storytelling tradition. The analysis of the context in Mark is based on the assumption that the audiences have just heard the preceding stories and will have those sounds and experience of those stories freshly in mind.[19]

There are also new elements of performance criticism exegesis. The most immediate and the most difficult to teach is the sound mapping of

---

18. For further exposition of performance criticism, see the Biblical Performance Criticism Series, edited by David Rhoads and published by Cascade. In particular, see Kelly R. Iverson, ed., *From Text to Performance: Narrative and Performance Criticisms in Dialogue and Debate*, BPC 10 (Eugene, OR: Cascade, 2014). Also see Rhoads, "Performance Criticism."

19. The identification and telling of some of the stories that would have been in the minds of Mark's audiences can help to sharpen the exposition of the meaning of the stories then. See Boomershine, *Messiah of Peace,* where the exposition of those remembered elements is an integral part of the exegetical process.

Mark's stories. The analysis of the sounds of Mark's story is based on the descriptions of cola and periods in the Greek grammatical and rhetorical literature. The mapping of the sounds is not unlike writing out the sounds of a musical composition. But there are no conventions of manuscript arrangement of these stories as there are with music (rests, volume markings, accents, indications of tempo, and mood identifications).[20] The major problem is that the current arrangement of Mark's composition in English prose sentences and paragraphs virtually blinds us to recognizing the rhythms and structures of the sound of Mark. In most instances, sound mapping biblical compositions will be done either by a professor or by an outside support community such as GoTell Communications.[21]

There is great value, therefore, in reforming Markan manuscripts in the structures of sound. While necessarily ambiguous at this stage of our communal research, the sound mapping of Mark restructures the basic conception and experience of Mark's story. Thinking of the sound map as a script for the story is sometimes helpful to students doing a sound map for the first time.

Another element of performance-criticism exegesis that is initially difficult for students is the analysis of the dynamics of the story as a story. Because virtually all of the exegetical works on Mark and, therefore, the models of exegesis focus on the identification of the theological and historical meaning of the story, students need help in identifying the meaning of Mark as a story. All of the elements of narrative criticism—point of view, characterization, plot, norms of judgment—are important dimensions of performance criticism. But there are also distinctive elements to the performance-criticism study of Mark as an oral narrative rather than as an ancient novel read by readers.[22]

The most important of these distinctive elements is the relationship between the storyteller and the audience. The basic facts of audience address are relatively easy to identify.[23] The storyteller addressed the

---

20. It may be that there are melodic signs implicit in the Greek manuscripts just as the masoretic editors made the traditional chant melodies in the Hebrew text explicit by the development of the trope markings. The traditions of Byzantine chant may afford some clues about this subject area, but at this point little is known.

21. See Boomershine, *GoTell Communications*.

22. Mary Ann Tolbert, *Sowing the Gospel: Mark's World in Literary-Historical Perspective* (Philadelphia: Fortress, 1989).

23. Thomas E. Boomershine, "The Medium and Message of John: Audience

audience, usually as Jesus addressing various groups in his teaching (e.g., 3:23–29; 4:3–9, 11–32; 8:34–9:1; 10:42–45; 13:4–36) but sometimes as himself addressing the audience as themselves (e.g., 1:1; 6:52; 7:3–4). The extension of those basic facts, however, to the identification of the impact of the story is outside the experience and training of most students. It is, therefore, important for the professor to provide a steady stream of performance-criticism demonstrations in the classes so that students have something to work with. But students await the production of full performance-criticism commentaries in order to have a wider range of models to work with in their exegetical study of Mark as performance literature.[24]

Student Production of Digital Storytelling of Mark

The reconception of Mark as performance literature also opens the possibility of Mark's being told with the full range of digital production resources. This is an area of potential creativity for which we have few models but that has great potential for creativity and a truly new hermeneutic. Potential elements of these productions are:

1. Videos of an individual person or a group telling the stories of Mark; if a group, the stories are divided between persons in episodes rather than by character as in a drama.
2. Archaeological pictures, maps, and other images from the first century.
3. Film clips that have related themes to Mark's story.
4. Videos of personal stories of the meaning of Mark's stories for individual persons.
5. Music videos of the dynamic equivalent contemporary images and music that are invited by Mark's story.
6. Musical background for the digital performance of Mark's story.

Address and Audience Identity in the Fourth Gospel," in *The Fourth Gospel in First-Century Media Culture*, ed. Anthony Le Donne and Tom Thatcher (New York: T&T Clark, 2011), 92–120; Boomershine, "Audience Address and Purpose in the Performance of Mark," in *Mark As Story: Retrospect and Prospect*, ed. Kelly R. Iverson and Christopher W. Skinner, RBS 65 (Atlanta: Society of Biblical Literature, 2011), 115–44.

24. For a detailed performance criticism study of Mark's passion-resurrection narrative, see Boomershine, *Messiah of Peace*.

Because of the ready availability of high-quality digital production technology, a new world of hermeneutical possibilities is now available for creative engagement with Mark's story.

Performance of Mark in Worship

Student performance of Mark by heart in worship services as the Scripture recital for the day brings the study of Mark as performance literature to another level of knowledge and experience. This is most frequently done in the context of theological seminaries, but it is also appropriate in university and, of course, local church contexts. I am an advocate of the performance of the Scriptures by heart without a manuscript. The current performance of Mark in particular and the Bible in general is done in an emotionally distant style with which we are all familiar. Telling the story by heart brings a new level of vitality and interest to the performance of the Scriptures in a worship service. The frequent response of congregation members is something akin to "I feel like I never heard the story before." The performance needs to be steadily rehearsed with supervision and direction by the professor. But, if done well, the telling of Mark and the performance of the Bible by heart in worship profoundly deepens the worship experience.

A Communal Performance of Mark

A concluding communal performance of Mark is an excellent ending for a course on Mark. The students and professor divide up the story and tell it in sequence. It is possible to invite the academic community as well as interested persons from the wider community to such a performance. If an audience is invited, the students need to practice the stories intensively as they would in preparation for the performance of a play. The professor functions as the director of the performance. It is important for the director to provide clear feedback and direction for the individual students. This work can be done best in individual coaching sessions, but that is very time-intensive work. Managing the mix between positive encouragement and reinforcement and suggestions/directions for ways of improving the telling of the story requires sensitivity and courage for the professor.[25]

---

25. Doug Lipman, *Improving Your Storytelling: Beyond the Basics for All Who Tell Stories in Work or Play* (Atlanta: August House, 1999).

These communal performances for invited audiences have been highly energizing experiences for students and audiences that are unforgettable. They do, however, require a lot of preparation.

It is also possible for this concluding performance to be an "in-house" event in which the members of the class tell one another the stories they have learned. We have told Mark in a classroom, the community chapel, and a private home or apartment. I have invited classes to my home, and we have sat on the floor around the living room and told Mark in the circle. We have passed around food and/or put various dips, fruit, crackers, and bread in the middle of the group where everyone can reach it in the ancient style. These celebrations of the learning of Mark by the class have been universally positive experiences. Students discover a lot about themselves and about Mark in this process, and the ante is much lower than for an external audience. But the benefits from a public performance are greater because of the higher investment of time and energy. Whichever the format, the students talk about it even years later as a transformative experience.

Conclusion

This essay is a case study on teaching Mark as a particular example of approaches that are applicable to the full range of biblical literature. I have used these approaches in the teaching of the other canonical Gospels, the Pauline and pseudo-Pauline letters, the Revelation to John, as well as Psalms, Jeremiah, and the narratives of the Pentateuch. The same benefits of a more historically accurate and experientially interesting encounter with the literature have been the results.

While I have explored the teaching of the Bible as performance literature for many years, we are only at the beginning of the formation of this new framework of biblical interpretation as a research and teaching community. This pedagogical shift is built on the foundation of the exegesis of biblical compositions as performance literature. More of that work has been done on Mark than any other biblical composition, hence the focus of this essay. Further research, pedagogical experimentation, and curriculum development on the Gospels and the rest of the biblical tradition are needed. The conclusion here is that the full inclusion of performance by faculty and especially by students in the teaching of biblical literature establishes a pedagogical process that is congruent with biblical literature in its original cultural context and in contemporary digital culture.

5
How to Hear and Teach Textual and Contextual Echoes in Mark 10:42–45

Alberto de Mingo Kaminouchi

The Gospel of Mark bears the marks of the storytelling practices of early Christianity. One of these features is the repetition of certain motifs I call "echoes." In this essay, I will explain one exercise I use in the classroom to teach students to listen to these echoes using Mark 10:42–45. Not only does this exercise provide a better understanding of the rhetorical strategy and meaning of Mark, but it also introduces students to the important theological topic of the relationship between Scripture and tradition.

Mark and Oral Performance

"Biblical performance criticism" is the name of a methodology rooted in the assumption that some biblical texts emerged from oral performance. One of the New Testament books more intensely studied using this approach is the Gospel of Mark. Today, however, there is a heated scholarly debate about the validity of some of the assumptions upon which performance criticism is based.[1] For the purpose of this essay, I do not need

---

1. Probably the best place to start a study of biblical performance criticism is David M. Rhoads, "Performance Criticism: An Emerging Methodology in Second Temple Studies," *BTB* 36 (2006): 118–33, 164–84. Larry W. Hurtado has recently published a critique of performance criticism: "Oral Fixation and New Testament Studies? 'Orality,' 'Performance' and Reading Texts in Early Christianity," *NTS* 60 (2014): 321–40. Other relevant works on the oral character of Mark include Joanna Dewey, "Oral Methods of Structuring Narrative in Mark," *Interpretation* 53 (1989): 32–44; Dewey, "Mark as Interwoven Tapestry: Forecasts and Echoes for a Listening Audience," *CBQ* 53 (1991): 221–36; Dewey, "The Gospel of Mark as an Oral-Aural Event: Implica-

to analyze in detail these hypotheses but to affirm two facts that I believe can safely be accepted by both proponents and opponents of performance criticism alike. First, Mark was composed to be read aloud. I do not deny that Mark could be read privately, but this Gospel was redacted having in mind public reading in Christian gatherings as its main function. Second, the Gospel of Mark presents "features of an oral 'register.'"[2]

Since the 1990s, some scholars have pointed out that Mark shows some traits that are typical of oral literature: sentences tend to be connected paratactically, redundancies and repetitions abound, concrete examples are preferred to abstract formulations, and so forth. Larry Hurtado has affirmed that the presence of these features is "a choice by the author, precisely in order to give the text a certain storytelling 'air.'" Having studied these features in my own research, however, I think that it is a simpler hypothesis to state that the text of Mark presents these traits not because of some editorial intention of the author, but because it was in its origin connected to storytelling.[3] By this I am not saying that the text of Mark is merely a transcription of an oral performance, but I affirm that the Gospel of Mark was also not the result of a one-time creative act by a solitary writer. I suggest that a storytelling tradition about Jesus existed that somehow helped to shape the text we now call Mark.

The origin of Mark is related to repeated events of telling the story of Jesus before listening audiences. Something similar to the story we now call the Gospel of Mark was read or recited aloud and evolved with the feedback of those listening. The oral features we find in Mark are the marks left in the text by this process. I propose that public proclamations of Jesus's story contributed to shape the final form of Mark. This hypothesis assumes that Christian communities not only preserved discrete pieces of information in particular settings—*Sitze im Leben*—as Rudolf

---

tions for Interpretation," in *The New Literary Criticism and the New Testament*, ed. Elizabeth Struthers Malbon and Edgar V. McKnight, JSNTSup 109 (Sheffield: Sheffield Academic Press, 1994), 145–63; Christopher Bryan, *A Preface to Mark: Notes on the Gospel in Its Literary and Cultural Settings* (New York: Oxford University Press, 1993); Elizabeth Struthers Malbon, "Echoes and Foreshadowings in Mark 4–8: Reading and Rereading," *JBL* 112 (1993) 211–30; Malbon, *Hearing Mark: A Listener's Guide* (Harrisburg, PA: Trinity Press International, 2002).

2. Hurtado, who has seriously questioned the validity of performance criticism, admits, however, that these features are present in Mark (*Oral Fixation*, 339).

3. I have studied these features in *"But It Is Not So among You": Echoes of Power in Mark 10.32–45*, JSNTSup 249 (London: T&T Clark, 2003), 52–56.

Bultmann thought, but they also transmitted a more complete portrayal of the Christ.

Early Christians did not understand that their mission and identity consisted mainly in preserving a pool of information about Jesus. They thrived to embody who he was. As Paul wrote to the Philippians, Christians should "have the same practical thinking [φρονεῖτε] as Jesus Christ" (2:5). This entails not only "knowing things" about Jesus, but also having some understanding of his character. If this is true, it is reasonable to assume that early Christians should have had storytelling traditions about Jesus that went beyond the preservation of disjointed logia or facts about his life. They must have had clusters of stories that enabled them to imagine the kind of person Jesus was. These sessions of storytelling probably happened in lively liturgical contexts where the figure of Jesus portrayed in narrative resonated with believing audiences that, with their reactions, helped to fine-tune the image of Christ being presented.

My departing position for this essay is that oral features of the Gospel of Mark, concretely the presence of some repeated motifs—echoes—in the text, are marks of these oral origins and that the study of these echoes helps us to understand the process through which an image of Jesus was preserved and transmitted before listening audiences.

The awareness of the oral character of much of the New Testament concerns not only performance criticism. A broader group of scholars than those engaged in this particular form of criticism is investigating the process through which Jesus's memory was preserved and transmitted orally.[4] I think that it is not a coincidence that this renewed interest in the relationship between oral storytelling and written gospel is happening in this moment of history when Western culture is accessing a new stage that some observers have called a *second orality*.

---

4. James D. G. Dunn, *Christianity in the Making*, vol. 1 of *Jesus Remembered* (Grand Rapids: Eerdmans, 2003); Dunn, "Altering the Default Setting: Re-envisaging the Early Transmission of the Jesus Tradition," NTS 49 (2003): 139–75; Samuel Byrskog, *Story as History—History as Story: The Gospel Tradition in the Context of Ancient Oral History*, WUNT 123 (Tübingen: Mohr Siebeck, 2000); Richard Bauckham, *Jesus and the Eyewitnesses: The Gospels as Eyewitness Testimony* (Grand Rapids: Eerdmans, 2006); Birger Gerhardsson, "The Secret of the Transmission of the Unwritten Jesus Tradition," NTS 52 (2006): 319–36; Gerhardsson, *The Reliability of the Gospel Tradition* (Peabody, MA: Hendrickson, 2001).

Walter Ong classified the variety of historical and existing cultures into four stages, according to their relationship with writing. In the first stage are the primary oral cultures, those that have not achieved written expression. The second group is composed by the literate cultures in the manuscript stage. In the third stage are those that are using print. Ong thought that Western civilization was entering a fourth period, called secondary oral stage, a new kind of orality thanks to the development of electronic media.[5] In this new environment, books are still part of the cultural landscape but do not occupy any longer the entire stage by themselves; rather, they must be understood as one more "information technology device" among others in the intricate web of human interactions.

During the print age, a fixed form of text—the book—was enshrined as the primary repository of knowledge. In the university classroom where I used to sit as a student two or three decades ago, education was understood primarily as learning information contained in books. Being able to reproduce memorized pieces of knowledge was an important part of the learning process. This paradigm was based on the assumption that learning was the acquisition of a scarce resource: information. Today we no longer feel that information is a scarce good; on the contrary, we perceive it as overwhelmingly abundant. Learning today has more to do with how to use information than with retaining or memorizing it. In this new paradigm books are perceived more as one kind of tool among others—textual, audio, and video—than as a repository of information to be retained.

This situation of second orality in which we find ourselves today has similarities with the manuscript stage in which the Gospels were written. Mark was produced as a manuscript or series of manuscripts in a fluid relationship with the oral traditions behind them. The study of the oral features still present in the text is a path we can take to imagine the complex interactions of the text within a web of practices through which it came to exist: people were shaped by the story told by the reciters of Jesus's life, but they also helped to shape the story being told by their reaction to it. This awareness of the process of interaction between story and listening audience and the production of manuscripts helps us to realize that Mark is not just a body of information, but a tool that was formed by a living community.

---

5. Walter J. Ong, *The Presence of the Word* (New Haven: Yale University Press, 1967), 1–110.

My proposal is that the shift in higher education from an information-centered paradigm to one based on skills and practices may offer an opportunity to rethink the relationship between books and the lives that shaped them and were shaped by them. Learning today is no longer only about memorizing content; it is rather about understanding books as part of a web of practices and interactions. This relationship put in theological terms is nothing less than the very important question of the relationship between Scripture and tradition.

Scripture and Tradition Revisited

During the first half the 1960s, a revolution in the theological understanding of the relationship between Scripture and tradition took place in the church at an ecumenical level. Breaking with a narrow understanding of the *sola scriptura* principle, the Fourth World Conference on Faith and Order of the World Council of Churches, which took place in Montreal in 1963, spoke about tradition in the following terms:

> Our starting point is that we are all living in a Tradition which goes back to our Lord and has its roots in the Old Testament, and are all indebted to that Tradition inasmuch as we have received the revealed truth, the Gospel, through its being transmitted from one generation to another. Thus we can say that we exist as Christians by the Tradition of the Gospel (the *paradosis* of the *kerygma*) testified in Scripture, transmitted in and by the Church through the power of the Holy Spirit.[6]

When this declaration was released, the Catholic Church was immersed in its most important event since the sixteenth century: the Second Vatican Council (1962–1965). In preparation for it, the Theological Commission appointed by Pope John XXIII redacted a document called *De Fontibus Revelationis* (*On the Sources of Revelation*) to be discussed by the conciliar fathers. The aim of this document was that the council would define the "material incompleteness" of Scripture. This doctrine stated that some revealed truths were contained only in tradition but not in Scripture. On

---

6. World Council of Churches Commission on Faith and Order, *Faith and Order Findings: The Final Report of the Theological Commissions to the Fourth World Conference on Faith and Order* (London: SCM, 1963), sec. II, n. 45. Quoted by Roger Schutz and Max Thurian, *Revelation, a Protestant View: The Dogmatic Constitution on Divine Revelation; A Commentary* (Westminster, MD: Newman, 1968), 28–40.

20 November 1962, the council voted to refuse such a proposal and a commission was created to compose a new document that should formulate Catholic doctrine on the matter. The result was the *Dogmatic Constitution on Divine Revelation, Dei Verbum*.[7] The theologians working in this document realized that *De Fontibus Revelationis* assumed a propositional model of revelation: God had revealed truths, some of them through tradition, some of them through Scripture. Inspired by thinkers like Martin Buber and Emil Brunner, *Dei Verbum* moved away from this doctrinal model of revelation, which had prevailed since the Council of Trent (1545–1563), to another model in which revelation is understood primarily as a personal encounter between God and human beings.[8] *Dei Verbum* presents this renewed understanding in this passage:

> In His goodness and wisdom, God chose to reveal Himself [*Seipsum*] and to make known to us the hidden purpose of His will (cf. Eph. 1:9) by which through Christ, the Word made flesh, man has access to the Father in the Holy Spirit and comes to share in the divine nature (cf. Eph. 2:18; 2 Pet. 1:4).[9]

Dei Verbum no longer considers tradition and Scripture "sources of revelation" (*fontes revelationis*), as *De Fontibus Revelationis* assumed; there is only one source of revelation: Jesus Christ. Tradition and Scripture are complementary means that witness to this unique man in whom God revealed *Seipsum*.[10]

The constitution *Dei Verbum* does not offer a clear-cut definition of tradition, but it says that "the Church, in her teaching, life, and worship, perpetuates and hands on to all generations all that she herself is, all that she believes."[11] Here tradition is identified with the total life of the church

---

7. John W. O'Malley, *What Happened at Vatican II* (Cambridge: Harvard University Press, 2008), 141–52.

8. Avery Dulles, *Models of Revelation* (Maryknoll, NY: Orbis, 1992), 26–52; Alister E. McGrath, *Christian Theology: An Introduction* (Oxford: Blackwell, 2001), 202–8.

9. *Dei Verbum*, art. 2. Cf. Joseph Ratzinger, "Revelation Itself," in *Commentary on the Documents of Vatican II*, ed. Herbert Vorgrimler, trans. Lalit Adolphus, Kevin Smyth, and Richard Strachan, 5 vols. (London: Burns & Oates; New York: Herder & Herder, 1967–1969), 3:170–80.

10. *Dei Verbum*, arts. 7–10.

11. *Dei Verbum*, art. 8.

(doctrine, ethics, worship); tradition perpetuates and transmits the whole of Christian life and faith.

The Montreal Conference on Faith and Order and the Second Vatican Council converge in a way of understanding tradition: God's revelation in Christ was not only a disclosure of information; it was, and is, an encounter with God that sustains a way of life. Tradition is but another name for this way of life transmitted from generation to generation. According to one of the great theologians behind the Second Vatican Council, Yves M. Congar, the way in which tradition transmits revelation "is not that of discourse, with its precise and defined formulations: it is that of life and the concrete and familiar experience of the realities out of which one lives."[12]

The research in the oral past of the Gospel of Mark helps us to imagine how the interaction between Scripture and tradition took place during the formative period of the Christian faith. The Gospel of Mark emerged organically from a community that was shaped by the witness of Jesus. Even before Jesus's story was fixed in written form, it was already shaping Christian lives. Those who believed in Jesus *through hearing* did not devote their lives simply to memorizing his logia; they let Jesus's memory configure their lives through practices like prayer, the celebration of the Eucharist, works of mercy, and nonviolent resistance to persecution. People whose character was shaped by these practices listened repeatedly to the proclamation of Jesus's story and through their reactions to it helped to shape the story being told. This two-way process can be described as tradition shaping Scripture and Scripture shaping tradition: Jesus's story created a way of life, but the actual realization of this life helped to give final form to a story that was eventually committed to writing and recognized as Scripture.

Let us not forget that the true title of the book we are studying is not "Gospel according to Saint Mark" but Ἀρχὴ τοῦ εὐαγγελίου Ἰησοῦ χριστοῦ [υιου θεου] (Mark 1:1).[13] This document we call the "Gospel of Mark" does not claim to be the gospel, but the beginning of the good news.[14] Jesus's

---

12. Yves M. Congar, *La tradition et la vie de l'Église* (Paris: Cerf, 1984), 24.

13. I have put "Son of God" in brackets just as the critical text of NA[28] does, due to the well-known text-critical problem. See Bruce Metzger, *A Textual Commentary on the Greek New Testament* (Stuttgart: United Bible Societies, 1975), 73.

14. Joel Marcus, *Mark 1–8*, AYB 27 (New York: Doubleday; New Haven: Yale University Press, 2002), 145–46; Malbon, *Hearing Mark*, 11–14.

life, death, and resurrection that it tells is the ἀρχὴ of a εὐαγγελίον that continues in the lives configured by the one narrated by the story.

The writer of the Gospel of Mark and his first hearers and readers understood their stories as part of the story of the gospel that was inaugurated by Jesus. Their listening to the stories about Jesus was a means of configuring their own personal lives and the life of the community to the image of Christ. On the other hand, their responses to the storytelling influenced the configuration of the story being told until it was fixed in a written text.

Oral tradition is not a new discovery. The moment it is established that there is a gap of several decades between the life of Jesus and the composition of the oldest Gospel, it becomes clear that the oral transmission of Jesus's words and deeds during that period of time played an important role. Until recently, however, a propositional model of revelation and an information-centered paradigm of tradition hindered a more comprehensive understanding of the way in which the life of the Christians who kept that tradition alive contributed to the formation of Scripture.

The model of oral composition applied to Mark makes us aware that in the origins of this Gospel there was a process of interaction between a community that tries to *live* Jesus's gospel and storytellers that *tell* Jesus's story as the ἀρχή—beginning and foundation—of those lives that are being configured by Christ. This interaction was not limited to the preservation (and eventual modification or creation) of logia and short narratives, as the *formgeschichtliche Schule* affirmed one century ago; it affected the configuration of the overall narrative of Mark as a portrait of Jesus.

The corollary of what I have said so far is that we are in a privileged moment to improve our understanding the Gospel of Mark both as a piece of literature and as a work of theology. If Christianity is not mainly a set of beliefs but a way of community life adopted by those who have responded to God's revelation in Christ, learning to be a Christian is not mainly about content but about the skills needed to sustain such a life. Lives that were shaped by the direct contact with Jesus started a tradition that within some decades gave birth to the written Gospels. The study of the oral composition of the Gospels can help us to understand how Scripture emerged organically from tradition and how tradition and Scripture are meant to be forever intertwined. Let us now get down to the business of listening to textual and contextual echoes in Mark 10:42–45.

Textual Echoes

"Echo" is a useful metaphor for exploring the oral composition of the Gospel of Mark.[15] A feature of oral literature pointed out by pioneers of this field such as Milman Parry, Ong, and Eric Havelock is the use of modulated repetitions that give coherence to the narrative.[16]

Oral composers of stories (a different trade from storytellers who tell memorized stories written by themselves or by others) create their work without the help of ink and paper. They use unaided memory as the only tool to produce stories that are sometimes quite long and complex.[17] This is a process of creation that is closer to that of a musician than to that of a writer. After showing the unsatisfactory nature of the outlines proposed for Mark, Howard Clark Kee suggests: "It would appear that Mark no more lends itself to analysis by means of a detailed outline developed by simple addition of components than does a major contrapuntal work of music." Kee compares Mark to a fugue in which the great motifs of the Gospel are repeated again and again.[18]

In oral cultures, only memorable knowledge is useful, and therefore important thoughts must be worded in a way that facilitates memorization. The most common technique for memorization, used in a great variety of cultures, is the use of formula and repetition. But *echoes* are not only a mnemonic resource for the speaker; they also help the hearer to follow the discourse. Oral audiences expect to hear echoes in the speech and are trained to follow the story line helped by this mnemonic aid. The repetition of motifs assists the hearer in his or her appropriation of the text as it unfolds throughout the plot.

An echo, however, is not an exact repetition. It is not a duplicate. Echoes change and are modulated according to different contexts in fresh statements; the subtle but significant variations make the plot advance

---

15. Kaminouchi, *But It Is Not So among You*, 56–95.

16. Milman Parry, *The Making of Homeric Verse: The Collected Papers of Milman Parry* (Oxford: Clarendon, 1971); Eric A. Havelock, *Preface to Plato* (Cambridge: Harvard University Press, 1963); Walter Ong, *Orality and Literacy: The Technologizing of the Word* (London: Methuen, 1982).

17. The *Odyssey* and the *Iliad*, studied by Milman Parry and Albert Lord, are the ultimate examples. See Albert B. Lord, *The Singer of Tales* (Cambridge: Harvard University Press, 1960).

18. Howard C. Kee, *Community of the New Age: Studies in Mark's Gospel* (Philadelphia: Westminster, 1977), 64, 75.

and the hearer deepen his or her understanding. In this way, by variation within the same scheme, new knowledge is introduced gradually.

I use a very simple exercise to help my students understand the importance of textual echoes in the Gospel of Mark. Their homework is to read or to listen to the section on journey to Jerusalem in Mark (8:22–10:52).[19] Then they must fill the blank cells in the table below with chapter and verse and look for similarities and differences among the repetition of motifs or echoes.

	Passion Prediction	Disciples' failure	Jesus's teaching
1			
2			
3			

The next day in class we speak about how these echoes modulate through the narrative. Students observe that the third passion prediction is more detailed than the previous two, which causes an effect of *crescendo*. The reader/listener has the feeling that the drumbeats that announce the passion sound louder in this third repetition. However, the motif that calls more of their attention is the *disciples' failure*. After the first prediction of the passion, the narrator reports that Peter took Jesus "and began to rebuke him" (8:32). What Mark does not tell is the content of Peter's reprobation. The hearer/reader must guess what Peter has said through Jesus's reaction to his words and the teaching he gives afterward: "If any want to become my followers, let them deny themselves and take up their cross and follow me" (8:34–38). After the second passion prediction, the Twelve as a group show that they are failing to be true followers of Jesus: questioned by Christ, they confess that they had been arguing who was the greatest (9:33–34). The third iteration of this motif is the scene in which the sons of Zebedee ask Jesus to sit "one at your right hand and one at your left, in your glory" (10:37).

---

19. An audio recording of the entire Bible is narrated by Max McLean, *The Listener's Bible*, Fellowship for Performing Arts, Listenersbible.com, 2006–2015, http://www.listenersbible.com/. Another possibility that I have not yet explored is to organize a reading of the section for the class. Other video and audio resources are listed in Malbon, *Hearing Mark*, 107–11. Another wonderful resource is *Network of Biblical Storytellers International*, 2010, http://www.nbsint.org/.

The triple repetition of the pattern *prediction-failure-teaching* makes progressively clear that the cause of the inability of disciples to become true followers of Jesus is their thirst of power: they want to be the first ones. As a teacher, I try to lead students as maieutically as possible toward this discovery: Which is the stone disciples trip on again and again? What is keeping them from truly following Jesus?

Then the class may continue with a detailed analysis of Mark 10:42–45, which culminates this section:

> You know that among the Gentiles those whom they recognize as their rulers lord it over them, and their great ones are tyrants over them. But it is not so among you; but whoever wishes to become great among you must be your servant, and whoever wishes to be first among you must be slave of all. For the Son of Man came not to be served but to serve, and to give his life a ransom for many.

The third passion prediction is longer and more detailed than the previous two; also, the third scene of the disciples' failure is more vivid and complete than the others. The third iteration of the teaching motif is, however, shorter and more concise, which makes the message even more focused: the discovery of Jesus's true identity as the redeeming Son of Man is open only to those disciples that are willing to serve. Only those who renounce power as lording it over others will become true followers of the Messiah who will suffer, be killed, and rise again after three days. This lesson, however, is not something disciples can learn just in theory. Only those willing to take up a real life of service can enter into the secret place where God's power is revealed as humble service.

The study of the textual echoes in the Journey to Jerusalem section is an effective way to teach in the classroom one of the main doctrines of the Gospel of Mark. The critical approach that takes into account the oral origins of the Gospel may actually help students get deeper into the message of the Gospel by bringing them closer to the experience of the original hearer.

Contextual Echoes

The best explanation of why Mark was so well received by early Christians (to the point of eliciting two "expanded versions" we now call Matthew and Luke) is because it *sounded true* as a portrait of their Jesus.

Mark was produced and was recognized as canonical in a tradition that was much more than "oral tradition" understood as a mere transmission of pieces of information. Early Christians were not concerned primarily with memorizing Jesus's words; they shared the Eucharist, they took care of the sick and the poor, they resisted persecution with nonviolence, they offered and received hospitality, and so forth. In their mutual interactions, they tried to embody the kind of power that was revealed in Jesus's life, death, and resurrection. Jesus is the Lord, but his power is not like the power of those who "apparently rule the nations" (δοκοῦντες ἄρχειν τῶν ἐθνῶν). He is the one who has come not to be served but to serve. The shape of the community they tried to build resonated with this image of Jesus that is present in the overall plot of Mark, especially in 8:27–10:45.

I continue the exercise on textual echoes with another one on contextual echoes. With this second exercise, the students' study of Mark 10:42–45 jumps from the world of the text to the world in front of the text, that is, to our world. I pose the following questions: How does Mark 10:42–45 resonate with the experience of the students about power both in the church and in the world at large? Is their perception of how power is exercised in the church different—as this passage assumes—from the way "rulers lord over nations"? How should a church be configured by a power such as the one described in Mark 10:42–45?

Answering these simple questions about the relationship between text and life helps students better to understand the relationship between Scripture and tradition. The Gospels did not only put into writing an "oral tradition" as a pool of information. Through storytelling, tradition—understood as life configured by the memory of the one who is the ἀρχή of the gospel—contributed to the creation of the earliest Gospel. Scripture was born out of tradition, and ever since it has been crucial in the shaping of Christian life. But in order fully to exercise its power, Scripture requires not only minds that understand, but men and women open to be configured by the good news that was revealed in Jesus Christ.

6
No Performance Criticism without Narrative Criticism: Performance as a Test of Interpretation

Geert Van Oyen

Introduction

Both performing the Gospels (and other biblical texts) and studying the art of performance have become part of recent biblical scholarship. The number of conferences and publications on the topic has increased over the last decade, as has the number of scholars and professional actors who perform biblical books or larger portions of the Bible. Is there a place for this recent discipline among the already diverse branches of the biblical exegesis tree? In this essay I will defend the thesis that both performing and participating in performances as an audience make sense and that performance criticism should be done on the basis of narrative criticism. Moreover, because performance is a helpful means of becoming aware of one's own interpretation and the impact of the story's message, it is a useful pedagogical tool.

In what follows, I begin by sketching the background and the place of orality in biblical scholarship in order to make a case that the reason to perform the Gospel of Mark (or the Bible) today should not be that it was performed in antiquity but that it adds communication value for a modern audience. Next, since it is the *text* rather than oral methods that link early Christian communities to today's readers, I insist on the need to build a foundation of narrative-critical insights in order to become conscious of the decisions that are taken when a modern performance is done. In particular, narrative criticism illuminates subtexts—implicit layers of meaning in the text—so that performers may choose how to portray a text. Conversely, performance highlights thorny or ambiguous exegetical issues that require further discussion and investigation. Finally, I focus on a concrete teaching situation during one of my undergraduate classes in which I look at three difficult texts that illustrate the mutually interpretive relationship between narrative criticism and performance.

A Brief History of Orality before Performance Criticism

Performance criticism on the Gospel of Mark is based on the hypothesis that the Gospels were orally performed at an early stage, before and after they were written down.[1] The presupposition of an oral gospel tradition is not new. Interest in orality with regard to the formation of the Gospels can be divided into several stages. At the beginning of critical exegesis, Johann Gottfried Herder defended the hypothesis of oral tradition as a solution to the Synoptic problem in the eighteenth century, followed by Johann Karl Ludwig Gieseler in the nineteenth century. Herder believed that Mark wrote an oral "apostolische Sage" in Aramaic (between 34 and 40), of which Peter was the origin, and later in Greek (between 63 and 68).[2] Gieseler defended the hypothesis of a primitive oral gospel. The evolution toward a "fixed" oral tradition happened automatically ("wie von selbst").[3]

---

1. David Rhoads, "What Is Performance Criticism?" in *The Bible in Ancient and Modern Media*, ed. Holley E. Hearon and Philip Ruge-Jones, BPC 1 (Eugene, OR: Cascade, 2009), 86: "The Gospel of Mark was probably composed orally and performed many times before it was transcribed at some point in its performance life."

2. Johann Gottfried Herder, *Vom Erlöser der Menschen: Nach unsern drei Evangelien*, vol. 2 of *Christliche Schriften* (Riga: Hartknoch, 1796), 149–223; Herder, *Von Gottes Sohn, der Welt Heiland: Nach Johannes Evangelium; Nebst einer Regel der Zusammenstimmung unserer Evangelien aus ihrer Entstehung und Ordnung*, vol. 3 of *Christliche Schriften* (Riga: Hartknoch, 1797), 382: "Mit Evangelienschreiben fing also das Christentum nicht an, sondern met Verkündigung vergangner und zukünftiger Dinge (Kerygma, Offenbarung), mit Auslegung, Lehre, Trost, Ermahnung, Predigt."

3. Johann Karl Ludwig Gieseler, *Historisch-kritischer Versuch über die Entstehung und die frühesten Schicksale der schriftlichen Evangelien* (Leipzig: Engelmann, 1818), 90: "Durch nichts lässt es sich so bequem als durch die Annahme einer gemeinschaftlichen mündlichen Quelle erklären, wie es gekommen ist, dass die Erzählungen, je wichtiger sie den Schülern scheinen mussten, desto übereinstimmender vorgetragen werden. Natürlich wurden diese am häufigsten vorgetragen, und ihre ursprüngliche Form erhielt sich also durch die öftere Wiederholung reiner, als die der übrigen Erzählungen, von denen mehr die Materie als die Form in dem Gedächtnisse der Einzelnen bewahrt werde."

In most of the introductions to the New Testament, one normally jumps from this first stage in the research of orality to the second one, form criticism, which arose in the 1920s. But one should not forget that before form criticism, scholars in the period between 1900 and 1919 had already shown an interest in orality.[4] Johannes Weiss, Julius Wellhausen, and Paul Wendland emphasized the oral origin of the gospel tradition.[5] For them, however, unlike recent performance critics, the oral character of the tradition did not form a complete gospel. It was rather limited to individual pericopes (or small collections). The founders of New Testament form criticism, Rudolf Bultmann and Martin Dibelius, explicitly referred to Herder.[6] In this period, shortly after the Great War, they developed their ideas by emphasizing the oral evolution on the level of pericopes and the social conditions in the *Sitz im Leben*. While acknowledging the individual differences among the *Formkritiker*, Walter Schmithals notes a commonality: "It is a common conviction in all different manifestations of this method of research that between Jesus's activity and the gospel messages an anonymous and unliterary tradition existed."[7] The link of this oral tradition with the preaching activity (especially in the work of Dibelius) is of interest to performance critics, since both form criticism and performance criticism focus on the transmission and on the communicative aspect of the tradition.

---

4. On this period see, among others, Maurice Goguel, "Une nouvelle école de critique évangélique, la *Form- und traditionsgeschichtliche Schule*," *RHR* 94 (1926): 114–60.

5. Johannes Weiss, *Die drei älteren Evangelien*, 3rd ed., SNT 1 (Göttingen: Vandenhoeck & Ruprecht, 1917), 31–71; Weiss, "Literaturgeschichte des Neuen Testaments," *RGG* 3:2175–2215. Julius Wellhausen, *Einleitung in die drei ersten Evangelien* (Berlin: Reimer, 1905), 43: "Die letzte Quelle der Evangelien ist mündliche Überlieferung, aber diese enthält nur den zerstreuten Stoff"; see also Wellhausen, *Einleitung in die drei ersten Evangelien*, 2nd ed. (Berlin: Reimer, 1911), 32, 37, 45, 48. Paul Wendland, *Die urchristlichen Literaturformen*, HNT 1.3, 2nd and 3rd eds. (Tübingen: Mohr Siebeck, 1912), 257–405.

6. The link between the predecessors and the form critics has especially been emphasized by Erich Fascher, *Die formgeschichtliche Methode: Eine Darstellung und Kritik; Zugleich ein Beitrag zur Geschichte des synoptischen Problems*, BZNW 2 (Giessen: Töpelmann, 1924).

7. Walter Schmithals, *Einleitung in die drei ersten Evangelien* (Berlin: de Gruyter, 1985), 261: "Allen Ausprägungen dieser Forschungsrichtung ist die Überzeugung gemeinsam, dass zwischen dem Wirken Jesu und den evangelischen Berichten darüber eine anonyme und unliterarische Tradition steht."

This *formgeschichtliche* stage was followed in the 1960s and 1970s by what is sometimes called the Scandinavian school, represented by Harald Riesenfeld and Birger Gerhardsson.[8] The emphasis this time was put on the role of Jesus, who, as an authoritative rabbi, taught his disciples in such a way that they could easily memorize the words he had given them. Jesus is called a "parabolist" (Heb. *moshel*), who repeats again and again short, didactic, and well-constructed logia that are easy to remember. One could say that more recent publications by Samuel Byrskog on the role of eyewitnesses in the transmission of the tradition share a similar view.[9] Orality is considered to be a guarantee for a trustworthy and reliable transmission and conservation of the words of Jesus.

Werner Kelber's *The Oral and the Written Gospel* is considered a milestone in the research of orality. Kelber first makes an evaluation of earlier literature on orality and—under the influence of the Anglo-American oralist school[10]—he clearly explains that "the circumstances of performance, the composition, and the transmission of oral versus written materials are sufficiently distinct so as to postulate separate hermeneutics."[11] His idea of "oral synthesis" is particularly noteworthy and of interest for performance criticism: it describes a characteristic of oral communication that implies that the words pronounced are actualizing their content for the audience. Orality according to Kelber's approach becomes a much more dynamic concept because the axis of communication is more accentuated.

In the second chapter of his book ("Mark's Oral Legacy"), he explains that the aim of oral transmission is not to be found on the level of historical reliability. The success of this tradition depends on the authority of the narrator and the acceptance by the audience: "In sum, orality's principal

---

8. Harald Riesenfeld, *The Gospel Tradition and Its Beginnings: A Study in the Limits of "Formgeschichte,"* 2nd ed. (London: Mowbray, 1961); Birger Gerhardsson, *Memory and Manuscript: Oral Tradition and Written Transmission in Rabbinic Judaism and Early Christianity*, 2nd ed., ASNU 20 (Lund: Gleerup; Copenhagen: Munksgaard, 1964).

9. Samuel Byrskog, *Story as History—History as Story: The Gospel Tradition in the Context of Ancient Oral History*, WUNT 123 (Tübingen: Mohr Siebeck, 2000).

10. In the United States: Milman Parry, Albert B. Lord, Eric A. Havelock, Walter J. Ong, Berkley Peabody; in the United Kingdom: Ruth Finnegan, Jack Goody.

11. Werner H. Kelber, *The Oral and the Written Gospel: The Hermeneutics of Speaking and Writing in the Synoptic Tradition, Mark, Paul, and Q* (Bloomington: Indiana University Press, 1983), 14.

concern is not to preserve historical actuality, but to shape and break it into memorable, applicable speech."[12]

In chapter 3 ("Mark as Textuality"), Kelber explains the changes that take place during the *textualization* of the oral gospel. According to him, this process is to be considered as a reaction to the oral transmission. Key words are *transmutation, linguistic disorientation,* and *reorientation.* The isolated elements of the text receive a new meaning through a "process of intersignification." Textuality offers the possibility to create a plot: "The result of Markan textuality is thus not a copy of the Jesus of history, but rather an artistic recreation. Art, one remembers, does not produce but illuminate nature, not copy but re-create actuality."[13] Kelber has been largely criticized for this exaggerated, artificial opposition between orality and textuality.

In 1986 Robert Culley concluded his overview on "Oral Tradition and Biblical Studies" with the following words: "After many decades of discussion, much remains unresolved. Almost all agree that the Bible probably has oral antecedents, but there is little agreement on the extent to which oral composition and transmission have actually left their mark on the text or the degree to which one might be able to establish this lineage."[14] It seems to me that the situation has not changed since then. After having reviewed the authors mentioned above, and some more recent evolutions since Kelber's book, Eric Eve makes the following conclusion: "No attempt has been made to come up with one definitive model as *the* way of understanding the oral Jesus tradition. There is probably no way in which such a definitive model could be arrived at, given both the great variety of ways in which oral tradition has been observed to operate under other circumstances and the absence of much specific evidence for how it actually operated in primitive Christianity."[15]

---

12. Ibid., 71.

13. Ibid., 116. In his conclusion Kelber mentions the difficulty of imagining the original target group of Mark's Gospel, since there is no continuity in the process from orality toward textuality.

14. Robert C. Culley, "Oral Tradition and Biblical Studies," *Oral Tradition* 11 (1986): 56.

15. Eric Eve, *Behind the Gospels: Understanding the Oral Tradition* (Minneapolis: Fortress, 2014), 184. See also the section on "Tradition and Performances," 103–7.

Performance Criticism as a New Research Method on Orality: Some Reflections

Performance criticism is the latest offspring in the genealogy of orality.[16] The history of research on orality after Kelber can be read in several contributions.[17] The representatives of this new method recognize themselves as the heirs of their predecessors. But performance critics (in general) also keep their distance from what precedes. I mention three differences: (1) Many performance critics do not want to be associated with those scholars who use orality to defend the reliability of the text in the sense that the Gospels preserve Jesus's words or traditions. This certainly has to do with their affiliation to narrative criticism. (2) Performance criticism includes more profound research on oral *communication* in antiquity and in modern times that—with regard to its application to the Bible—goes much further than anything that has been said before: "performance as a method of research."[18] This research goes hand in hand with a renewed interest in the hermeneutics of "storytelling." (3) Performance theory walks hand in hand with the practice of performing. This adds a new and enriching dimension to the method. In this context, one could also point to the interest in the *real* addressee(s) of the Gospel (and not only the implied reader as in narrative criticism).

In a critical article, Larry Hurtado considers the idea of a storytelling performance of the Gospels (or other biblical texts) before they were written down in their "final" form (qualified by performance critics as "composition in oral performance") to be an oversimplification in many ways.[19] Hurtado argues instead that "the Roman period is better characterised as a time of rich interplay of texts and readers (both private and to/before groups), writers and speakers, and appreciation of both oral/aural

---

16. Antoinette C. Wire, *The Case for Mark Composed in Performance*, BPC 3 (Eugene, OR: Cascade, 2011), 15: "The most recent wave of research on the gospels as oral tradition began with Werner Kelber's 1983 study, *The Oral and Written Gospel*."

17. Wire, *Case for Mark*, 17–18.

18. This is the title of an important contribution by David Rhoads, "Biblical Performance Criticism: Performance as Research," *Oral Tradition* 25 (2010): 157–98, esp. 169–70.

19. Larry W. Hurtado, "Oral Fixation and New Testament Studies? 'Orality,' 'Performance' and Reading Texts in Early Christianity," *NTS* 60 (2014): 321–40. For literature on the topic of "performance" based on the memorization of the text, see the notes in Hurtado's article.

and written expressions of thought and entertainment, and it is a fallacy to make the one subservient to the other in any generalising way."[20] The role of written texts should not be underestimated: speeches were studied in written form; texts were read not only aloud and in public but also individually and in silence; people were trained to read the *scriptio continua* in the manuscripts; elite manuscripts made some "concessions" to readers (for example, the use of small columns); and readers prepared their reading with markers (accents, punctuation, and paragraph markers). The degree of literacy at the beginning of the Common Era is sometimes underestimated. In short, "As was the case for other Roman-era authors, [New Testament] writers often (typically?) composed their texts with a view to them being read aloud to groups and experienced aurally. But [New Testament] texts are the products of authors who wrote for readers and for those who would hear their texts read out."[21]

Hurtado's critical remarks weaken the methodological considerations about the oral composition and performance of the Gospel during the first century both before and after the written composition would have taken place. The reasons to think of an oral performance of the entire Gospel by heart are hypothetical and cannot be based on any strong argument in the contemporary sources. The only thing we have in hand is the written text. Oral tradition—in the sense of the form critics—was certainly the first step in the formation of the Gospels, but this is something completely different than the statement that the Gospels were composed in oral performance.

Moreover, many elements of the text that performance critics argue are characteristic of oral tradition and of oral transmission can be explained by other means. I am still impressed by the catalog of so-called duality (but in fact it contains all forms of repetition) that Frans Neirynck made in 1972.[22] He clearly showed how Mark (in Neirynck's redaction-critical analysis, the anonymous author of Mark wrote the text, not the storyteller Mark, who performed the story) created a homogeneous text at the redactional level by using the literary device of repetition. This homogeneity is a sign of a conscious author-writer whose hand is recognized by a *reader* of the *written text*.

---

20. Ibid., 325.
21. Ibid., 340.
22. Frans Neirynck, *Duality in Mark: Contributions to the Study of the Markan Redaction*, 2nd ed., BETL 31 (Leuven: Leuven University Press; Peeters, 1988).

Does this imply that there were no performances in the early Christian communities? We do not know. Maybe there were. But if so, it is difficult to answer more concrete questions with regard to the time, place, or mode of performance. When did these performances take place? Between 30 and 40 CE? Between 60 and 70? Between 70 and 90? Or later? And were the Gospels performed every week, every month, once a year? How can we know if the whole of the Gospel was performed or only single pericopes or larger sections? Where and in which communities would these performances have taken place? Could we really say that the Gospel of Mark survived thanks to the oral transmission of the text? Or did it survive, on the contrary, because it was written down? And what could have been this "oral text" that was read and learned by heart? It certainly would have existed in many forms, but then what are we really talking about when we study performance in antiquity, since in "performance as research" one always starts with the standardized latest edition of the Nestle-Aland text? The key word in performance criticism is *oral composition*, but whatever exegetical method is used, one always has to start from the *written* text. Even if one would accept the influence of oral culture upon the way any particular author wrote, the written text is always a starting point, and it is this text one must study first.

It is almost impossible to reconstruct the original situations and conditions in which the stories about Jesus and the words of Jesus were transmitted from one generation to another in that first period of early Christianity. We simply do not know what happened and how it happened. In this sense, I agree with Hurtado's conclusions about oral performance in antiquity. But since the author does not want to "engage" the matter of oral performance today,[23] this field remains open for discussion. The question about the contribution of performance and performance criticism today is a valuable one, even when we recognize that we are not able to find strong support for it in the first century. I therefore would propose that performance critics would use other useful arguments in favor of performance today. The intention of performing the Gospels today lies in the added value with regard to the communication of the biblical message. The initial challenge at the basis of performing the Bible is how to improve certain aspects of the communication of those ancient texts for a modern audience. Good performance together with a thorough reflection on how

---

23. Hurtado, "Oral Fixation," 322 n. 3.

performance works helps to illuminate the way the "text" functions today. In other words, there is a unity between the methodology (performance) and the objective and intention of the approach (added value to the communicative aspect of the "text"). It seems to me that the main objective of performance criticism is the effective transmission of the message to real readers/listeners today. I would like to quote an emblematic example as a *pars pro toto* for the whole of performance criticism:

> No performer can control the response to the text any more than the implied author of Mark's gospel could. As I have said, the early Christians would not have experienced this gospel except as it was performed! And no performance will be the same as another. Still, one thing becomes clearer to me about the gospel of Mark as I perform it: The "action" of Mark's gospel is performed—that is, "carried through to completion"—in the *actions of the community* to which it is given. And what is that "action" of that gospel? First, the realm of God broke into the world in the wake of the ministries of Jesus of Nazareth and John the baptizer. Second, the realm of God breaks in through the faithful performance of the gospel by communities of faith. Finally, faithful performance of the gospel has the power to turn the world, as it is known by those communities, upside down and inside out. The complication of the action of Mark's gospel is this: The abiding presence of Jesus breaks the grip of evil but confounds even his most cherished intimates while evoking confession and faith from unexpected voices in unexpected places. Doesn't this "action" play itself out in our faith communities? And how does that action end? It ends as this gospel does—with followers like us who are perplexed and bewildered at the good news of Jesus' resurrection, who say nothing to anyone about it because of fear, and who do not know where to look for him.[24]

This quote clearly explains the intention of a performance-critical approach: performance in antiquity is the basis of modern performance. In the same sense, David Rhoads wrote his article on biblical performance criticism as "an in-depth exploration of ways in which performing the New Testament compositions may help in our understanding of these documents in the context of the first century."[25]

---

24. Richard F. Ward, "The End Is Performance: Performance Criticism and the Gospel of Mark," in *Preaching Mark's Unsettling Messiah*, ed. David Fleer and Dave Bland (St. Louis: Chalice, 2006), 88–101, esp. 100–101.

25. Rhoads, *Biblical Performance Criticism*, 169; see also 168: "Hence, I propose

I agree that both performing the Gospel today and understanding the story in its first-century context are valid aspects of exegesis, but is there not a danger in trying to harmonize them? Our knowledge of how the Gospel stories were transmitted in the first century is too uncertain to use it as the basis for modern performance. Moreover, the early Christian context and our twenty-first-century situation are very different, making a transplantation of how performance in antiquity would have taken place to how it should be done today ill advised. Studies on performance criticism seem to mix up the original *Sitz im Leben* and the modern context, as if both contexts necessarily have to be identical. I propose that in performing the Gospel today we put in parentheses the question of the performance within the original context, not only because the contexts are absolutely incomparable, but also because—as performance critics acknowledge themselves—every performance is a new experience, created by the circumstances, audience, and not at least the performer himself or herself. If we are performing the Gospel today—and once again, why shouldn't we do that?—let it be for pedagogical, catechetical, or missionary activities. Rhoads writes, "Interpretation lies at the site of performance,"[26] but—convinced as I am that exegetical methods should be used in a complementary way—I think one should rather say "*also* at the site of performance." The complementary element of performing the Gospels is the justified revaluation of the communicative aspect of the message through its lively presentation. This revaluation makes sense, even without a theory of oral performance in antiquity. Oral communication of the Gospel contributes positively to the appropriation of the text today: it is a direct way of communication between the performer and the audience; it does not take too much time for an audience to hear a complete story; it creates the opportunity to bring together people from different backgrounds (like people coming together in a concert hall to hear Bach's *St. Matthew Passion*). And, as I will try to illustrate later on, in a class situation, for instance, it can create pedagogical moments through interactive discussions among the

---

that we can experiment with twenty-first-century performances as a way to explore the first-century performance event"; and 170: "If the goal of interpretation is to understand a New Testament writing in its ancient context, contemporary performing can open us exegetes to fresh dynamics of the text that will have an impact on our interpretations."

26. Ibid., 192.

students and the teacher about the content of the text and the interpretive skills needed to explicate it.

Narrative Criticism and Performance Criticism

Of course, from an academic perspective the success of telling the story of a Gospel will not (or not only) depend on the quality of the play or performance or performer[27] but also on two other aspects: the narratological insights that are at the basis of the performance and the continuing debate with the audience on matters of interpretation (which may be both historical and narratological). It is beyond the scope of this essay to address the question of the continuing debate. I just want to say that assisting at a performance could be an excellent trigger for people to become interested in biblical studies and that it could open doors for them to learn more about the historical and literary contexts of the Bible. The first point, however, on the relationship between performance and narrative criticism, requires further exploration. I do not pretend to address something completely new here. I only want to put more emphasis on a specific element that one has to take into account when performing the Gospel. Richard Ward has written that performance criticism is the child of narrative criticism ("literary criticism").[28] This necessary connection between narration and performance is well described by Rhoads:

> In order to perform, the interpreter/performer must make judgments about the potential meanings and the possible rhetorical impacts of a New Testament composition—taking on the roles of the characters, moving in imagination from place to place, interacting between one character and another, recounting the narrative world from the narrator's perspective and standards of judgment, and so on. I regularly discover new meanings of a line or an episode or a point of argumentation in the course of preparing for a performance and in the act of performing itself. In this way, performances can confirm certain interpretations,

---

27. I even think that a "too good" performance that leads the attention of the audience to the performer and not to the text does not necessarily serve the pedagogical aim of the method.

28. Ward, "End Is Performance," 93: "The performance critic is the child of the literary critic."

can expand interpretive possibilities, and can set parameters on viable interpretations.[29]

The performer has a capital role to play. He or she is an exegete, an interpreter, a mediator of the text to the audience. Every move, every emphasis, every look, every moment of silence, every position on the scene, every gesture, every use of rhythm—they all are the result of a (voluntary or involuntary) exegesis of the story. But the story is not a simple connection of single short pericopes. It is above all characterized by a unified plot based on some specific choices made by the narrator. These choices concern the overall presentation of characters, of conflicts, of time, of values, and so forth. The word used to talk about the global perspective behind these choices is *subtext*. Subtexts create coherence in the story and provide the implicit layers of meaning and themes in the text. In Mark, for instance, the narrator does not explicitly state that the disciples are ambivalent characters. But the idea is there, underlying every mention of the disciples in the text.

The *text* of the Gospel itself is what links the early Christian communities and the readers today. Moreover, *subtext* seems to me to be the connective word between performance criticism and narrative analysis. And that is why the performer today should first analyze the story, or more specifically the "subtext," before performance can take place. The performer is challenged to transfer to the audience the subtext of the Gospel through every action of the performance. Once again, Rhoads is a good guide to understand the function of subtext in performance:

> Perhaps the most generative feature of performance for research is that of the "subtext." The subtext refers to the message and impact that the performer conveys in the way a line is delivered. In performance, whether ancient or modern, the subtext represents a layer of meaning that is present in every line. Subtext is a level of exegesis largely unexplored in biblical studies, because silent reading in print does not require one to address the issue of subtext. Yet all performers have to decide what they will convey by *how* they say each line. Consider Jesus's manner of relating to the disciples in Mark. Take, for example, the line "Don't you understand yet?" in which Jesus addresses the disciples (Mark 8:17). Does the question imply inquiry, patience, impatience, sarcasm, disappointment, disdain, resignation? This is an obvious example, even to

---

29. Rhoads, "Biblical Performance Criticism," 170.

readers, but *every line* requires this kind of reflection. Listen to two different performances of the same passages and experience how differing inflections change the meaning and impact of the text.

A performer must seek to infer the subtext from the context and then try different subtexts to determine which approaches work best. There is no way to do a performance without conveying a subtext message with every line, no matter how badly done or ill-informed it is. Subtext can be conveyed both by voice and by physical expression (see below). For the most part, however, subtext is conveyed primarily through the voice—what tone to convey, where to put the emphasis, what pace to say it, whether there should be a pause, how loud it should be, and so on. It is a common exercise in oral interpretation to take a simple line and attempt to say the same line in as many different ways as possible. Or take any episode in Mark or a passage in a letter of Paul and try each line with different subtexts to see what works and how it works. This is an exercise well worth doing, if only to see how important the subtexts are and what a difference they can make.

The subtext is not an add-on. Rather, it is integral to and determinative of the meaning and rhetoric of a text. In performance, the subtext is an implicit part of the "text." There are many clues in a script that suggest how a line can be delivered, and the immediate clues are assessed in relation to the composition as a whole. To look for clues in the text that suggest appropriate subtexts for every line is to see a dimension of the text that may otherwise not even be part of the interpretation.[30]

"A performer must seek to infer the subtext from the context." The significant ideas here are first of all that performance through the communication of the "surface layer" (that is, the text) aims to transfer the deeper stratum of the text (that is, the subtext). Second, in order to understand the subtext of a particular verse or passage, one should take into account the immediate context and assess this in relation to the text as a whole. That is where narrative criticism comes into the picture. In the 1980s, one of the major innovative aspects of New Testament narrative criticism (together with the idea that the Gospels are stories) was the idea that the Gospels should be read as a whole. The meaning of every single verse had to be discovered against the background of the complete text. Once all the narrative elements, such as characterization, plot, conflict, rhetorical technique, stylistic features, and standards of judgment, are joined together so as to form one great puzzle, the subtext of the text can be discovered.

---

30. Ibid., 185.

That is why when students are learning to perform they should first of all become aware of the subtext in the story.

The Subtext and the Practice of Performing

The subtexts of the Gospel of Mark are complex, and scholars have differed in the description of it. The reason is clear: Mark is known for its use of indirect rhetorical strategy, recognizable through literary techniques such as paradox, irony, enigmatic metaphor, open ending, ambiguous characterization. This explains why so many different, even opposite, interpretations exist on Mark, particularly about his Christology or the role of the disciples. Rhoads is convinced that performing the Gospel can function as a test of interpretation: "Through performances, we may be able to identify which interpretations have a consensus, which interpretations are controversial but permitted, and which interpretations constitute a fundamental misconstrual of the possibilities of the text. In this way, performance may be an important way to test the limits of viable interpretations and provide criteria for making critical judgments in adjudications over interpretation."[31] Rhoads's point is that narrative criticism has first revealed that sometimes the story has multiple meanings. The same text could hide different subtexts. Performance forces one to opt for one out of several subtexts, and in order to make this choice one should be aware of the different readings presented through narrative analysis. In making choices performers are forced to limit themselves to one way of interpreting the text, that is, to one particular subtext. This could be considered as a certain weakness of performing, and this is why we need a continuing debate before or after the performance. Nothing, however, prohibits a performer from shifting to a different subtext in subsequent performances.

The Experience of the Classroom

All that I have written above is largely theoretical. The quest for the subtext(s) opens a new box of exciting challenges. One of them is how we could apply this in a teaching situation. In order to make it more concrete, I would like to share how I built up my own class around these

---

31. Ibid., 191. Rhoads is referring to Ronald Pelias, *Performance Studies: The Interpretation of Aesthetic Texts* (New York: St. Martin's, 1992).

reflections on the relationship between narrative criticism and a concrete performance of the Gospel of Mark. During the academic year 2014–2015, I taught a class on the Gospel of Mark for undergraduate students at the Faculty of Theology at Louvain-la-Neuve (Belgium). We had twelve meetings of two hours each, and the whole course was accessible through a digital learning environment. Fifteen students took the class: five regular undergraduate students, two "free" students, and eight students who took the course as part of their program to become a certified teacher of religion in the secondary school (ages 13–18). This last group was composed of students who had already some experience in teaching (religion and other courses) in a secondary school. One of the learning outcomes of the course was to make the students acquainted with different exegetical methods and how these could be useful when they are applied in a complementary way. A second learning outcome was to understand how narrative criticism (and the search for a subtext) could help with a performance of the Gospel. By appropriating these insights, students could also learn how to use these principles themselves in their own classrooms. I organized the class as a flipped classroom in which we would start from what the students themselves discovered to be problematic elements in the text of Mark. This pedagogy seems to have contributed considerably to the success of the course.

Since not everything we did in the class is relevant for this article's topic, I want to describe how we proceeded and focus on some particular elements. First, I asked the students to read the Gospel from A to Z at home. I asked them to read it attentively and to choose a single passage that they would like to study more deeply in the weeks thereafter. Any reason that would ground their choice was good: maybe they found it a difficult passage or maybe they liked it very much or maybe their fellow students in other classes always asked questions about miracles or exorcisms. They also had to formulate two or three spontaneous questions about the passage they had chosen and try to give their own spontaneous answers to these questions.

At the next meeting, we discovered together that we had a representative sampling of questions on Mark. Apart from the evident questions (What are Pharisees? What is the temple? Why did Jesus ask the healed people to keep silence?), students discovered stylistic elements (change from singular to plural, repetition, sandwich constructions) or posed questions on the content (Why is it that he "had to suffer"?). This was an illuminating experience since we could see that the spontaneous answers—especially with regard to contents—were not unanimous. Some of the students spontaneously adhered to a rather "apologetic" reading in order to defend a historical or even theological accuracy of the evangelist. Others were more open to accepting enigma and uncertainty. One could say that the first group thought that Mark should *contain* truth, while the second thought that Mark's reader should *discover* truth.

The next step was for the students to find out how *scholars* are answering these questions and to compare these scholarly approaches with their own answers. So every student had to search in at least three international commentaries on Mark what the exegetes were thinking. In doing so, the students could see that scholars as well did not agree on the interpretation of the difficulties in the text. Especially for the first group of students, this experience was very fruitful. They saw how scholars on the one hand tried to study the text "objectively" but still differed among each other in many ways. Through their own small research work, students were confronted with the fact that there is a debate about almost every word in the Gospel and that there is no such a thing as one single interpretation of the text. All this was nothing more than preparatory work for a narrative-critical approach of the text.

The first step toward narrative criticism was to find out that many stylistic features and many themes occur throughout the Gospel. This meant that we likely had to do with a coherent text that was written by one single author. One of the students who had studied Romance languages brought up the notion of "point of view": Is it possible that we could speak about a narrator who had a specific way of looking at the "events" and who had constructed his own Jesus? What would that particular point of view be? And do all students recognize the same point of view? They also learned that there seemed to be contradictions in the text: some students had chosen a text for deeper study in which the disciples or Peter were described in very positive terms, while other students had chosen one in which the disciples were "dumb." The question of the subtext came up automatically. If the Gospel of Mark is written in that strange particular way, what is the deepest underlying message that it wants to transfer after all?

This question—what kind of message does the narrator want to transmit by not saying it?—led to a rather strange formulation of Mark's overall "subtext." Since the subtext is communicated indirectly by all kinds of narratological elements in the text (characters, time, topography, style), narrative criticism helped students to investigate. They found out that it was not easy to find *the* subtext of Mark. They mentioned at least two reasons. First, their own preparatory work (questions and answers) and the reading of commentaries had revealed that Mark is situated in a specific political and religious context (represented, for example, through different characters in the Gospel) and that it was difficult to decide what exactly Mark was focusing on. To give just one example: What does μετανοία mean (1:4, 15)? The same could be said about Mark's theology and Christology: Who is God and who is Jesus?

These last questions are at the heart of the second reason why it is difficult to find *the* subtext, namely, that the narrator creates confusion in the mind of the reader. Unexpected and surprising reactions of Jesus or other characters, ambiguous sayings, gaps in the text, asides, and parabolic language make it almost impossible to catch at first sight the metamessage of Mark. One of the conclusions we reached was that we could not impose one single specific subtext for all students. Every student was allowed to search for a unifying subtext in the Gospel, as long as she or he was able to give arguments from the entire text of the Gospel.

As I stated above, at the end of the first class I had asked the students to learn by heart the text of the pericope they had chosen. They did not know at that moment that I would ask them to perform their story in front of the other students. I proposed this to them only one month before the last two lessons. Initially, they were surprised: Should we, students between twenty and forty years old, perform this text? In front of the other students? And how does it help us to understand the text?

In order to convince them of the added value of performing a passage as the result of the research work they had done, I told them that I myself would perform three passages from Mark that witness to the complexity of the subtext and where the discussion about the meaning should necessarily precede or follow the performance. It was my suggestion to them that performance is not a simple thing to do but that it is based on a long process of studying the text. Also, it is not always possible to perform the story in such a way that the tensions of the complex written text are transmitted to the audience. I would like to help them understand that a performance of these three "difficult" texts raises the question of the relation between narrative criticism (the subtext) and performance. The three passages served as an invitation to a debate on the interpretation of the subtext of Mark. Two questions are in permanent dialogue: *what* to perform and *how* to perform. Below, I present my three choices and represent myself as the performer to my students.

Mark 15:34: "My God, My God, Why Have You Abandoned Me?"

How to understand and how to perform this verse?[32] In exegesis I find two very different, almost opposite, interpretations of this verse. The positive one considers the verse to be an expression of hope by Jesus, who intends to pray the whole of Ps 22. The other one emphasizes Jesus's feeling of complete abandonment by his Father; he is praying only the first verse of the psalm. Does the performer depict hope or abandonment, just to mention the two extremes of a wide range of emotions in between?

I performed the two possibilities in front of the students. They immediately understood that the question has very important christological consequences. The performer must determine which content she or he wants to transmit. Difference in tone, rhythm, gesture, look, volume, and speed will offer the possibility to the performer to transmit a different kind of portrait of Jesus to the audience. The subtext here is of major importance: Which is the global image of Jesus the performer has in mind when performing the story? The way one performs 15:34 will be the result of how one has characterized Jesus in front of one's audience in the story that precedes this verse. If one has presented a self-confident Jesus who is master of all situations, even the difficult ones, one will be tempted to play 15:34 as a saying of trust in the good result of this tragic moment. The perspective of the resurrection is already there; the characterization of Jesus is dominated by his authority and power, which are characteristic of the Son of God. If, however, the performer has thought of a Jesus who is a human person, "one of us," who shares the human condition and who is characterized also by fear and uncertainty, one will perform 15:34 as an expression of anxiety and abandonment. Both interpretations seem to be possible, but it is through narrative criticism that the performer will discover them. Then one has to choose. Which subtext will dominate: a suffering, abandoned Jesus or a suffering, trustful Son of God? When I performed the two possible options, it became clear for the students what the challenge was about. They felt the need to search the Gospel for other passages on the characterization of Jesus in order to know how to perform 15:34.

---

32. For a recent study on the history of the interpretation and on the role of the background of the real reader for the interpretation, see Geert Van Oyen and Patty Van Cappellen, "Mark 15,34 and the *Sitz im Leben* of the Real Reader," *ETL* 91 (2015): 269–99.

Mark 15:39: "Truly, This Man Was God's Son"

The same situation occurs in the performance of the confession of the centurion at the moment of Jesus's death. Once again, the christological and theological impact of the interpretation of this verse became immediately clear when I performed the verse in two different ways, first as if I stood in a sacred place full of devotion, then with a kind of mocking ironical tone. Are the words of the centurion really a positive recognition of Jesus's divine sonship? Or could they be understood as an ironical (that is, sarcastic) mockery by the centurion? Once again, these are two extremes and in between them we find many more nuanced interpretations. But the challenge for the performer is clear: he discovers two different ways of reading. Will he play the text in such a way that the centurion becomes one of the Roman soldiers who are mocking at Jesus, because it is unthinkable and unacceptable that a son of God should be crucified? Or will he opt for acting as if the centurion represents the first (pagan) Christian who is confessing that Jesus is the Son of God (and who unlike Peter in 8:29 will not be corrected by Jesus and will not be asked to keep silence)? Once again, the choice of a subtext is important. The discussion with the students in the class received a new dimension: What precisely in the Gospel of Mark is it that could make people recognize in a correct way that Jesus is Son of God? It is certainly not the miracles, but is it his passion and his death? Or does a true confession implicitly presuppose the experience of the empty tomb story? Or even an encounter with the risen Lord (not told by Mark!)? Or should the audience learn to live with the fact that there is no human person at all who is able to recognize the exact meaning of Jesus's divine sonship? Having the direct experience of both ways of performing raised a number of fundamental questions on Mark.

The End of Mark

The panorama of interpretations of the provocative ending of Mark in 16:8 is endless. The threefold attitude of the women (fear, flight, silence) after they had heard the announcement of the resurrection of Jesus by the young man is surprising. How could this verse be understood as "good news"? So many themes of the Gospel are joined together in this paradoxical finale that the performer is confronted by an enormous challenge. What elements of the text will she pay most attention to? What kind of effect does a performer want to provoke within the audience? What is the fundamental message she wants to transfer to the audience? Is it the resurrection of Jesus? Then in what sense does the threefold reaction of the women (silence, fear, flight) help to transmit this message? Is their reaction positive (awe) or negative (incomprehension)?

It was not easy for me to perform two different versions of 16:8. It was mostly by my facial expression that I tried to show the difference. The first time I did it with a firm voice and almost no facial expression, so as to give the impression that the story had come to an end. The second time I tried to show while I was pronouncing the words that I was puzzled by them.

A new debate started among the students about the meaning of the end of Mark. It seemed to them that there are too many elements in the text to make them visible or audible in one single performance. The subtexts, or underlying layers of this handful of words, is richer than the oral performance can show. The most important thing—they found—is that the performer should be aware of the narrative debate going on about the end of Mark and that she should be aware of the choice she is making. One of the students said: "Mark wants us to continue to talk about the story."

Conclusion

After having seen my performances, the students understood that performing a passage of Mark demands an understanding of the whole of the Gospel. They felt more relaxed and better prepared to perform their own pericope. We took about thirty minutes for each student. They were asked to play their short passage and to try to integrate the insights they had found through the preceding study of the narrative. It is impossible in this article to explain all the individual choices students made to perform the Gospel passages, but some of them were creative. One student simply put a mask on the back of his head and turned around every time the narrator spoke. Another one looked into the eyes of the audience when Jesus spoke. Still another one took different positions on stage depending on whether the narrator, Jesus, or other characters were speaking. The effect of the course was that through small techniques they all tried to bring in something they had learned from narrative criticism. To the question if and what they had learned in the course, I received several and varying answers that could be classified in two groups.

The first group concerns learning by heart:

- Having learned the text by heart I am able to meditate on it easier.

- I could not overlook the smallest detail of the text, and I heard an echo of the text the whole day long.
- I noticed details I never noticed before (characters, space, movement).
- Knowing the text by heart makes it easier to understand the exegetical literature.
- The repetitions (of sentences and of words) became apparent.
- I am used to drilling my courses aloud. Doing the same thing while learning by heart made me discover different ways of performing the text.
- I was struck by the conciseness of Mark's style ("I would have made Jesus much angrier in the temple!").
- I could create more suspense when I paused from time to time.
- Knowing the text by heart made me much more comfortable in discussing the text with my own students.

The second group concerns the link between narrative criticism and performance criticism:

- The gestures I had to make allowed me to get closer to the meaning of the text.
- I had to pay attention to who was talking: Jesus or the narrator.
- Narrative criticism gave me a more solid basis to preach or teach about the text I performed.
- Through narrative criticism I learned that the emotions should receive a place while performing (When do I have to talk loud? When do I have to change the tone? When do I have to pause?).
- The different points of view in the passage were very important: the disciples do not think like Jesus.
- Through performance it was easier to make clear to the audience that there were three groups in my scene (Jesus, disciples, opponents).
- Through narrative exegesis I learned to discover the plot of my passage and I could perform it easier.
- The advantage of performing was that I could dramatize the text better. I could give more emphasis to the words of Jesus.

After each performance the other students were allowed to ask questions from what they had experienced (and also about the contents of the text). These discussions were fruitful, because we discovered another completely overlooked dimension of performing: the role of the audience! The performance made clear that the impact of a certain way of performing provoked direct reactions and emotions within the audience. This immediately brought up a very interesting question: Should we add a new item in the course, something like *audience criticism*? Just like there is reader-response criticism as a logical consequence of narrative criticism, audience criticism would be an indispensable addition to performance criticism. What are the expectations of the audience? What are their presuppositions? Why does the same performance provoke different reactions in the audience?

Though the evaluation of the course was rather positive, we all regretted two things: first, that there was not enough time for the students to make a second tour of their performances in which they would have played once more the same passage taking into account the remarks of their classmates; second, that there was no profound discussion about how to deal with the fact that more subtexts seemed to be possible. In what measure does the identity of the reader/performer him- or herself contribute to the "discovery" of a subtext? Could it be possible that the choice of the subtext that is used is influenced by the kind of audience and community? These are questions that would need further reflection.

But the construction of the course is a work in progress, and we agreed upon several positive outcomes afterward: (1) Performing a story means enrichment for both performer and audience. (2) The performer should be aware of the subtext that is underlying the performance. (3) This subtext should be discovered through narrative analysis of the story. (4) Discussion before or/and after the performance (on the subtext or on other more concrete items of the story) is a welcome complement to deepen the immediate and unique experience of a performance.

7
TEACHING THE MOST DIFFICULT TEXT IN THE GOSPEL OF MARK: MARK 9:42–50

Francis J. Moloney, SDB, AM, FAHA

The Gospel of Mark contains puzzling sequences, raising questions about what they mean in themselves and how they function within the narrative as a whole. One of the most puzzling is 9:42–50: "Readers may well feel slightly bewildered after a first glance at these verses."[1] In this text, Jesus's words initially warn against "scandalizing" (σκανδαλίσῃ) one of "these little ones" (ἕνα τῶν μικρῶν τούτων, v. 42). From that point on "the little ones" are forgotten, and the possible causes of personal sin are challenged. Jesus recommends the violent elimination of parts of the body that "cause *you* to sin" (σκανδαλίσῃ σε, vv. 43–47). This is followed by a chain of sayings that seem to be linked by the catchwords "fire" and "salt" (vv. 48–50b). Without any immediate warning, Jesus closes the saying with a recommendation to be at peace with one another (v. 50c). The narrative takes another direction in 10:1: "He left that place and went to Judea and beyond the Jordan."[2] NA[28] prints Mark 9:42–50 as a self-standing literary unit.[3] A majority of commentators also sets it apart from the surrounding narrative, though it forms part of Jesus's instruction of the disciples across verses 33–50. Among others, Joel Marcus has rightly recognized that the instruction embedded in 9:33–50 is similar to passages that follow each

---

1. Dennis E. Nineham, *The Gospel of Mark*, Pelican Gospel Commentaries (Harmondsworth: Penguin Books, 1963), 250.
2. NRSV, tentatively accepting the reading "and" (καί), missing in the Western and Antiochene texts.
3. At this point, a teacher should point out the secondary value of the printed editions of the New Testament and the medieval background to chapters and verses.

of the passion predictions in 8:31; 9:31; and 10:32–34.[4] What approach, therefore, should a teacher take in addressing this difficult passage? Perhaps no single approach can claim to communicate what intelligent students need to know.[5]

Using an eclectic approach, the teacher can consider the text's literary history and possible creative links that generated the Markan version of a complex of Jesus-sayings made up of apparently unrelated statements. Moreover, the teacher who hopes to render this first-century Christian text relevant must communicate more than "history." That is, the teacher must not ignore the inner dynamic of the narrative but employ some audience-oriented approach in order to test whether a text now almost two thousand years old, written in Greek, has an enduring impact on the minds and hearts of a classroom of students in the third millennium.

Mark 9:42–50 offers itself to an eclectic approach in a number of ways. For example, it is an excellent text for instruction on the intricacies of textual criticism. It is notoriously jumbled across the witnesses, and verses 44 and 46 are universally regarded as additions to the original, an attempt to insert some clarity into these "bewildering" verses.[6] It is also an excellent passage to use as the starting point for a teacher to examine the vagaries of the Synoptic problem. Traditions found in Mark 9:42–50 are variously used, in different literary and theological settings in Matthew 18:6–9 (little

---

4. See Joel Marcus, *Mark 9–16*, AYB 27A (New York: Doubleday; New Haven: Yale University Press, 2009), 671–73.

5. In this essay, I presume throughout that the Gospel of Mark was written from and into a believing context, that it was eventually accepted as sacred Scripture in a believing context, and that it has maintained its place because of a community of believers. Today's classroom, however, may be composed of believing and unbelieving students. The expression "what needs to be known" is deliberate. No one can hope to discover "what can be known." Students must be made aware of this hermeneutical issue at an early stage of their biblical studies curriculum.

6. The complexity of the passage and the obvious nature of the textual manipulation by copyists make it a very clear example of scribal practices. Both v. 44 and v. 46 in the Textus Receptus are missing from all the major witnesses. They are clearly added by copyists from v. 48 (v. 44) and v. 43 (v. 46). The introduction of "salt" in v, 49, regarded by Marcus as "perhaps the most enigmatic logion of Jesus in the NT" (*Mark 9–16*, 698), also has a disturbed textual tradition. The scholarly commentaries offer helpful information. See, for example, Adela Yarbro Collins, *Mark: A Commentary*, Hermeneia (Minneapolis: Fortress, 2007), 442–43; William L. Lane, *Commentary on the Gospel of Mark*, NICNT (Grand Rapids: Eerdmans, 1974), 346–47 n. 76; Craig A. Evans, *Mark 8:27–16:20*, WBC 34B (Nashville: Nelson, 2001), 68–69.

ones, causes for sin, cutting off); 5:13 (salt); Luke 17:1–2 (causes for sin); and 14:34–35 (salt).[7] I will argue that a text is best illuminated by an eclectic approach that encompasses historical-critical, redactional, literary, and performance approaches. Using Mark 9:42–50 as a test case, I will suggest how an eclectic approach to exegesis can lead students to a discovery of the meaning of a passage, both then and now.

Historical Approaches

Source and Form Criticisms

Those who identify a number of redactional stages and interpolations into that redaction begin by pointing to the wider narrative context. Rudolf Bultmann has suggested that the material originated in some form of pre-Markan instructional catechism on the question of greatness, beginning with the gathering "in the house" at Capernaum in 9:33–35.[8] The passage has been constructed from pre-Markan tradition in the author's attempt to produce rules of piety that distinguished the church from Judaism.[9] While the details of Bultmann's theory have been widely rejected, historical critics have accepted his approach to the history of the passage, with variations. Stated simply, Mark has inserted at least three originally independent pre-Markan collections into Jesus's instruction of his disciples that follows hard on the heels of the second passion prediction (see 9:31). Some suggest an original triad of sayings that were concerned with children (vv. 37, 41, 42), a further triad that dealt with causing sin (vv. 43, 45, 47), a final parable on salt, leading to the command to be at peace with one another (vv. 49–50), and a Markan conclusion that looks back to the contentious silence that immediately followed the passion prediction in verses 33–34.[10]

---

7. For a helpful discussion, see W. D. Davies and Dale C. Allison Jr., *Matthew*, ICC, 3 vols. (Edinburgh: T&T Clark, 1988–1997), 2:752–53.

8. Rudolf Bultmann, *The History of the Synoptic Tradition*, trans. John Marsh (Oxford: Blackwell, 1963), 149–50.

9. See ibid., 146.

10. See, for example, Joachim Gnilka, *Das Evangelium nach Markus*, 5th ed., 2 vols., EKKNT 2 (Zurich: Benziger; Neukirchen-Vluyn: Neukirchener Verlag, 1999), 2:63–67, esp. the summary on p. 67.

Redaction Criticism

This final remark, that verses 49–50 form a type of "inclusion" with verses 33–34, indicates a turn to redaction criticism.[11] Depending upon the results of the research that identified traditions that were used to generate the text as we have it today, redaction critics ask a further historical question: what theological agenda (among many possible) led an early Christian author to gather these prior traditions *in this way*? In our case, why were originally independent sayings gathered together and placed side by side within the literary frame of verses 33–34 and verses 49–50? As one of the founding figures of the approach, Hans Conzelmann, put it: "A variety of sources does not necessarily imply a similar variety in the thought and composition of the author. How did it come about that he brought together these particular materials?"[12]

Redaction critics strain to uncover the theological perspectives that drove the final composition of Mark, Matthew, Luke, and John. These are important *historical* questions and belong to the world behind the text. But a class must be led to understand that the printed text they have before them, generally in their own language, not in the original Greek, came from a real-life situation in the early church. In an eclectic approach, an initial historical investigation is the first stone to be put in place in order to arrive at the more audience-oriented contemporary approaches. We "stand upon the shoulders" of those who went before us.

Literary Approaches

Narrative Criticism

Without disregarding the historical background that must be understood for an appreciation of the story, a narrative commentary attempts to trace the intended impact of that story upon its readers. This reading and interpretive process attempts to uncover the literary structure of the narrative as a whole and traces the unfolding of the narrative, allowing it to speak for itself. The interpretation of difficult texts like Mark 9:42–50 must be

---

11. For a summary, see Francis J. Moloney, *The Gospel of Mark: A Commentary* (Grand Rapids: Baker Academic, 2012), 6–8.

12. Hans Conzelmann, *The Theology of St Luke*, trans. Geoffrey Buswell (London: Faber & Faber, 1960), 9.

determined by the narrative as a whole. Keys for unlocking interpretation are found *within the narrative*. Readings that focus upon the flow of the narrative must always consider the longer story.[13] The Gospel of Mark begins with a prologue (1:1–13) and ends with an epilogue (16:1–8).[14] Mark 1:14–15:42 contains two major narrative developments that deal, in the first place, with the question that surrounds the person of Jesus (1:14–8:30), followed by the Markan response to the question. Jesus is presented as the crucified and risen Son of Man, the Christ, and the Son of God (8:31–15:47). Mark 9:42–50 is located in a section of 8:31–10:52 that focuses intensely upon what it means to be a disciple of Jesus.

Set between two miracles where a blind man is cured (8:22–26; 10:46–52) and dominated by Jesus's three passion predictions (8:31; 9:31; 10:32–34), the same literary pattern is repeated three times.[15] It can be summarized as follows:

8:31–9:29: Passion prediction (8:31). The disciples cannot or will not accept Jesus's self-revelation as the suffering and vindicated Son of Man (vv. 32–33), and Jesus instructs his failing disciples on the cost of discipleship (8:34–9:29: the cross).
9:30–10:31: Passion prediction (9:30–31). The disciples cannot or will not accept Jesus's self-revelation as the suffering and vindicated Son of Man (vv. 32–34), and Jesus instructs his failing disciples on the cost of discipleship (9:35–10:31: service).
10:32–10:45: Passion prediction (10:32–34). The disciples cannot or will not accept Jesus's self-revelation as the suffering and vindicated Son of Man (10:35–37; see also v. 41), and Jesus instructs his failing disciples on the cost of discipleship (10:38–40; see also vv. 42–44: the cross and service)

Closing this threefold development of Markan Christology and its subsequent idea of discipleship, one finds "one of the most important"

---

13. For what follows, see Moloney, *Gospel of Mark*, 16–22. These pages attempt to uncover the plot of the Gospel of Mark on the basis of markers within the text itself and then develop a literary structure that best carries that plot.

14. This division accepts that the original Gospel closed at 16:8. See further ibid., 354–62.

15. On the literary "bridge" out of 1:14–8:30 into 8:31–15:47 generated by 8:22–30, see ibid., 162–68.

sayings in the Gospel, summarizing 8:31–10:44: "For the Son of Man also came, not to be served but to serve, and to give his life as a ransom for many" (10:45).[16] A classroom exposed to this section of the Gospel of Mark can be called upon to share their experience of revelation, failure, and Jesus's ongoing teaching and accompanying presence. Whatever the history of the passage, it can be taught as a narrative expression of age-old Christian experiences.

Contemporary postmodern critics have rightly insisted that an interpreter take into account his or her particular social and religious "location." They necessarily impose limitations upon any teacher who can do no more than communicate her or his interpretation.[17] Humility should be a key virtue for any interpreter of ancient texts. Belief that the Gospel of Mark is part of the Christian "sacred Scriptures" presupposes that this story made an impact in their original setting and telling (or performing) in the life of the church.[18] A narrative interpretation attempts to uncover a communication process that has gone on between writers/tellers and readers/listeners across the Christian centuries.

A Narrative Interpretation of Mark 9:42–50

Within the thrice-repeated literary pattern of passion prediction, failure, and teaching, 9:42–50 forms part of the "teaching" section that follows hard on the heels of the second passion prediction (9:31), the disciples' lack of understanding and fear (v. 32), and their weak responses to Jesus's self-revelation (see vv. 33–34; v. 38). Essential for the narrative interpretation of verses 42–50 are the indications of verses 33–34. On arrival at Capernaum, when Jesus asks what they were discussing on the way: "they were silent, for on the way they had argued with one another [πρὸς ἀλλήλους γὰρ διελέχθεσαν] who was the greatest" (v. 34). In verse 35, Jesus adopts the position of a teacher ("he sat down, called the twelve, and said to them") and begins to instruct them on the greatness of service. In verses 36–37,

---

16. The statement about the importance of the saying is from Vincent Taylor, *The Gospel according to St. Mark*, 2nd ed. (London: Macmillan, 1966), 444.

17. See, among many, the helpful pages of Jonathan Culler, *On Deconstruction: Theory and Criticism after Structuralism* (London: Routledge, 1983), 31–83.

18. On this process, see Francis J. Moloney, *Reading the New Testament in the Church: A Primer for Pastors, Religious Educators, and Believers* (Grand Rapids: Baker Academic, 2015), 57–61.

he uses the image of a child to teach the disciples the need for service and receptivity. This is immediately followed by John's witness to the *lack of service and receptivity* among the Twelve, who reject an exorcist "because he was not following us" (v. 38). This passage features sayings linked by the catchphrase "in my name" (vv. 39, 41). They are wrong to insist that the exorcist must follow them (v. 38), since he is acting in the name of Jesus.

Within this broader setting, the noun changes from "child" to "little one," but Jesus's words on receiving "one such child" (v. 37) become a threat in verse 42.[19] Jesus warns his disciples: "Whoever causes one of these little ones who believe in me [ἕνα τῶν μικρῶν τούτων τῶν πιστευόντων εἰς ἐμέ] to sin." The argument is ongoing.[20] John's remarks and Jesus's answer raise an issue concerning those who belong to Jesus, and the community that "bears the name of Christ" in verses 38–41 (see esp. v. 41) determines the storyteller's use of earlier traditions to continue his presentation of Jesus's teaching. This passage is a collection of originally independent sayings from pre-Markan tradition, gathered on the basis of two principles. The first of these principles is the problem of sin within the community, the theme stated in verse 42a. People who considered themselves "great" (see v. 34) may not concern themselves overly with "the little ones" (v. 42). Such people would be better eliminated from the community. The image of the millstone around the neck of such a person cast into the sea speaks eloquently of total annihilation, a practice used in antiquity (v. 42b).[21] If a violent death by drowning, with a millstone attached to the neck to assure death, is *better* (καλόν ἐστιν αὐτῷ μᾶλλον) than giving scandal, one can only imagine how devastating would be the punishment for causing a member of the community to sin. The use of the verb σκανδαλίζω in verse 42 brings

---

19. For what follows on 9:42–50, see Moloney, *Gospel of Mark*, 190–92.

20. An important exegetical decision is called for in interpreting the change from "child" (vv. 36–37: παιδίον) to "one of these little ones" (v. 42: ἕνα τῶν μικρῶν) as a continuation of Jesus's use of children (see Evans, *Mark*, 70) or as a change of direction in the argument, with the "little ones" being "a reference to Christians, perhaps again Christian missionaries" (Marcus, *Mark 9–16*, 695). The ongoing nature of the argument from 9:33–50 points to the former as the most likely meaning. However, the overall argument of 9:31–10:30 raises the possibility that *all* the innocent and frail members of the community are indicated.

21. This form of execution is taken from Roman practice and was not unknown among the Jews. Thus we see the importance of "history," even in literary interpretations. See Marie-Joseph Lagrange, *Évangile selon Saint Marc*, EBib (Paris: Gabalda, 1920), 234–35.

into play the second generative principle in this passage: link-words. This literary process was already part of the author's technique in the immediately previous verses 38–41.[22]

From the "causing to sin" (σκανδαλίσῃ) in verse 42, the author uses the same verb to consider other parts of the body, the hand (v. 43), the foot (v. 45), and the eye (v. 47), which might lead a believer to sin (σκανδαλίζῃ). If a part of the body causes sin (vv. 43, 45, 47: σκανδαλίζῃ), then it is to be cut off and cast away. One is better to enter life maimed than to go to the unquenchable fire of hell. These demands are regularly explained as Semitic hyperbole—cutting off hand and foot, plucking out the eye—but this is not the case.[23] The teacher should point out that Jesus's words mean what they say. They teach the unsurpassable blessings available in the kingdom. "God is even more important than the most important parts of our body."[24] It is better (καλόν ἐστιν σε) to be without a hand, a foot, or an eye, than to lose the opportunity to enter the life of God's kingdom.[25] This point can only be appreciated when one takes into account that women and men normally have *two* hands, *two* feet, and *two* eyes. One can do without a hand, a foot or an eye; but one cannot do without the gift of life in the kingdom. To have both hands, both eyes, and both feet, but to have allowed them to lead you into sin and death, forever in the unquenchable fire of hell, is unthinkable for the Markan Jesus. The classroom situation can be used to generate a realistic understanding of this Christian truth. This would be especially true in a classroom that had experience of people with physical incapacities who are able to function quite well.

---

22. Some commentators link v. 42 with vv. 38–41, but the link generated by σκανδαλίζω locates it firmly as the opening statement in vv. 42–50. There is also a *reprise* of the call for oneness in v. 50, recalling the necessary care for the "little ones" in v. 42. For an even more extensive suggestion of "link-words" across vv. 33–50, see Marcus, *Mark 9–16*, 672–73.

23. See, for example, Morna D. Hooker, *The Gospel according to St Mark*, BNTC (London: Black; Peabody, MA: Hendrickson, 1991), 232.

24. Eduard Schweizer, *The Good News according to Mark*, trans. Donald H. Madvig (London: SPCK, 1971), 198.

25. In vv. 43 and 45, Jesus speaks of entering "life," while in v. 47 he speaks of entering "the kingdom of God." For Mark they are the same, although Mark indicates the richness of "life in the kingdom" by using both expressions. See Dale C. Allison Jr., *Constructing Jesus: Memory, Imagination, and History* (Grand Rapids: Baker Academic, 2010), 168–90.

The extreme measure of cutting off and plucking out attests to the unparalleled richness of the life offered to those "little ones who believe in Jesus" (see v. 42).[26] Whatever these sayings may have meant originally, in their present context they refer to sin that brings scandal and further sin into the community.[27] This meaning is determined by the introduction, verse 42, where causing the little ones who believe in Jesus to sin is the theme. The same message is taken up in the conclusion of verses 49–50, where living in peace with one another is stressed, returning to the theme of the tense and conflictual silence among the disciples concerning who was the greatest in verses 33–34.[28]

A description of Gehenna closes the rhetoric of verses 43–47, dominated by the possibility of the choice of entering the kingdom maimed, or the never-ending pains of Gehenna physically intact (see already v. 43). Mark cites Isa 66:24: "where the worm does not die and the fire is not quenched" (v. 48).[29] These words lead the author to link other originally independent sayings. The word *fire* (πυρί) in the citation of Isaiah leads to the addition of a further saying: "For everyone will be salted with fire [πυρί]" (v. 49).[30] The word *salted* in verse 49 (ἁλισθήσεται) leads to a fourfold play on "salt" in verse 50 (ἅλας, ἅλας, ἄναλον, ἅλα). Salt was a most widespread precious commodity in antiquity, giving ongoing life and flavor to food. We are again dealing with a past reality that has an impact upon a present reading in the hands of a good teacher. In our own time, salt is an essential ingredient to so many foods and even to drinks. Once it is in food and drink, it permeates everything and cannot be removed. Such is the comprehensive presence of "fire," which, in contrast to salt that enlivens, destroys entirely.

---

26. The sayings are therefore a strong affirmation of the life offered by following Jesus, cost what it may. Commentators rightly see the link with 8:34–9:1.

27. For this case, see Allison, *Constructing Jesus*, 186–88.

28. The use of the verb διαλογίζομαι in v. 34 carries the meaning of "arguing" among themselves. See BDAG, 232, s.v. διαλογίζομαι.

29. "Gehenna" was the name given to a valley to the southwest of Jerusalem where human sacrifices had been offered to the gods Moloch and Baal. After the reform of Josiah (see 1 Kgs 23:10), it became the city rubbish dump, where fires burned continually.

30. This enigmatic saying, which crosses from the punishing fire to the blessing of salt, has a complicated textual history. For the discussion, and the establishment of the above text, see Charles E. B. Cranfield, *The Gospel according to St Mark*, CGTC (Cambridge: Cambridge University Press, 1959), 314–15.

The threatening image of the penetrating and destroying fire of Gehenna (v. 49) has been transferred to refer to the life-giving uniqueness of the believers. The move from the destructive power of fire to salt as a source of life may run the danger of overmixing metaphors; but, paradoxically, it gives unity to the message. Like fire, salt is an agent of purification (Ezek 16:4; 43:24); it can also bring desolation and destruction (Judg 9:45; Zeph 2:9). But unlike fire, salt is a source of life (2 Kgs 2:19–22); it can be used to preserve food from putrefaction. However mixed the metaphor, the idea that people can be salted with fire sums up exactly the message of verses 43, 45, and 47: the purificatory process may destroy, but it can also preserve.[31]

Having salt in themselves, believers are penetrated by belief in God and openness to God's ways (v. 50).[32] Once this salt, which gives sense and flavor to the believer's commitment to follow the way of Jesus, is lost, nothing can replace it. Whether this happens or how it might happen is irrelevant;[33] the image retains its power, as one cannot imagine what a salted object might be like without its saltiness. "An image of communal harmony ('be at peace with one another') is counterposed to the portrait of lonely horror."[34]

Integration: History, Redaction, Narrative

By the conclusion of the second major step in an eclectic approach to Mark 9:42–50, students are aware that a collection of originally independent sayings is drawn together in concluding words that could lay claim to motivating the whole of verses 33–50. Having salt, the driving force that makes sense of Christian life and gives it flavor, is described as being at peace with one another (v. 50b). The issue that opened these sayings returns, the demand that none of the little ones who believes in Jesus be led into sin

---

31. Hooker, *Mark*, 233.

32. The καί, linking having salt and being at peace, indicates consequence: "have salt in yourselves, *and then* you will be at peace among yourselves." See Ernst Lohmeyer, *Das Evangelium des Markus*, 17th ed., Meyers Kommentar (Göttingen: Vandenhoeck & Ruprecht, 1967), 197; Taylor, *Mark*, 414.

33. See Hooker, *Mark*, 233. She regards the discussions about salt losing its taste as "pedantic." For a contrary view, reading the combined use of salt and fire as powerful eschatological language, with its roots in the wisdom tradition, see Marcus, *Mark 9–16*, 698–99.

34. Marcus, *Mark 9–16*, 699.

(vv. 42, 50). This theme, in turn, looks back to Jesus's criticism of John's description of the divisive practices of the Twelve that would never produce peace (vv. 38–41). The storyteller has used this complex gathering of traditions and somewhat bewildering linking of images by means of catchwords and catchphrases to expand further upon Jesus's teaching to the Twelve, after their initial failure (vv. 32–34) and their continued arrogance (v. 38).

By now the classroom is aware that Mark had concerns for the original audience of this story of Jesus, who wondered about authority and care for the more fragile members of the community. Mark's concerns remain within any single Christian community and the Christian community as a whole. Disciples are to be the least of all and the servants of all, like children themselves, receptive to the least of all (vv. 35–37), never judging anyone who works in the name of Jesus (vv. 38–41), never endangering the faith of even the most fragile (vv. 42–50). They are to be at peace with one another in the kingdom (v. 50). Disciples, including the students in the classroom, are called to receive Jesus and the one who sent him (vv. 35–37).[35]

Performance Criticism

This contemporary approach to biblical narratives has gained a great deal of ground in recent Gospel scholarship in the United States of America.[36] For a number of reasons (for example, the immediacy of the Markan narrative [everything happens "immediately"] and the brevity of the story that makes it easier to commit to memory) the Gospel of Mark has proved to be the most used text in this emerging discipline.[37] Performance criticism

---

35. See Gnilka, *Markus*, 2:67.

36. For a history of the development of the adoption of performance criticism from the broader academy, see Kelly R. Iverson, "Performance Criticism," in *The Oxford Encyclopedia of Biblical Interpretation*, ed. Steven McKenzie, 2 vols. (New York: Oxford University Press, 2013), 2:97–98. See the most helpful and comprehensive essay of David Rhoads, "Performance Criticism: An Emerging Methodology in Second Temple Studies," *BTB* 36 (2006): 118–33, 164–84.

37. For an influential study that sets the Gospel of Mark within performance expectations in antiquity, see Whitney T. Shiner, *Proclaiming the Gospel: First-Century Performance of Mark* (Harrisburg, PA: Trinity Press International, 2003). See also Antoinette C. Wire, *The Case for Mark Composed in Performance*, BPC 3 (Eugene, OR: Cascade, 2011), who argues that the text of Mark is the result of repeated performance.

attempts to appreciate the intellectual and emotional response from the audience. In this respect, it is more radically oriented to "hearers and viewers" than narrative criticism, which depends upon "reading" a written text for its impact. The close, direct relationship that a skilled performer can create between him- or herself and the audience is clearly witnessed by the gasps, laughter, and other responses that one can hear in filmed versions of good performances.[38]

This is not the place to debate the possibilities of the long-term scholarly contribution of performance criticism.[39] The obvious problem is the "objectivity" of the interpretation of the performer. In a scholarly tradition that was born in a post-Enlightenment world determined to establish objective criteria for "truth" in every aspect of human thought and activity, a performance that generates emotional reaction from an audience on the basis of the interpretive and dramatic skills of an actor will be regarded as suspect.[40] This may create less of a problem if we take more seriously the fact that many of the biblical traditions, and perhaps especially the Jesus story, originated in an oral context. Moreover, a teacher can link the text with its past by employing performance in the classroom.

Approximately 5 percent of the population of the first century was literate.[41] Even the form critics recognized this, but the scholars of that time, especially in Germany, "were unable to disentangle themselves from

---

38. For example, performances are available on DVD by David Rhoads, *A Dramatic Presentation of the Gospel of Mark* (1992); and Philip Ruge-Jones, *The Beginning of the Good News* (2009), available for purchase from *Select Learning*, http://www.selectlearning.org/.

39. See the questions raised by Larry W. Hurtado, "Oral Fixation and New Testament Studies? 'Orality,' 'Performance' and Reading Texts in Early Christianity," *NTS* 60 (2014): 321–40.

40. Theorists and practitioners of performance criticism, products of the postmodern era, are not troubled by this classical objection. As Philip Ruge-Jones puts it: "every performance is an original and no single, pristine specimen ever existed. Rather these disciples can aid in the construction of credible performance scenarios that are generative in understanding the multiplicity of ways the narrative may have made an impact in the ancient world" ("Orality Studies and Oral Tradition: *New Testament*," in McKenzie, *Oxford Encyclopedia of Biblical Interpretation*, 2:70).

41. See, among several studies, Alan Millard, *Reading and Writing in the Time of Jesus* (New York: New York University Press, 2000); Catherine Hezser, *Jewish Literacy in Roman Palestine*, TSAJ 81 (Tübingen: Mohr Siebeck, 2001). But see the critique of Hurtado, "Oral Fixation," 323–33.

a literary mindset."[42] Things are different now, but the question arises as to whether we are better served by sharing in "performances" of the whole text, which is the majority approach, or by mapping issues in the Gospel narrative as we have it that point to the world of orality and tracing there something of the learning experience that cannot be captured on the printed page. These options are not mutually exclusive. The following reflections accept the primacy of the oral transmission of the Jesus story and test how the "oral performance" of one of its component parts (Mark 9:42–50) might impact upon the players and their audience in a classroom. It will also indicate, however, that performance can enhance the classroom's awareness of the results of the earlier historical and literary approaches to the text.[43] For the purposes of this study, the classroom, already possessed of such awareness, is the place of the performance, and the students are the players.

A particular aspect of oral transmission of narrative that can enrich the interpretation of Mark 9:42–50 calls for attention: the relationship between the narrator and the audience. To this point, the students in the classroom will have encountered a written text on a page, an essential element to the interpretive processes. In an oral transmission, however, there is no printed text. The narrator is "in your face," speaking directly to the hearers, looking them in the eye, judging their response (approval, joy, horror, fear, disappointment, expectation) as she or he tells the story. The narrator, although not a character *in* the story, assumes the role of a character and is thus the major player in the communication *of* the story. This immediacy creates an element essential to a performance by eliminating the "time" element central to a report from the past in a written text. As Kelly Iverson has pointed out:

> Although in any given performance off-stage time and stage time may refer to temporal periods that are chronologically distant, *the temporal dimensions converge in the oral arena*. Despite the temporal distinctiveness of the narrative and performance worlds, the "liveness" of performance fuses the horizons, transforming the audience's perception

---

42. Iverson, "Performance Criticism," 97.
43. In order not to overburden the text of this essay, the mutuality across the different methods will be indicated in footnotes. Despite their appearance in the footnotes, however, these indications are an important part of the overall argument of the essay.

of the drama. Because the story unfolds in the direct spatio-physical presence of the audience and performer, the relative distance between events and discourse is compressed. This proximity has the effect of seamlessly converging the off-stage and stage times so as to thrust forward (or backward) the world of the narrative into the world of the performance.[44]

This process of rendering the past world of the narrative "present" to the audience in a performance adds considerable vigor to an understanding of Mark 9:42–50.

Aspects of a Performance of Mark 9:42–50 in a Classroom

The "wholeness" of a narrative teaches that the performance of Mark 9:42–50 must be part of the performance of what precedes and follows this instruction over a series of class meetings. But there are obvious "breathing moments" in any performance, and the moments that circumscribe this passage are the passion prediction in 9:31 that opens Jesus's instruction of his disciples and the further passion prediction, introduced at length by a description of Jesus and the disciples on their journey to Jerusalem in 10:32–34. This lengthy resumption of the brief prediction in 9:31 introduces the episodes that lead to arrival in Jerusalem (11:1). To use the language of theater, the students in the classroom, with the teacher acting as director, might enact 9:31–10:31 as one of three "scenes" played out within the "act" of 8:22–10:42. The others are 8:22–9:30 and 10:32–52. Together they form an act entitled: "Jesus on the way to Jerusalem with his disciples" (8:22–10:52).[45]

However, the performer faces a further challenge in the scene of 9:31–10:31. *Only here* in the whole "act" of 8:22–10:42 (with the exception of the two blind men who mark the opening and closing of the act [8:22–26; 10:46–52]), characters other than Jesus and the disciples appear. This is an

---

44. Kelly R. Iverson, "The Present Tense of Performance: Immediacy and Transformative Power in Luke's Passion," in *From Text to Performance: Narrative and Performance Criticisms in Dialogue and Debate*, ed. Kelly R. Iverson, BPC 10 (Eugene, OR: Cascade, 2014), 138. The theory articulated in Iverson's essay (131–57) is the experience of anyone who has been part of an audience at a good theatrical performance.

45. The "breathing moments" provided by the passion predictions in 9:31 and 10:32–34; the role of 9:31–10:31 as a "scene" within an "act" made up of 8:22–10:52, come to the performers from prior awareness of both historical and literary interpretations.

important feature of the drama that the performing students must negotiate in light of their earlier exposure to the historical and literary analyses of the text. Although the role of Jesus, whose words dominate the passage, must be central, the rest of the class is involved, providing "reactions" from the disciples not found in the written text.[46] This observation raises the point that student performers must negotiate a number of challenges, from the ambiguity of the text to the participation of the audience. Below I discuss a number of challenges that performers might face in playing the scene of 9:31–10:31.

The Presence of Children

Children appear in 9:31–41 (see vv. 36–37) and in 10:1–31 (vv. 13–16) in such a way that leads the students into and out of their enactment of 9:42–50 (see the reference to children in v. 42).[47] Aware of the narrative links between 9:31–41 and 10:1–31 with 9:42–50 from their literary analysis, the student audience accepts *the same gestures* to indicate that the children, and Jesus's affection for them is an important feature of this scene in the performance. Once the performing student repeats the gestures used for 9:35–37 in verse 42, the presentation of Jesus and the children in 10:13–16 repeats *identical gestures*. In this way, what has been performed in 9:32–50, highlighting Jesus's affection for the children, casts a shadow over the performance of Jesus's discussion of divorce with the Pharisees and his subsequent teaching to the disciples "in the house" (10:1–12) and over his encounter with the rich man and his subsequent teaching to the disciples (10:13–31).

---

46. The entrance of two unexpected "characters" into 10:1–31 is something that has been noticed by the redaction critics, and especially the narrative critics, for whom "character" is a particular concern. The stimulating essay in this volume by Richard Swanson, "Hiding in Plain Sight: Performance, Pedagogy, and Mark 15," introduces an element that would impact considerably upon such a performance: the use of multiple characters.

47. As we have seen, the association of v. 42 with "the children" of vv. 35–36 and the relationship between vv. 35–36 with 10:13–16 was a feature of Bultmann's work on the history of the tradition. Literary and performance criticism can build upon these associations. Another obvious link with traditional exegesis is the decision that "the children" of 9:35–36 and 10:13–16 are to be associated with "the little ones" of v. 42. See above, n. 25. As we will see, this decision is important for a performance.

Especially important for this "shadowing" is the gesture of embracing in 9:36 and 10:16, used to indicate an invitation to the audience about the importance of "receiving" Jesus and belonging to the kingdom of God (9:36–37; 10:14–16). Neither the Pharisees nor the rich man are able to "receive" in this way. "The force of the argument is that the rich who cannot let go of their security in goods have already lost the security of God's kingdom where the children are at home."[48] This element of the performance also adds gentleness and a demonstration of affection to the instruction of disciples that throws into relief and contextualizes the violent acts performed in verses 42b, 43–47. The classroom of "disciples" recognizes the sharp contrast between warmth and affection through the performance of the sullen silence of verses 33–34. This contrast motivates the performance of Jesus's request that those gathered for the performance "be at peace with one another" (v. 50). As the world of the narrative and the world of the audience have converged in the performance (Iverson), a classroom of disciples that acts out and responds to the performance are instructed on the need for service and receptivity. One would hope that they nod approval.

The role of the children makes a major dramatic impact on the classroom in the performance of scenes that indicate arrogance (9:38–41), sinfulness and causing to sin (vv. 42–47), and the rejection of Jesus's invitation (10:1–9, 17–22). It also serves as a key to Jesus's explicit instruction of his disciples in 9:35, 50; 10:10–12, 23–31. By bringing the contrast between warmth and affection to life in the classroom, the performance overcomes the temporal distance between the past episodes of the written text and the present situation of the audience.[49]

The Location in the House

A further aspect of the performance that generates a close relationship between the student performers and the classroom audience is the regular reminder that they are sharing in a discussion between Jesus and his

---

48. Wire, *Case for Mark*, 159.
49. A performance that plays out Jesus's consistent affection for the children (9:36; 10:16), his defense of them (9:42; 10:14), and his use of them to instruct on "reception" and entering into life and the kingdom of God (9:37; 10:14–15) also makes a christological point about the coherence of the person of Jesus. His response to children is consistent, and through them he points with authority to the kingdom of God.

disciples that takes place in "the house" (9:33).⁵⁰ This is an important historical-, redactional-, and narrative-critical issue, since Mark uses "the house" elsewhere as the location for Jesus's instruction of his disciples (see 7:17; 9:28). But Mark also uses it in the domestic sense of a place where a person lives (see 2:1, 11; 3:20; 5:19, 38; 7:30; 8:3, 26). The setting for 9:33–50, including the report from John on the disciples' arrogant rejection of the unknown exorcist (vv. 38–41), is "in the house" (v. 33). A performing student has earlier shown that Jesus has been regarded as insane by the family of his "house," another group of students in the classroom (3:20–21).⁵¹ The student performing Jesus has turned away from "his own family," created a "new family" who will be "with him" (3:14–19), and indicated that the brother, sister, and mother of Jesus is one who "does the will of God" (3:31–35).⁵² In performing 7:17 and 9:28, the student performer has shown her or his colleagues in the classroom that the "house" Jesus uses for the instruction of his disciples is a "new place," quite unlike anything else the disciples (the students in the classroom) have experienced.

Their earlier experience of a discussion between the new family of Jesus (see 3:13–14) that no longer follows the accepted codes for family (see 3:35–37) has led to their awareness that there is another "house," where Jesus is "with his disciples" (see 3:14; 7:17; 9:28, 33). This is a different "house" than the culturally accepted domestic household. As the performance of the scene of 9:31–10:31 comes to closure, the theme of a "house" returns. The Jesus figure instructs his followers in the classroom that to be part of Jesus's household, they must be prepared to abandon any comfortable experience of house and family (see 10:29–31). This may be especially challenging for anyone who comes from a stable family or traditional "household."

---

50. As we have seen, this was important for Bultmann's identification of the passage as a type of catechism on piety that separated the church from Judaism.

51. This would be an important moment for a performer and depends upon what she or he makes of the exegesis of οἱ παρ'αὐτοῦ and the verb ἐξέστη in 3:21. The position taken above is that the former refers to his family, and the latter indicates that they thought he had "gone out of his mind." Both are rendered as such in the NRSV. See also Moloney, *Gospel of Mark*, 80–82. An awareness of traditional critical methods is required for a good performance.

52. Literary and narrative readings of 3:21–35 point out an inclusion between Jesus's blood family in 3:20–21 and 3:31–35. Between the inclusion, a new family has been founded in 3:13–19. See Moloney, *Gospel of Mark*, 80–84.

The Violent Images

Especially powerful in a performance of this text are the violent and even angry gestures of casting into the sea with a great millstone hung around one's neck (v. 42) and the cutting off of hand, foot, and eye (vv. 43–47). The Jesus performer can generate gestures that point to the Markan meaning of this passage, drawing that meaning into the "now" of the participating audience. In the case of anyone who causes little ones to sin, death through drowning—accompanied by the gesture of pushing a heavily laden object over a cliff—indicates that there is no place in a believing audience for the one who has breached the embrace between Jesus and the children (v. 37). An initial response of the class might be a gasp. But the loss of one hand, one foot, or one eye can be performed in such a way that indicates that a hand, a foot, and an eye *remain in place*. The performer balances the gestures of cutting off and casting away parts of his or her body with the equally important positive gesture that he or she *still has a hand, and an eye, and a foot*. This is all one needs to "enter life" (vv. 43, 45), that is, enter the kingdom of God (v. 47). Such gestures may generate a sense of relief and comfort in the classroom.

The performer can show the *positive result* of such violent action to lead a classroom to recover from an initial shock that the violent gesture of cutting off generates and to tell the audience of the fundamental importance of the life that is to be had from God's gift of the kingdom.[53] The threefold repetition of these contrasting gestures, performed deliberately and slowly, each time concluding with an indication of the remaining one hand, one eye, and one foot that one takes into the life of the kingdom, generates an impression. The classroom not only learns but experiences that all is not lost; indeed, the only thing that is important is gained. The destruction by drowning of the one who causes scandal of verse 37 is mitigated by the promise of life in the kingdom to those who sin but are instructed on the way to avoid such sin. The message is positive, even though by means of

---

53. In the discussion of this paper at the International Society of Biblical Literature meeting in Vienna, Alberto de Mingo Kaminouchi suggested that a humorous note could also be added to the performance of tying a large weight around the neck of an offender. He rightly indicated that there are "many" performances possible. See above, n. 40. However, I would argue that "any" performance is not acceptable. See above, n. 5. I would argue that the interpretive tradition should play a role in determining the "many," and excluding others.

the performance of verses 43–47 the classroom is warned that they may have to pay a hefty price for it. The performer asks, what do you prefer, total elimination because you cause others to sin (v. 42) or life and the kingdom by sacrificing something you may regard as precious but that is not essential (vv. 43–47)? Performing a text from *the past*, this question is asked of the classroom audience *now*.

Ambiguous Metaphors

The final association between hellfire that salts those who choose to retain two hands, feet, and eyes (vv. 48–49) can be highlighted by the text's use of the image of a never-dying worm that weaves its way through the innards of the person in question. The student-performer simulates "worming" as a negative permeation of fire that could make a powerful, perhaps comical, and even sinister, negative impact upon the class. Again, following Mark's narrative, she or he can turn this into a positive image, as the destructive salting of the condemned turns into the permeating goodness of the salt that does not lose its flavor (v. 50a). By playing on the negative and positive use of "salt" and "saltiness," making a feature of the steady repetition of the word *salt* across verses 49–50a, the classroom is not surprisingly faced with the challenging punch line of this brief performance, so dominated by opposites: violent death versus life in the kingdom; severed bodily member versus those that remain intact; hell versus the kingdom; insipid salt versus salt that produces peace with others.[54]

Jesus's Sayings and the Larger Context

The classroom has witnessed a performance of the disciples' silence and division when Jesus asks them what they have been discussing on the way to Capernaum (vv. 33–34). They are now aware that this sullen silence is the loss of saltiness; their discipleship no longer has taste or value. This must be reversed, as is obvious from the location of these words in a performance that follows immediately upon Jesus's "teaching his disciples" of his forthcoming death and resurrection (v. 31). The well-instructed

---

54. The dilemma for some historical critics, that there is no such thing as salt without flavor, could even play into a performance, as surprise could be manifested that the impossible has happened. Things are different in the world imagined and taught by Jesus, then and now.

student-performer makes the audience aware that insipid salt is not what Jesus seeks from them. Indeed, they are warned that such a response to Jesus will lead to their being "salted with fire" (v. 49). Jesus, the performer, communicates that there is no place in this classroom for discussions over greatness (vv. 34–35) by taking little children into his arms to show that service and receptivity are the marks of the true disciple (vv. 36–37). But arrogance continues among the performers (vv. 38–41), so a member of the class instructs fellow students in the audience on the avoidance of actions that generate sin in others and in themselves (vv. 42–47). There are radical remedies for these problems, and they produce life, the gift of the kingdom, and disciples of quality (vv. 43–50a). Jesus, the performer, instructs the classroom: "Be at peace with one another" (v. 50b), having instructed them on the price of that peace.

Conclusion

Anyone teaching Mark 9:42–50 might justifiably ask: why am I bothering with this text? So many other more interesting, and certainly less convoluted, literary productions that deal with Christian discipleship are available, both ancient and modern. The obvious response is that the teacher and the class regard this passage as part of its accepted sacred Scripture. The Gospel of Mark has come down to us read within Christian history and its faith tradition. Recent scholarship has affirmed that "'canonicity' lies in the progressive and mutually forming relationship between certain texts and the Church: a relationship which is complex, historical, but not beyond the bounds of grace."[55] We ignore this at great risk as we pass on the serious analysis of biblical texts from our generation to the next.

I suggest that a teacher ask questions that lead from the origins of a text down to its contemporary appropriation and reception, as in the following examples.

Questions for an Eclectic Approach to a Biblical Text

1. What are the historical origins of this passage?
2. Do we have an assured original Greek text?

---

55. Morwenna Ludlow, "'Criteria of Canonicity' and the Early Church," in *Die Einheit der Schrift und die Vielfalt des Kanons/The Unity of Scripture and the Diversity of the Canon*, ed. John Barton and Michael Wolter, BZNW 118 (Berlin: de Gruter, 2003), 71.

3. How did the text being taught assume its somewhat puzzling present form, and are there other places in the New Testament where these supposed "sayings of Jesus" are found (e.g., Matt 5:13; 18:6–9; Luke 14:34–35; 17:1–2)?
4. Do these other New Testament locations enlighten our understanding of Mark 9:42–50?
5. Does this passage add anything to our understanding of Mark the theologian?
6. Where does this passage come within the overall theological and literary unfolding of the Markan narrative?
7. Does the narrative of the Gospel of Mark as a whole throw light on the meaning of 9:42–50?
8. Does the final step into a performance staged with students shaped by their historical-critical and narrative-critical investigations generate spontaneity?
9. Does the performance impinge intellectually and emotionally on the audience in the classroom?
10. Do the words of Jesus articulated in Mark 9:42–50 add anything to a contemporary appreciation and practice of Christian discipleship? The test of the value of the eclectic approach advocated here is authentic performance of the text as it is lived out in a Christian community.

It is intellectually dishonest to use a text we regard as sacred Scripture without asking something akin to these questions. What I have proposed might serve as a paradigm for the teaching of any such text within the classroom. The Gospel of Mark had its origins in an original and originating experience of Jesus.[56] It was most likely recorded *in a written form* in and for a believing Christian community.[57] Given the world in which it

---

56. As already indicated, Wire (*Case for Mark*) has argued the unlikely scenario that Mark is an orally composed tradition, told by several storytellers over a period of time.

57. In making this affirmation, I disagree with Wire's suggestion that Mark was "composed" in performance. Hurtado recognizes that Mark "seems to preserve features of an oral 'register' (e.g., frequent use of καί), and that may well have been a choice by the author, precisely in order to give the text a certain storytelling 'air'" ("Oral Fixation," 339), but he continues: "there is no Roman-era example of such an extended prose literary text *composed* in 'performance,' and no basis for positing that Mark was so composed" (340).

was produced, it would have been generally *communicated* orally. It was most likely read and perhaps performed for a population that neither read nor wrote.

From our location, however, the Gospel of Mark has been used predominantly as written text for two thousand years, generating a long tradition of remarkable, and at times beautifully presented, manuscripts. From the invention of the printing press by Johannes Gutenberg (ca. 1449), it has been widely dispersed as a book. Translations that challenged the Latin Vulgate became a matter of crucial importance in the sixteenth-century European Reformation. Confessional differences still play a role in contemporary versions. These developments, with their contrasts, similarities, and mutual enrichment, should be taught as a newer generation learns a relevant interpretive process. Ignorance of the past produces shallow answers to the questions of the present.

The teaching of ancient texts requires many skills, ranging from those of the historian to the sensitive performer. Most importantly, however, responses to questions that focus upon reception (8–10) must be *the fruit of a long process* (1–7). They cannot be answered honestly without responses to the historical, redactional, and narrative-critical questions that preceded them.

I chose the text considered in this essay, Mark 9:42–50, because of its complexity at every stage: its historical origins, its transmission, its theological and literary reception, and its performance. If an eclectic teaching process enables us to communicate the meaning of the most difficult text in Mark, it could prove to be a helpful pedagogical tool to approach all texts, most of which are not so complex.

8
HIDING IN PLAIN SIGHT:
PERFORMANCE, PEDAGOGY, AND MARK 15

Richard W. Swanson

Some years ago, as the result of an unexpected invitation to perform as a storyteller for a large youth gathering, I began experimenting with performance as a mode of biblical interpretation. Now, almost twenty years later, this experimentation has led me to places I would never have imagined. There have been many surprises, some successes, and also some (mostly productive) failures.

My first experiments with performance (in a seminar I taught for senior religion majors) grew into an ongoing collaboration with a few students in the class. Out of that exploratory collaboration came some initial public performances here and there around the United States—from Albuquerque to Chicago to Atlanta—and out of those performances came what we have called the Provoking the Gospel Storytelling Project, a continuing group of students, alumni, and colleagues who have committed to exploring the insides of biblical texts through performance. Out of this exploration has come even more experimenting, both in pedagogy and in performance. In collaboration with the latest members of this exciting project, I have created performances of the *St. Mark Passion* and of the book of Job. As a result of this work, I have written a set of storyteller's commentaries on the Gospels,[1] and I have changed the way I study biblical texts and the way I teach biblical narrative.

---

1. Richard W. Swanson, *Provoking the Gospel of Mark: A Storyteller's Commentary, Year B* (Cleveland: Pilgrim, 2005); Swanson, *Provoking the Gospel of Luke: A Storyteller's Commentary, Year C* (Cleveland: Pilgrim, 2006); Swanson, *Provoking the Gospel of Matthew: A Storyteller's Commentary, Year A* (Cleveland: Pilgrim, 2007); Swanson,

This essay has two main parts: in the first, I will consider pedagogy and performance, focusing especially on how they might relate to each other and what they might offer to each other, both in terms of possibilities and problems; in the second, I will apply the method to a portion of the death scene in the Gospel of Mark. In the essay, I aim to ask and answer a basic question: what does performance add to pedagogy? I have asked this question repeatedly throughout the explorations of my research over the past years, and I expect that it will be important to anyone who is considering using performance as a pedagogical tool.

Pedagogy and Performance Considered

What Is Pedagogy?

Every generation asks this question, usually with some evident distress. Every generation also usually answers this question with some active disdain for the answers given by earlier generations. In the late days of the Second World War, C. S. Lewis argued that the contemporary world and its educational industry were seeking the "abolition of man."[2] A quarter century later, in the midst of the war in Vietnam, Neil Postman and Charles Weingartner argued that "teaching [was] a subversive activity."[3] These two very different books have sharply different authors and assumptions, but they share key elements, particularly their diagnoses of the problems facing pedagogy. Both argue that degraded pedagogy sought not to initiate but to "condition"[4] the next "generation of inadvertent entropy helpers."[5] I am not sure that Lewis would enjoy being made an ally of Postman (nor would Postman, in his turn, accept this arrangement), but both

---

Provoking the Gospel of John: A Storyteller's Commentary, Years A, B, and C (Cleveland: Pilgrim, 2010). See also Swanson, *Provoking the Gospel: Methods to Embody Biblical Storytelling through Drama* (Cleveland: Pilgrim, 2004), a "how-to, why-to" study of the method.

    2. C. S. Lewis, *The Abolition of Man, or Reflections on Education with Special Reference to the Teaching of English in the Upper Forms of Schools* (New York: Macmillan, 1947).

    3. Neil Postman and Charles Weingartner, *Teaching as a Subversive Activity* (New York: Delacorte, 1969).

    4. Lewis, *Abolition of Man*, 32.

    5. Postman and Weingartner, *Teaching as a Subversive Activity*, 15.

distrust any educational scheme that aims at indoctrination, even as both have doctrinal commitments that drive their analyses.

Now, writing in the midst of yet another generation that reflects on pedagogy, I find myself considering performance as a teaching tool. If pedagogy is simply a matter of passing on preprocessed information, well known and well digested, then performance will be simply a tool used to catechize, to indoctrinate, to inform. It surely can work for such a task, though that is not a task that I value very highly. If, on the other hand, pedagogy is about drawing students into productive modes of encounter and analysis, into ways of engaging and productively studying biblical texts, if it is in some sense an apprenticeship, then performance is a mode of pedagogical engagement to the extent of being a productive mode of critical engagement for the professor. This yields a very different understanding and practice for both performance and pedagogy and yields a different task for this essay. If pedagogy involves apprenticeship, then my task must be to demonstrate the productive value of performance-critical analysis for interpretive work and, therefore, for teaching.

What Is Performance?

The impact of performance on pedagogy will also depend on how seriously one takes performance. Performance is much discussed these days (and in many fields besides biblical studies), but some of the theoretical discussions elaborate performance and neutralize it in the process. For instance, Paul Scott Wilson argues that even silent reading is a performance of text.[6] While the theoretical reasons for this abstract argument are comprehensible, this kind of abstraction removes the very physicality that makes performance significant for textual interpretation.

Performance Is Physical

My discussion of performance is rooted in solid physicality. For my purposes, performance occurs when real actors really perform a text in real time in a real place. This focus on physical performance links the present practice of performance criticism to the ancient practice of performance.

---

6. See his interesting and useful essay, "Preaching, Performance, and the Life and Death of 'Now,'" in *Performance in Preaching: Bringing the Sermon to Life*, ed. Jana Childers and Clayton J. Schmit (Grand Rapids: Baker Academic, 2008), 37.

In the ancient world, texts (including biblical texts) were performed aloud. This is significant for my discussion, but it must also be noted that I am not aiming to re-create ancient performance practice. My understanding of performance grows out of my experience working with an ensemble of actors who perform together. This surely does not replicate ancient practice, except insofar as it chooses to perform narratives in a form adapted to the present-day audience. Whitney Shiner (among many others) has studied ancient rhetorical performance and has used that as a lens to study what might have been a mode (among others) of solo performance of Gospel texts in the ancient world.[7] I have studied present-day theatrical performance and have used that as a lens to examine biblical narratives. Both Shiner and I understand performance to be an appropriate medium for engaging texts that had their origin in performance. Both modes of performance (solo and ensemble) yield, we believe, productive understandings of the texts and their reception. I have found contemporary exploratory performance by an ensemble to be especially helpful, both in interpreting texts and in teaching them to my students. For both Shiner and me, however much we may disagree on the matter of reproducing ancient practice, the solid physicality of performance is crucial.

Performance Involves an Audience

As Bernard Reymond notes in an important discussion of theatrical performance, performance requires both actors and an audience.[8] For performance to be physically real, the actor and the audience must be physically present in the same physical space at the same time. This simple (but crucial) recognition flows into a discussion of the role of the audience in creating the meaning and message of anything that is performed. Theater studies spend considerable time noting how much influence actors have on the meaning of a performance—how much influence and how little control.[9] At a basic level, this is simple communication theory. Reception

---

7. Whitney Shiner, *Proclaiming the Gospel: First-Century Performance of Mark* (Harrisburg, PA: Trinity Press International, 2003).

8. Bernard Reymond, *Théâtre et Christianisme* (Geneva: Labor et Fides, 2002), 76: "le théâtre suppose à la fois des acteurs et des spectateurs. S'ils ne sont pas là ensemble, le fait théâtral ne peut avoir lieu."

9. For instance, see Jacques LeCoq, *The Moving Body: Teaching Creative Theatre* (New York: Routledge, 2001), 18.

is not a passive event. This is true when two people are engaged in a casual conversation, but it is crucial to the theater. Every member of the audience brings assumptions, hopes, and fears to the performance of a play. The whole audience, therefore, participates in creating the meaning of what is performed. The intentions of the author or the actors (though crucial and powerfully effective) do not eliminate the creative activity of the audience. We would do well, in our theological and pedagogical discussion of performance, to note this matter of influence and lack of control.

Performance Resists Regimentation

We would also do well to note that theater studies have spent considerable time arguing that ideological theater, which attempts to control completely the meaning of the stories that are presented, is bad theater. Peter Brook, in *The Empty Space*, calls this "The Deadly Theatre." Brook sees the danger of "Deadly Theatre" especially in performances of the works of Shakespeare, because such performances cater to what Brook calls the "deadly spectator," a chief example of which being "the scholar who emerges from routine performances of the classics smiling because nothing has distracted him from trying over and confirming his pet theories to himself, whilst reciting his favourite lines under his breath."[10] Bernard Reymond notes that the dangers of ideological theater are especially pressing for theology, because theological interpreters pick up performance with an ideological goal too clearly in mind. The performer of the text will act as herald or witness, and this overriding intention ignores the first and most important injunction offered by the arts: "Now, be silent and watch; be silent and listen."[11] The problem, says Reymond, is that theological use of performance too often asks whether the result is edifying or encourages "good feelings" and too seldom considers whether the result is good theater, which Reymond (and not him alone) understands to require the active presence of both "cruelty"

---

10. Peter Brook, *The Empty Space* (New York: Atheneum, 1968), 7–8.
11. Reymond, *Théâtre et Christianisme*, 22: "Le plus difficile, pour un théologien, est de prendre les arts tels qu'ils se donnent, sans les transformer peu ou prou en instruments de quelque idéologie théologique ou religieuse. Le premier défi qu'une oeuvre d'art peut addresser à la théologie est bien de lui dire implicitement: 'Maintenant tais-toi et regarde. Tais-toi et écoute. Laisse ce que tu entends, ce que tu vois ou ce que tu lis faire en toi son chemin.'"

and "monstrosity"[12] (the terms are drawn, of course, from the work of Antonin Artaud).[13] The clear implication is that, for performance to take place, actors and audience must be present in the same physical space, and that neither emerges from that space unchanged. Both are transformed.

Performance resists regimentation because performers make choices. So, what is performance? It is a mode of engagement with a text that changes both actors and audience and that therefore changes also the text that is performed. This creates a textual fluidity that is radically real. This fluidity has two independent dimensions: one related to the interpretive power of the audience (noted above), and one related to the improvisatory openness created by the work of the actors. The work of David Rhoads may be taken as indicative here. Note the time he spends in his essay, "What Is Performance Criticism?," discussing the choices he must make when he prepares to perform a biblical text.[14] For every line he must decide pacing and tone, emotion and gesture, continuity and discontinuity. And, as Rhoads notes, every decision interacts with all of the other decisions a performer must make. This matter of interlocking decisions is discussed at length in theatrical studies. Performing is about deciding, and every moment of decision could change the flow of the text decisively. This is true for performance in general, and it is therefore also true for the performance of biblical texts.

Some discussions of biblical performance imagine that it all comes down to selecting an ideological framework and letting that framework determine everything. Given the very real power of performance to influence an audience, it is guaranteed that ideologues of every sort (including theological) would adopt it. If such ideologues grant the existence of textual and hermeneutical fluidity, it is only at an early stage in the development of a performance. Everything is open until you close it, and the governing ideology of the performer or the community is understood to

---

12. Ibid., 168. "Le problème prioritaire n'est pas de savoir s'il est Chrétien ou non, mais quand il est le fait de chrétiens, s'il est du bon theâtre—s'il a toute la 'cruauté' et toute la 'monstruosité' voulues, pour reprendre encore une fois ces tremens, et non s'il est suffisamment 'édifianté' ou s'il éveille assez de 'bons sentiments.'"

13. Antonin Artaud, *The Theater and Its Double*, trans. Mary Caroline Richards (New York: Grove, 1958). See especially his second manifesto on the Theater of Cruelty (122): "The Theater of Cruelty has been created in order to restore to the theater a passionate and convulsive conception of life."

14. David Rhoads, "What Is Performance Criticism?" in *The Bible in Ancient and Modern Media: Story and Performance*, ed. Holly E. Hearon and Philip Ruge-Jones, BPC 1 (Eugene, OR: Cascade, 2009), 83.

function properly when it closes off any interpretive possibility that does not directly serve the predetermined purposes of the performer.

Such attempts to close off textual and hermeneutical fluidity run into at least two sorts of problems. The first is textual. As poststructuralist studies have made clear, there are always tensions with texts, always forces that flow in different directions, always voices that sing in slightly different keys, even (maybe especially) in texts that aim themselves to be tightly controlled and controlling. To appropriate the words of the American poet Robert Frost, "Something there is that doesn't love a wall."[15] For all their regularity, texts will not be regulated, at least not completely and finally. Every wall that a writer builds will be pulled down by forces internal to the wall itself. Texts fight with themselves. Such fluidity may be inconvenient for interpreters (and for performers), but it is always present, and any attempt at textual interpretation will engage it. More on this presently.

The second problem for ideologues who wish to limit textual fluidity arrives in the form of the bodies of the performers: *Performance resists regimentation because of the space between bodies.* If there is only a single performer, textual fluidity exists simply because of the webs of choices that the performer must cast over the text. The problem of textual and hermeneutical fluidity is intensified (and not just increased) when one works (as I have for almost twenty years) with an ensemble of actors. When an ensemble performs a text, the lines of the story are not just open to the range of an individual actor. Now they are shaped also by a group of performers, each with a specific range of bodily nuance, each with a set of decisions to be made, all of which interlock with the other decisions that are made continually. Now the text is made fluid not only by decisions, but also by the actors' reactions to those decisions. The variables multiply beyond easy reckoning.

This matter of reaction and interaction is a factor of the space between the bodies of the players. Actors do not stand in rigid lines speaking their words in regimented rote. They listen to each other, they consider each other, they regard each other, and they react.

Performance negotiates stability in the midst of fluidity. As Emmanuel Levinas made clear, the space between bodies is the field on which ethics

---

15. Robert Frost, "Mending Wall," in *The Poetry of Robert Frost: The Collected Poems, Complete and Unabridged* (New York: Holt, 1969), 33.

becomes real.[16] Levinas was concerned about the ethical stability of a complex world. This stability is not accomplished by isolated moral actors, sequestered Cartesian thinkers, but by human beings who encounter the face of another and negotiate obedience to the crucial commandment, you shall not kill. This same negotiation of stability and reliability may also be seen in the work of Richard Bernstein.[17] In the face of multiple points of view and multiple construals of reality, human society negotiates stability, even in the seemingly utterly objective field of scientific inquiry.

This negotiation of stability, of course, is nothing new for the theater. Every line is an interaction, a negotiation between characters, and every character must be real, alive, plausible, historical, and loved (at least by the actor). This has always been the case. For our current discussion, however, it should be noted that this increases and intensifies the fluidity and openness for the audience because the space between the characters, and the distinctions among them, make it possible for viewers to agree with some characters and disagree with others, regardless of what might be the "approved" pattern of agreement and disagreement. Audiences watch the patterns of conflict and consonance among the characters onstage. They identify with some of the characters and not with others. They agree with some, or sympathize with them, and reject others. This is what the ethical response of the audience is constructed out of. In a properly performed scene from the Gospel of Mark, therefore, audience members might, at points, even disagree with Jesus.

And this heightened fluidity increases also the need to negotiate stability. Actors must do it individually as they develop the character they will play, and then they must do it again among themselves on stage. The audience, with its multiplicity and complexity, must also enter the negotiation. The members of the audience see and hear the performance, seeing and hearing always in the context of everything else they see and hear, hope for and fear, and they respond. They respond in order to make order, to make stability, to make sense. And out of this effort to make sense comes such stability as we are ever likely to get.

---

16. Emmanuel Levinas, *Totality and Infinity: An Essay on Exteriority*, trans. Alphonso Lingis (Pittsburgh: Duquesne University Press, 1998).

17. Richard J. Bernstein, *Beyond Objectivism and Relativism: Science, Hermeneutics, and Praxis* (Philadelphia: University of Pennsylvania Press, 1983).

What Are the Problems with Performance?

The key question, therefore, is this: Can performance function as a productive mode of analytical engagement with biblical texts, one that a professor would choose to model for students who are being drawn into the practice of the discipline? This is a question fraught with some difficulty.

Performing Is a Risk

It may be easy enough to argue that the texts themselves demand engagement through performance, since they are, in their origins, performance texts. There are many studies that one might cite to argue this point: the work of Joanna Dewey, for instance, or that of Holly Hearon, of Whitney Shiner, or of the many participants in the Society of Biblical Literature section, The Bible in Ancient and Modern Media.[18] It may even be easy to argue that such engagement amounts to good pedagogical practice, since research seems to indicate that multisensory engagement yields better retention of material to be mastered.[19] But even after such things are granted, there still remains the difficulty involved in actually doing the performance. There are risks and reasons to avoid the vulnerability that attends such risks; and professors, in the main, may well finally avoid the whole matter.

The risks are real. John Miles Foley noted his experience of viewing a "performance" of Serbian traditional tales done by academics wearing academic robes and intoning the texts in the safety of a television studio and contrasted this static and finally off-putting performance with the experience of watching a traditional *guslar* engage a crowd by performing the same traditional tales, only this time the performance worked. It involved chanting texts learned by heart and improvised upon in response to the

---

18. See Joanna Dewey, *The Oral Ethos of the Early Church: Speaking, Writing, and the Gospel of Mark*, BPC 8 (Eugene, OR: Cascade, 2013); Holly E. Hearon, *The Mary Magdalene Tradition: Witness and Counter-Witness in Early Christian Communities* (Collegeville, MN: Liturgical Press, 2004); Shiner, *Proclaiming the Gospel;* for The Bible in Ancient and Modern Media, see, for instance, Hearon and Ruge-Jones, *Bible in Ancient and Modern Media*.

19. There are many detailed studies one might cite, but Jacques LeCoq, founder of the International School of Mime and Theater, makes one of the more evocative arguments for this position in *Moving Body*.

input of a live audience.[20] Even if biblical texts are indeed begging for just this sort of live, improvisatory performance, most academics will choose the safety and shielding of academic robes and television studios over the risks of audience engagement. It will not do to pretend that this is not true. We are academics, and abstraction is our bulwark against unmanageable risk. There are other risks, however, that are more significant.

Performance Risks Relinquishing Hermeneutical Control

The most significant risks, in my estimation, pertain to matters of hermeneutics. Even academics who grant that there is no single biblical text, no absolute original that can serve as an anchor for all interpretation,[21] even such students of biblical texts will recognize that engaging in improvisatory interaction with an audience will introduce a whole new kind of fluidity, and with that fluidity comes risk. Textual interpreters encountered this risk even before performance was considered as a mode of biblical interpretation. Literary readers of biblical texts found themselves reading Stanley Fish,[22] who asked them whether texts existed at all or whether all that existed was the reading process, which may be regulated but cannot be regimented, except through the imposition of external authority. Such regimentation, of course, breaks the reading process, makes it false and unfaithful, and thus suggests that if there is a text in the class, there is no reading allowed; and if there is reading in the class, there can be no text, at least not in the form of a frozen, fixed thing. And farther down that road, interpreters encountered deconstruction, which further destabilized the very idea of a fixed, controllable text.[23] It is surely easy to caricature the excesses of deconstruction, but it is hard to deny the recognition

---

20. John Miles Foley, *How to Read an Oral Poem* (Urbana: University of Illinois Press, 2002), 84.

21. See ibid., 143. See also Robert M. Fowler's essay, "Why Everything We Know about the Bible Is Wrong: Lessons from the Media History of the Bible," in Hearon and Ruge-Jones, *Bible in Ancient and Modern Media*, 3. See esp. Antoinette C. Wire, *The Case for Mark Composed in Performance*, BPC 3 (Eugene, OR: Cascade, 2011).

22. Stanley Fish, *Is There a Text in This Class? The Authority of Interpretive Communities* (Cambridge: Harvard University Press, 1980).

23. For an especially skillful example, see Stephen D. Moore, *Mark and Luke in Poststructuralist Perspectives: Jesus Begins to Write* (New Haven: Yale University Press, 1992). The entire study is worth close reading, but the introduction provides a useful (and quick) sketch of this approach to texts and interpretation. Moore begins: "Leaf

of intractable fluidity even (especially!) in the most firmly fixed of texts. And with that come risks that have led some interpreters to set aside the task of literary-critical analysis and return to the task of historical study. Of course, history has its own insistent fluidity, but somehow such study seems safer and more stable, at least to many.

Performance Risks Fluidity for the Sake of a Fluid Future

Our reaction to this fluidity deserves careful study, both as it affects us as textual interpreters and as it affects us as teachers. As soon as performance is considered as a mode of engagement (if Foley is correct), fluidity becomes inescapable. A solo performer must know the traditional tale well enough to improvise responsively, to become what John Niles calls a "strong tradition bearer," a lover of the tradition who can, out of that love, even attack and warp that tradition. Niles says that a strong tradition bearer "appropriates the preexisting materials of literary expression and stands against, subverts, or even wrecks them, not in a paroxysm of rejection, but so as to fashion these materials into bold new creative shapes."[24] The risks at this point are much higher.

The risks are higher still for one, like myself, who picks up ensemble performance, not simply solo performance. Now the text inhabits not only a single human body but also the spaces among bodies, the spaces in which the messy business of life is invented and conducted.[25] Now anything could happen. The risks are real.

Even if the performers choose to control and simplify the performance by having only one authoritative body, that of the all-controlling narrator, still there are interpretive and ethical issues to be solved. If there is really only one body that matters, then all the other characters, even Jesus, are only puppets, and the audience will see that. The audience may love the puppet show, but that only means that they share the governing ideology and submit to it. There are important hermeneutical implications here. Such performance requires prior agreement as to what the text is

---

through this book, recently a tree. Penned to its trunk are two readings. One is of Mark, 'The Gospel of the Mark,' the other is of Luke, 'The Gospel of the Look'" (xiii).

24. John D. Niles, *Homo Narrans: The Poetics and Anthropology of Oral Literature* (Philadelphia: University of Pennsylvania Press, 1999), 177–93, esp. 179.

25. See my discussion of this in "Taking Place/Taking up Space," in Hearon and Ruge-Jones, *Bible in Ancient and Modern Media*, 129.

allowed to mean, and the audience must participate in this prior limiting of potential meaning. The text in such a setting (and its performance) can never challenge either the audience or the actors, except in ways that are subject to prior approval. Dale Savidge, in an admirable book written with Todd Johnson, comments on the problem of incorporating performance into the life of the church:

> When art is at the service of a religious organization, however, a degree of submission is called for, and the artist may be expected to sacrifice some artistic autonomy in order to serve the ends of the organization. In the theatre, this tends to result in more discursive and less ambiguous (more priestly and less prophetic, more Pauline proposition and less parabolic, more sermon and less story) theatre.[26]

Savidge and Johnson bring to their task a well-earned understanding of both theater and congregation, and this strengthens their work. Savidge is giving good, pragmatic advice. But the prior limitation to which he points is telling: this sort of submission will be (at a minimum) stultifying to performance, and it is hard to imagine that a biblical interpreter ought to surrender both parable and story in order to serve the interests of a religious organization.

Life and text and tradition are not that simple, as Gerhard von Rad and the tradition critics made clear long ago. Biblical tradition, whether possessed in memory or inscribed in text, points "straight into the void."[27] And, at the same time, all tradition exists as it interacts with changing circumstances. Something there is in tradition, therefore, that loves not prior restraint, to return to Robert Frost. Emil Fackenheim has argued that this old truth is even more true now that Jews and Christians must read their Bibles after the horrifying events of the Holocaust, which complicated forever simple biblical assertions about a God who "neither slumbers or sleeps" (Ps 121).[28] The proper interpretation of tradition, therefore, lives

---

26. Todd E. Johnson and Dale Savidge, *Performing the Sacred: Theology and Theatre in Dialogue* (Grand Rapids: Baker Academic, 2009), 131.

27. Gerhard von Rad, *Old Testament Theology*, trans. D. M. G. Stalker, 2 vols. (Louisville: Westminster John Knox, 2001), 2:321. Von Rad is quoting Karl Barth, *Church Dogmatics*, ed. G. W. Bromiley and T. F. Torrance, trans. G. T. Thomson and Harold Knight, 4 vols. in 13 (New York: T&T Clark, 2010), 1.2:89.

28. Emil L. Fackenheim, *The Jewish Bible after the Holocaust: A Re-reading* (Bloomington: Indiana University Press, 1990), esp. 45–48, and 65–70.

and works in the tense intersection of the void of the open future and the (often painful) constraint of the concrete present.

And, of course, the audience may not love the puppet show. Audiences that do not love shows do not attend shows. The implication of such an outcome would be that the community of faith that left no room for any reading other than its own would, in isolation, perform its stories by itself, for itself. This is not a formula for the future vitality of either the story or the community of faith gathered around the story. But even more troublesome: this isolated performance of biblical story refuses to engage obvious public interest in biblical story, in terms of both themes and narrative structures. Attention to the matter of performance makes it clear: the future life of biblical narrative depends on performers and audiences, and the future is therefore characterized by insistent fluidity that is textual and, more importantly, interpretive. This fluid future is best prepared for through exploration of ensemble performance of the biblical text because that makes the matter of hermeneutical negotiation central to the interpretive process. If there is more than one body involved in the performance of the text, then every line is an interaction, open to several possible interpretations, for the actors, for the audience, and for the text itself. Performance provides the occasion for this open fluidity and is therefore itself the arena in which this openness provokes thought.

Are the Risks Worthwhile?

Judgments about these risks will finally have to be based on an assessment of the gain brought about by an interpretive, analytical method. Finally, a method must pay for itself.

I contend that performance-critical work is worth the risk, that it yields a strong return, both for the interpreter and for the teacher, and that this particular mode of engagement interweaves scholarly analysis and pedagogy in a way that benefits both. To be sure, no matter how well we perform and learn from it, still theological analysis and pointed critique will be necessary. Performance by itself is not theological critique, but it can strengthen such critique, and if it does, it will strengthen pedagogy that dares to bear the risks that come with an increase in fluidity. The answer to the question about risk hangs on one's understanding of how pedagogy and control affect each other.

To summarize: the success of our exploration of pedagogy and performance will depend on how seriously we take both pedagogy and performance. Performance, taken with proper seriousness, involves the creative activity of both actors and audiences. This creative activity generates (and reveals) a kind of textual and hermeneutical fluidity that defeats any notion of interpretive control. This becomes particularly clear when the matter of embodiment is taken seriously. Bodies, and the spaces among them, create the necessity of negotiating stability in the midst of textual fluidity.

Application of Performance to the Interpretation of a Text: Mark 15

The fruitfulness of an exegetical method for interpretation determines whether it will be used for pedagogy. Any method judged to be unproductive may appear as an item in a sketch of the history of interpretation, but it will not significantly shape teaching. The analysis of a portion of Mark 15 that follows grows out of my experience in courses that I teach at Augustana University. It grows also out of the work of the Provoking the Gospel Storytellling Project, which itself started as a pedagogical tool. And this specific investigation of the death scene in the Gospel of Mark was conducted using the mode of ensemble performance, both in class and beyond.

In the courses that I teach using ensemble performance as a mode of engagement, every Friday is a text workshop day. Students form performance groups (consisting of three or four students) and perform the text assigned for the week for an audience, composed of the rest of the class. The texts are short, and several groups perform in the course of the class-hour. After each performance, the members of the class analyze the performance that they have just seen.

Initial Discoveries

Mark 15:22–41 has been read closely from the beginning. Interpreters have amassed a standard set of discoveries, and these discoveries have driven standard interpretations, sermonic and otherwise. Students who are new to biblical interpretation make the same discoveries. These discoveries, while certainly basic (and even obvious), are a necessary starting point.

Jesus Dies Abandoned

A first discovery, made by students and experienced interpreters alike, is that when Jesus dies in the Gospel of Mark, he dies abandoned by the men who have shared almost every scene with him. The main group of disciples was last seen as they ran from the story, as they "forsook him and fled." Peter, the last persisting member of this group, was last seen weeping bitterly. The story has been structured so that the supporting characters are steadily stripped away and Jesus is left alone, surrounded by Roman enemies and their collaborators; and once he is completely alone, he dies, abandoned even by God.

But Women Are There

Having accomplished this isolation and execution, the storyteller pulls the focus of the story back, revealing a wider scene. In this wider picture, we discover women, there at the crucifixion, women who were watching, and we discover that there are many of them.

In the history of the interpretation of this passage, these watching women are often (even generally) disembodied. Vincent Taylor devotes only a short paragraph to them.[29] Rudolf Bultmann grants them an existence only as legendary accretions in the crafted story.[30] Raymond Brown acknowledges their presence but argues that, though they were there, they were perhaps not disciples, certainly not successful ones.[31] The main body of the interpretive tradition makes it clear: the women who were watching were not historical; or if they were historical, they were not disciples; or if they were disciples, they were not significant.

There is, of course, a counterargument. Some interpreters have argued that the women are present precisely to recognize, and even valorize, their courage.[32] Others argue that their presence reveals important characteristics of the community of faith out of which the Gospel of Mark originates.[33] Some argue that they may even reveal the identity, and suggest the gender, of the storytellers who originated this compelling story.[34]

---

29. Vincent Taylor, *The Gospel according to St. Mark*, 2nd ed. (London: Macmillan, 1966), 598.

30. Rudolf Bultmann, *The History of the Synoptic Tradition*, trans. John Marsh (Oxford: Blackwell, 1963), 274.

31. Raymond Brown, *The Death of the Messiah: From Gethsemane to the Grave*, 2 vols. (New York: Doubleday, 1994), 2:1156–58.

32. Here Brown points to the work of Luise Schottroff, particularly her "Maria Magdalena und die Frauen am Grabe Jesu," *EvT* 42 (1982): 3–25.

33. Dewey, *Oral Ethos of the Early Church*, 146–47.

34. See Wire, *Case for Mark*, 168.

Students learning to interpret biblical texts will not know this history of interpretation, but they do (intriguingly) often replicate it. When the text is read silently, the abandonment of Jesus is clear, and the presence of women passes by in a dependent clause, noted mostly by people who are already sensitized to the presence or absence of women in public and in public discourse.

The Women Are a Surprise

If we are to take the whole text seriously as a whole story, we must embody the fact that the storyteller *chose* not to show these women to us until now. They were always there, the storyteller tells the audience. But the storyteller keeps this deeply silent until chapter 15. It is this deep silence that motivates the main body of the history of interpretation of this scene. Interpreters read the storyteller's silence as authorizing their own disembodying of the women who were watching.

But all of this creates real problems for performance and for interpretation. Ideology wishes these problems away. Serious hermeneutical engagement welcomes them as the beginning of proper interpretive provocation.

How Will This Scene Be Played?

One of the virtues of using performance as a tool for teaching is that these simple discoveries, once made, must finally be made part of a performance. In the case under consideration, the women will simply have to be present, and the performers will have to find a way to make this happen. This takes students beyond customary readings of the text and requires them to entertain the possibility that the text needs to be read, understood, and performed differently from the ways it is usually understood. This acquaints them with what I have called "hermeneutical fluidity." In a text that is customarily read as a male-only event, with women absent, insignificant, or not to be included among the disciples, performance requires them to read differently. This initial difference leads, in my experience, to the discovery of further oddities, more surprises. The text, imagined to be simply discursive, is revealed to be far more like a parable than they had imagined. This revelation takes them from accepting hermeneutical fluidity to expecting textual fluidity. This is a significant gain, for interpreters, for teachers, and for students.

Assume performance of the story by an ensemble of actors, an aggregation of bodies. Even if only the narrator speaks, still other bodies surround that narrator throughout Mark's story: the disciples, the crowds, Pilate, the Roman torturers. Now at the end of the story, the audience suddenly discovers that the narrator is surrounded by yet another group of bodies, many of them, all women, bodies that are watching. Students who are performing the text sometimes gesture to the empty space that surrounds them, suggesting that the emptiness is filled with women. Sometimes they choose women who are members of their performance group to step forward at this point and establish their presence. Sometimes they select women in the audience and create them as the watchers who surround the death scene. Whatever they do, the women are simply there. Antoinette Wire has noted that though there are many women's stories in Mark's Gospel, only in chapter 15 are they the focus of a scene, only in chapter 15 are their names mentioned, and only in chapter 15 are they given real bodily reality: their bodies outlive Jesus, and they see where his body is buried.[35]

More than that, if the revelation in chapter 15 is to be performed seriously, these many women have to be actively involved in following Jesus and in the work of *diakonia*. The storyteller has made "following" into the general requirement for those who are identified as disciples. *Diakonia* has been established as even more important. The word is not common in Mark's story, but it does describe the activity of angels and of Peter's mother-in-law. Elisabeth Moltmann-Wendel has noted that the word names the activity of a "deacon" in a community of faith.[36] A deacon in ancient communities connected need with resource, bringing the sick to a healer, or the poor and hungry to someone who could feed them. At least that is what a deacon does when the word names a male subject. When the subject is female, Moltmann-Wendel notes, the word is translated as "serve," or "cook," or "wait tables." Even were we to choose (inexplicably, I would say) not to agree with Moltmann-Wendel that this word ought to be translated evenly for male and female subjects, still any proper performance of Mark's whole story must embody this active engagement in every scene from the very beginning.

---

35. Ibid., 166.
36. Elisabeth Moltmann-Wendel, *The Women around Jesus*, trans. John Bowden (New York: Crossroad, 1982).

This is not an issue for weekly text workshop performances, because each week involves performing only a single scene, but the Gospels course that I teach culminates in the several performance groups creating long-form performances (approximately thirty minutes each) of condensed versions of the Gospel that has been the main focus of the course. Because of this, I have students begin thinking about how to incorporate women into every scene when the issue arises out of performing Mark 15.

Simple Presence

How might the presence of the women be played? There are several options. Performers might choose to create a simple, continuous presence for the bodies of the women who are revealed at the end of the story. These women could simply surround every scene, perhaps watching (as they do at the death scene), but also simply and continuously engaged in following and *diakonia*. They would always be simply, but inextricably, involved in the working of the story. Of course, this would irritate ideological audience members who could be counted upon to insist that the "text" never mentions the women who now surround each scene. But Mark's storyteller provides his or her own response to this ideological reaction: 15:40 insists that the women were always present. Students, at this point, encounter the business end of hermeneutical fluidity. No matter how the text has customarily been read, the women have to be present. Period.

Resentful Presence

The moment of revelation is complicated, even for the simplest way of playing the continual presence of the women. In the congregations in which I grew up, every significant gathering involved a moment near the end when the work of the Women's Auxiliary was acknowledged. Someone, always a male, would interrupt the flow of the evening and direct everyone's attention to the women in the kitchen. These women were called out into the main room to receive the applause of the assembly. Then they were sent back behind closed doors to complete the cleanup. They always looked a little pleased, and a little embarrassed, by the whole process. Perhaps Mark 15:40 is to be played as this sort of "kitchen curtain call."

But even this simple scene has some complexity. I have been in the kitchen after the curtain call, both as a child and as a pastor, and I have heard the comments people make after the doors again are closed. "I'd like to see them try to do this without us," my mother once said. Perhaps the women on the hillside, the women who were watching, the women who were, of real necessity, always there, must be seen to resent their long invisibility. Even if this irritation is confined to the single scene in chapter 15, it will create tension in the performance of the story.

Students who have recognized the necessity of hermeneutical fluidity will experiment with this way of playing the scene. They will typically be rather uncomfortable with portraying resentment, to be sure, but their willingness opens the text even further. They typically begin to ask about what other voices and bodies might have been obscured in customary readings of the text. There are even more discoveries in the offing.

Surprising Presence

Performance demands that one pay careful attention to the structured experience of the text. It will not do to simply gloss over moments of awkwardness, unless one has decided simply to edit the base text for smoothness, ideological or otherwise. I think that one of the great gifts offered by performance-critical work is that it creates a distrust of ideological smoothing. As noted earlier, ideological theater, theater in which all things are controlled, is bad theater. This is especially true with a text like the Gospel of Mark in which surprise is itself a major structuring element. This is the analytical argument put forward by a very skillful reader of Mark's story, Donald Juel. In Juel's reading, Mark's story is not rough and unfinished; it is built in order to surprise any imaginable audience. One might even say that surprise is itself the main structural member of the story and that any reading that is too tame or too controlled reveals a serious misunderstanding of the story.[37]

When the women are discovered, perhaps surprisingly still onsite and watching as Jesus dies, and when the storyteller informs the audience, certainly surprisingly, that the women have been in every chapter, then every scene, responsible for every development of the story, attentive performance must find a way to render this very real surprise palpable for the audience. The audience must be surprised as well. That means that making the women simply and steadily part of every scene, while it respects what

---

37. See Juel's argument in *A Master of Surprise: Mark Interpreted* (Minneapolis: Fortress, 1994).

the storyteller has now, lately, told the audience, this refuses the fact of the structural surprise in chapter 15. An attentive performance of the text will need to create an aggressive surprise for the audience. Surely Antonin Artaud meant many more things when he wrote about a "theater of cruelty," but one part of his argument applies here: the audience must feel the impact of the sudden discovery of the women; even if the audience does not understand the import of this discovery, it must feel the impact. Theater changes people, or it is not theater. Artaud wrote, "The theater like the plague is a crisis which is resolved by death or cure."[38] We may comfort ourselves with assurances that this is meant to be metaphorical, but we may not imagine that an audience walks away unchanged.

Performing the Surprise: "Eyes to See"

Some years ago while developing a performance of the Gospel of Mark, my student actors made the matter of surprise central to the entire story. We called the show "Eyes to See" and carefully caught every surprise in the story, looking always for ways to make the audience feel those surprises. My students chose to play the parables so that the reversals and exaggerations were unmistakable. The slow comprehension (and absent comprehension) of the male disciples they chose to play broadly. But how could we play the women? My students and I conducted several shared experiments, mostly unsatisfying. We had got as far as having the women silently watch, not just the death scene, but also all of the scenes in the Gospel. This was interesting but not enough. Then a student suggested that the women who were watching should wear masks. The effect of the masking was that they were invisible to the other characters on stage except when one of them removed her mask to approach Jesus with a request regarding her daughter or to touch Jesus from behind from among the crushing crowd. When these central scenes were completed, the woman replaced her mask and thus vanished from sight (at least for the male disciples). This allowed us to make sense of the way women emerge out of nowhere and approach Jesus, apparently (somehow) understanding him and his promise perfectly. This also allowed us to embody the namelessness of the woman who anointed Jesus: promised an everlasting memorial, she was masked before anyone bothered to learn her name.

---

38. Artaud, *Theater and Its Double*, 31.

At the end of chapter 15, when Jesus is surrounded by the Roman enemies who have murdered him, one by one the women remove their masks, revealing that they were present and that they had indeed seen what Pilate and his cohorts had done, revealing also that they were watching still and that there were very many of them. This way of playing honored the continuous reality of the presence of the women, and it embodied the surprise that comes when the story, almost complete, reveals one more crucial detail that must change the way every scene is played. The effect was powerful, and much remarked upon by the audience when we performed this both onstage and for the Annual Meeting of the Society of Biblical Literature in Toronto (2002). This way of playing the text also made a strong impression on the actors involved, all of them students at the university where I teach. Strong performance contributed to strong interpretation and to strong teaching. This moment of discovery is finally why I am convinced that performance has something vital to contribute to pedagogy and that all of the effort is finally more than worthwhile. The idea of the masks came into our performance as the result of a student's suggestion, a suggestion that began simply as an attempt to make sense of the interpretive puzzle that the performance of Mark's story was forcing us to consider.

Some Implications of Performance for Pedagogy

The mode of engagement is productive. It yields strong interpretive work for the same reason it strengthens teaching. The text is made fluid and the activity of discovery and analysis is distributed beyond the isolated interpreter. The structure of the text is experienced as an event, experienced by interpreter, actors, and audience. In the case of the death scene in the Gospel of Mark, it is the surprise revelation that becomes an event, not simply an idea. Students become allies in the work of analyzing and interpreting the text. As a consequence, the course becomes (at least in part) an exercise in project-based learning with all the advantages of shared responsibility and shared insight

This works, of course, for the Gospel of Mark. But it works also for any narrative text (biblical or otherwise). In the performance of the *St. Mark Passion* that I created with members of the Provoking the Gospel Storytelling Project, we worked not only with Mark but also with the texts (particularly from Isaiah but also from Lamentations) that form the mythical background for Mark's story. My students and I chose to hand these texts to the composer (Christopher Stanichar) who created the music for the *St. Mark Passion*. He chose to give those mythic texts to the choir, who sang all the parts of the story that burrow deep into the past or swirl high into the heavens. This choice also developed out of a shared process of investigation. No part of this was simply my creation or simply that of the students. Together we created something that none of us could have created alone. Once again, this reinvigorates my commitment to project-based learning in the courses I teach. The projects are smaller in a semester course, but the collaboration is essential.

When the Provoking the Gospel Storytelling Project created a performance of the book of Job (which we called "A Man, A Simple Man"), I worked for a year with two student collaborators to develop the script and libretto. When we handed the libretto to the composer (John Pennington), the students and I met with him to explore the ways his creation danced with ours. This open collaboration continued when we met with the choir that would sing the music and when we gathered and rehearsed a cast of actors who would perform the story.

In every case, I came to the project with a thorough knowledge of the language of the texts and of the history of interpretation. In every case, my own fixed ideas from my research were made fluid. In every case, I learned new things, the students learned new things, and the audience encountered strong texts from the Bible that they might well never have encountered otherwise.

The next project for the Provoking the Gospel Storytelling Project focuses on stories of creation and restoration in Jewish and Christian Scripture. My student collaborators (eight of them at this point) have indicated interest in incorporating also origin stories from other cultures in the performance. I do not know how (or if) this will work, but the shared process of developing a performance will answer this question. What I do know is that this shared work (which will be a course for some of the students, a show for some others, and a collaborative creation for us all) will change the way I look at these stories that I have studied for decades. It will also change the way I teach, and that is the enduring value of performance-critical work, in my experience.

PART 3
STRATEGIES: THE SECOND ORALITY FOR
RESEARCHING AND TEACHING MARK

9
Mark in a Digital Age:
The Internet and the Teaching of Mark's Gospel

Mark Goodacre

This Transitional Generation

Our generation is an unusual one, and the challenges of teaching today are serious. Almost all of those teaching in universities and colleges are digital immigrants while all of our students are digital natives.[1] We are, in other words, a generation in transition. The current cohorts of undergraduate students have never known a time when there was no Internet, while their instructors all grew up in an analogue world. Even those, like me, who began teaching in the 1990s, did our graduate work using books and papers. We may have written our theses on some of the first affordable home computers or word processors, but even those who had access to the Internet found little use for it in their research, still less in their earliest experiences of teaching. Our first students often had less idea about the Internet than we did.

There is now a curious dynamic between the teacher who is ill at ease with the Internet and the student who lives and breathes the Internet. This dynamic is not here to stay. Today's graduate students are themselves digital natives who have an instinctive feel for how to utilize the Internet in their teaching and research. For them, it is no more a learned skill to work

---

1. For the terminology, see Marc Prensky, "Digital Natives, Digital Immigrants," *On the Horizon* 9.5 (2001): 1–6; Prensky, "Digital Natives, Digital Immigrants, Part 2: Do They Really *Think* Differently?" *On the Horizon* 9.6 (2001): 1–6. Reproduced at http://www.marcprensky.com/.

out how to deal with blogs, websites, podcasts, and social media than it is for them to open a book.

The pace of transition is pretty remarkable. As recently as 1994, Robert Fowler wrote an essay on the dramatic differences that hypertext makes to our concepts of canon, exploring ways in which the secondary orality of the Internet era might shed light on our understanding of antiquity.[2] What he was not able to appreciate in 1994 was the extent to which the Internet and electronic resources would reach out beyond *text* to something still more dynamic and varied, with podcasts, video, and other forms of media created for and disseminated on the Internet. Indeed, the Internet has not just gone beyond printed text to hypertext but beyond hypertext to multimedia, where watching and listening become as important as reading.

In this essay, I would like to explore how the Internet is changing our teaching and how its challenges can become exciting opportunities when we embrace them rather than resist them. Given the pace of change, I expect this essay, like so much of the Internet that is its major focus, to be out of date pretty quickly. Given the scope of the topic, I will target it by providing examples from the teaching of Mark's Gospel, which is the subject of this volume.

The End of the Great Divide

When I began experimenting with academic Internet resources in the late 1990s, it was common for university instructors to deal with the Internet by avoiding it.[3] They would exhort their students that if they wanted to find good, academic resources, they would need to go to the library and

---

2. Robert M. Fowler, "How the Secondary Orality of the Electronic Age Can Awaken Us to the Primary Orality of Antiquity, or What Hypertext Can Teach Us about the Bible, with Reflections on the Ethical and Political Issues of the Electronic Frontier," paper presented at the Annual Meeting of the Society of Biblical Literature, Chicago, IL, 19 November 1994. Reproduced at *Homepages.bw.edu*, http://homepages.bw.edu/~rfowler/pubs/secondoral/index.html. On the misappropriation of the term *secondary orality* in recent scholarship on Christian origins, see Mark Goodacre, *Thomas and the Gospels: The Case for Thomas's Familiarity with the Synoptics* (Grand Rapids: Eerdmans, 2012), 135–40.

3. It is a sign of how massively things have changed to see that I was able to write in 1997, "At present there is actually relatively little on the academic study of the New Testament to be found on the world wide web, and given increased student access to the Internet, there is a market that is wide-open and waiting to be exploited" (Mark

to avoid the Internet. For some years, this advice worked reasonably well, even if we might suspect that it was sometimes motivated more by the instructor's laziness and lack of familiarity with the Internet than it was by an honest assessment of the relative merits of print and Internet resources. Recent years, though, have made that great divide between "print" and "electronic" resources seem somewhat naïve.[4] It is not simply that scholars have been forced to take the proliferation of resources created for the Internet seriously. It is also, and perhaps more importantly, that "print" is no longer necessary as the means of primary access to the age-old scholarly resources like monographs and especially journal articles.

It is akin to the change in the way we use money. More often than not, physical cash and written checks do not pass through our hands in our financial transactions. Similarly, when we now want to access the latest scholarly journals, we see them first online. It is much quicker to see the current volumes online than it is to wait for hard copies to appear in the library. The journals are searchable, and we can access them everywhere. For most journals, the entire archive is available digitally too. With this comes a massive advantage in teaching. When one has a large class, the availability of seminal articles in the journal in question drastically reduces the workload for the instructor and provides students with the chance to read what the scholars are reading and not just the synthetic and often bland textbooks that we insist on assigning.

In my New Testament class at Duke University in the fall of 2012, with 120 students, I set them a classic essay question, one that I did at university too, asking about Mark's vendetta against the disciples. My recommended reading list included the seminal pieces by Joseph Tyson, "The Blindness of the Disciples in Mark"; Robert Tannehill, "The Disciples in Mark: The

---

Goodacre, "'Drawing from the Treasure Both New and Old': Current Trends in New Testament Studies," *ScrB* 27 [1997]: 66–77).

4. The term *great divide* is commonly used with respect to discussion of orality versus literacy in antiquity, especially in conversation with Werner Kelber's work. See Werner H. Kelber, *The Oral and the Written Gospel: The Hermeneutics of Speaking and Writing in the Synoptic Tradition, Mark, Paul, and Q* (Bloomington: Indiana University Press, 1997). The reprint of Kelber's work features some of the author's own responses to the charge of his participating in a "great divide" understanding of the period.

I am adopting the term here to characterize the change in perceptions of the Internet by teachers in the humanities and the change from the way that "print" was characterized as acceptable while "electronic" was characterized as problematic, a great divide that is now no longer viable.

Function of a Narrative Role"; and Elizabeth Struthers Malbon, "Disciples/Crowds/Whoever: Markan Characters and Readers,"[5] all of which the students can simply pick up digitally from Duke's library subscriptions to the *Journal of Biblical Literature*, the *Journal of Religion*, and *Novum Testamentum*, respectively. The point may sound like a banal one, but it is only very recently that access to resources for large classes was a major headache, involving photocopying, scanning, and course packs, with the additional issues of understanding copyright and fair use of multiply reproduced resources for students.

The glory of easy electronic access to journal articles also creates a problem, though, for a generation that expects to find everything online. While for the scholar it is still a wonderful thing to be able to sit at home or in the garden or at the beach and access whole archives worth of journal articles, our students have never known a world in which such things are unusual. They assume that everything valuable must be available online somewhere. To an extent, we are complicit in the problem. Scholars' homepages as well as resources such as academia.edu can give the impression that all the really valuable materials simply must be online somewhere if only the student looks hard enough. If it is not available, the instructor may simply be wrong in thinking that it is valuable. Who would write something and then hide it? To those of us brought up on the challenge of seeking out articles in bound journal archives deep in the dustiest, darkest stacks of the library, such a viewpoint can seem unfathomable and obtuse, but unless we think ourselves into the contemporary student's experience of the world, with its oceans of available data, we will do them a disservice. It is pointless complaining about it. We will do our students a far greater service if we try to understand it and participate in it. After all, why should we expect their experience in the digital present to mirror our experience in the analogue past?

The Future of the Gateway Site

The end of the great divide has also compromised the value of the gateway site. Since 1997, I have maintained a site called *The New Testament*

---

5. Joseph B. Tyson, "The Blindness of the Disciples in Mark," *JBL* 80 (1961): 261–68; Robert C. Tannehill, "The Disciples in Mark: The Function of a Narrative Role," *JR* 57 (1977): 386–405; Elizabeth Struthers Malbon, "Disciples/Crowds/Whoever: Markan Characters and Readers," *NovT* 28 (1986): 104–30.

Gateway that aims to catalog and annotate valuable, freely available Internet resources.[6] One of the major challenges with maintaining the site in recent years has been the proliferation of high-quality resources available online. In the early years of the site, it was relatively straightforward to stay on top of the academic resources in the area because those creating them needed a mild degree of technical competence, like the knowledge of HTML. Those of us who created academic websites generally hand-coded them, so the creation of web pages remained the preserve of a handful of geeks. But now it is not only that minimal technical expertise is required to publish on the Internet, it is also that what we used to think of as "print" resources are seeping into the electronic domain.

Up until about 2002, it was still possible to be comprehensive in indexing and annotating Internet resources in a given area. If it was a high-quality, scholarly resource created especially for the Net, it made its way onto the site. But as the world of freely available, high-quality Internet resources proliferated, with legally adopted materials finding a new home on the Net, it became impossible to index everything. I can recall the watershed moment. In the early years of the *New Testament Gateway* I worked with the absurd pretence, as it now appears, that I could be exhaustive. When the journal *Biblica* placed all of their back-catalog online, for free, for all, I realized that there was no hope of listing everything related to the New Testament on the site.[7] It was simply too much work, and it was too tiring and uninteresting a prospect. It took the fun out of working on the site. Up to that point, there was something thrilling about embracing the new technology. It was exciting to be working with those who were not only publishing books and articles but who were also producing websites and material specially for the Web. As soon as the older world of print resources began to seep into the new world of the Web, the gloss went off working on the gateway site.

I was not alone in feeling overwhelmed. Torrey Seland's pioneering *Resource Pages for Biblical Studies*[8] also began to creak under the weight

---

6. Mark Goodacre, *The New Testament Gateway*, http://NTGateway.com. The site began as "Recommended New Testament Web Resources" for students on my home page in the Department of Theology at the University of Birmingham, but it soon outgrew that home and became a site in its own right.

7. *Biblica*, BSW, Biblical Studies on the Web, http://www.bsw.org/project/biblica/.

8. Torrey Seland, *Resource Pages for Biblical Studies*, Torreys.org, http://torreys.org/bible/.

of new materials, and a site that was once near exhaustive became highly selective.[9] Nevertheless, although it has not been easy, gateway sites have endured. The proliferation of resources has meant refocusing. Instead of the attempt to be exhaustive, to provide links to and annotations of every good resource out there on the Net, the gateway sites have become more akin to the reading lists that they were initially attempting to supplement. Their authors have tried to isolate the best resources on the Net with a special focus on undergraduate students, a goal that has provided a real challenge.[10] I know from correspondence, as well as conversations and university syllabi, that sites such as the *New Testament Gateway* are still considered useful by many college professors, but I suspect that their time is limited—and I say this with huge regret given the massive amount of time that I have ploughed into the site—because the nature of the Internet has changed.

The Internet is no longer an area of supplementary interest where we go to for some "value-added" materials in our teaching. It is now right at the heart of every student's research. The key issue now is no longer "print" resources over against "electronic" resources. It is a matter of accessible resources over against restricted resources, resources that require institutional subscriptions versus those that are available free for all, resources that are only available in print in selected libraries versus those that can be accessed by everyone.

Under these circumstances, one of the most interesting developments is something quite unexpected in the 1990s, which were dominated online by text and hypertext, and that is the revolution that makes watching video and listening to audio an everyday activity, not only on the computer but also on Internet TV, tablet, and smartphone.

---

9. "I find it close to impossible for one man to keep up with all the studies—books and articles—that are now being published on the Internet related to the New Testament" (Torrey Seland, "Resource Pages for Biblical Studies Resurrected!" *Philonica et Neotestamentica* blog, 13 October 2012, http://biblicalresources.wordpress.com/2012/10/13/resource-pages-for-biblical-studies-resurrected/).

10. I have often written about the topic on my blog; I have gathered several of these together under the label "NT Gateway Future" at http://ntweblog.blogspot.com/search/label/NT%20Gateway%20future. See the systematic treatment of the issues in "How and Why the NT Gateway Was Rebooted, Revitalized and Relaunched," *NT Blog*, 16–19 November 2009, http://ntweblog.blogspot.com/search/label/How%20and%20why.

Online Video

Long before the dawn of the Internet, the instructor might well use video in the classroom. Legitimately purchased or illegally recorded television documentaries, and clips from them, would often provide a means of introducing students to the issues and giving them the chance to see reconstructions of first-century sites as well as to some of the more TV-friendly New Testament scholars. But now on the Internet, with greater bandwidth, greater speeds, and ever-improving technology, the proliferation of online video has provided major new options for the instructor. Many of us will now assign our students a ten-minute YouTube video in addition to or instead of a reading assignment. Sometimes, the video clip communicates what we want our students to grasp far better than any available textbook or introductory resource, perhaps not least because of the immediacy and informality of the video over against bland textbook texts.[11]

One of the best examples of the utilization of the Internet in this way is the project from the University of Nottingham (UK)'s Department of Theology and Religious Studies. Their remarkable *Bibledex* project is a series of YouTube videos, featuring scholars discussing every book of the Bible, each a bite-sized five–fifteen minute piece.[12] I have occasionally used them in the classroom too. They are well produced, informative, terse, and often quirky and humorous; and for the American student audience, it is all the more enjoyable for displaying a range of British accents.[13] Their introduction to Mark's Gospel is an ideal way of exposing the undergraduate to some of the key issues in its interpretation.[14] Further, a four-minute video filmed at Caesarea Philippi provides a superb location for the discussion of the messianic secret in Mark.[15]

---

11. See further my section on online audio and video resources on the Gospel of Mark at "Gospel of Mark: Audio and Video," *The New Testament Gateway.* http://www.ntgateway.com/gospel-and-acts/gospel-of-mark/audio-and-video.

12. *Bibledex: A Video about Every Book in the Bible*, University of Nottingham, http://www.bibledex.com/index.html.

13. The academics involved are listed at "The Theologians," *Bibledex: A Video about Every Book in the Bible*, University of Nottingham, http://www.bibledex.com/team/theologians.html. Not all, however, have British accents.

14. See Brady Haran, producer, "Mark," *Bibledex: A Video about Every Book in the Bible,* University of Nottingham, http://www.bibledex.com/videos/mark.html.

15. "Caesarea Philippi," *Bibledex: A Video about Every Book in the Bible,* University of Nottingham, http://www.bibledex.com/israel/caesarea_philippi.html.

The success of projects like *Bibledex* will no doubt cause other university departments as well as individual scholars to provide this kind of teaching resource. Remarkably, a similar project emerged at the same time from the same area of the United Kingdom. St John's College, Nottingham, released a whole series of well-produced videos on the Bible featuring well-known scholars like Jimmy Dunn, N. T. Wright, Richard Bauckham, and the late Graham Stanton. These videos included one on the Gospel of Mark, also ideal for viewing by new students, presented by Paula Gooder.[16] To an extent, the same kind of thing is available via lectures captured for *iTunes U*, most notably Dale Martin's entire series of lectures, at Yale University, on New Testament introduction; but while the latter is nothing more than a filmed lecture[17] in the style of the "Great courses" project,[18] *Bibledex* and St. John's Nottingham are doing something produced specially for the Internet, with high production values.

The possibility of online video means that as well as accessing scholarly resources about the Gospel of Mark, students can also access the text itself in a new way, a way that nevertheless draws from one of the oldest forms of presentation, the full dramatic performance.

Performances of Mark

For some years, scholars have enthused about one-man shows (and it usually is a man) in which an actor will memorize and perform Mark's Gospel.[19] The advantages of such performances for biblical scholars are pretty

---

16. Paula Gooder, "The Gospel of Mark," *YouTube*, 20 July 2012, http://www.youtube.com/watch?v=XyV2tuE84FA; and Gooder, "The Gospel of Mark, Part 2," *YouTube*, 4 Sep. 2012, http://www.youtube.com/watch?v=P1tvW7t0WZY.

17. Dale Martin, *Introduction to New Testament History and Literature*, *iTunes U*, Yale University, 2009, https://itunes.apple.com/us/itunes-u/introduction-to-new-testament/id341652026; *YouTube*, http://www.youtube.com/course?list=EC279CFA55C51E75E0. The lecture on the Gospel of Mark is at https://itunes.apple.com/us/itunes-u/introduction-to-new-testament/id341652026 and http://www.youtube.com/watch?v=yd5sXfFboxA&list=PL279CFA55C51E75E0.

18. *The Great Courses*, http://www.thegreatcourses.com, sells specially filmed lecture courses by figures such as Bart Ehrman. Given the number of free resources now available through iTunes U and YouTube, it is possible that commercial resources like this will ultimately falter.

19. The most famous and well-respected version remains Alec McCowen's *The Gospel according to St. Mark*, which he performed widely to strong reviews across several years. Thames Television produced a version for ITV in 1979, and there was a VHS

striking, allowing them the rare opportunity to jump out of the scholar's text-dominated world and to see and hear Mark's Gospel afresh.[20] The ease of online video has now made this a major new reality in the digital age. It is no longer a matter of going to church or to an avant-garde theater or even an academic conference in order to witness such a show. Students can now go to YouTube to view Tom Boomershine performing the whole of Mark's passion narrative, in both Greek and English,[21] as well as several sections from earlier in Mark.[22] This is another area where we are at transitional stage since there is not yet available online a single officially released example of a complete performance of Mark in English. Earlier examples such as the one by Max McLean[23] have disappeared from YouTube.[24]

---

release also in 1990: Arthur Cantor and Alec McCowen, *Alec McCowen in His Solo Performance of St. Mark's Gospel* (New York: Arthur Cantor Films, 1990). The 1990 revival was subsequently released on DVD, *Alec McCowen in His Solo Performance of Mark's Gospel* (Oklahoma City: Daystar Foundation and Library, 2013). Although there are low quality "bootleg" versions of this on YouTube, there is no official online version.

20. For reflections on Mark as performance, see Kelly R. Iverson and Christopher W. Skinner, eds., *Mark as Story: Retrospect and Prospect*, RBS 65 (Atlanta: Society of Biblical Literature, 2011), in particular the essays by Thomas Boomershine, "Audience Address and Purpose in the Performance of Mark," 115–44; and Robert Fowler, "In the Boat with Jesus: Imagining Ourselves in Mark's Story," 233–58.

21. Cortney Haley, director and ed., "The Messiah of Peace: Mark 14–16 told in English by Dr. Tom Boomershine," *YouTube*, 25 Aprril 2014, https://www.youtube.com/watch?v=fnPtuXiYcBw; and Haley, "The Messiah of Peace: Mark 14–16 told in Greek by Dr. Tom Boomershine," *YouTube*, 26 April 2015, https://www.youtube.com/watch?t=43&v=3dwo3z9T7HY. See also Tom Boomershine, *The Messiah of Peace: A Performance Criticism Commentary on Mark 14–16*, http://messiahofpeace.com, which provides links to the videos and promises further updates.

22. I have gathered together the many links and added a playlist, "Tom Boomershine Performs Mark's Gospel," *YouTube*, 16 April 2009, 21 July 2001, 2 November 2011, 16 December 2011, 25–26 April 2014, https://www.youtube.com/watch?v=Aytp-1OpMVE&list=PL7DR0ecPG8I1WonZetQ6-Fj7gC4g4ED-L. An earlier version of the playlist is referenced and discussed at Mark Goodacre, "Tom Boomershine Performs Mark," *NT Blog*, 25 June 2013, http://ntweblog.blogspot.com/2013/06/tom-boomershine-performs-mark.html. See also Tom Boomershine's contribution to this volume.

23. Max McLean's "Complete Gospel of Mark" was published in sections on *YouTube* on 16 August 2010, but it was subsequently removed. The performance is commercially available. See further Max McLean, *Mark's Gospel on Stage with Max McLean*, http://www.markonstage.com/, which used to feature embedded video of the performance but which now only features a clip.

24. There is a well-produced full German performance available, Eric Wehrlin,

One of the advantages of assigning students a YouTube clip rather than a section in their study Bible is that it is a notorious difficulty to get students actually to read the primary text. This way, they may encounter Mark directly and not indirectly through what the textbook tells them to think. Moreover, the instructor can use a clip in the classroom so that the class can access the performance together and share the experience of seeing and hearing Mark performed together. The YouTube clip welcomes a guest into the classroom whose performance itself gives the students something extra to discuss, and this is the kind of area where theater studies and English majors can also make a contribution.

Moreover, one of the advantages of accessing Tom Boomershine's performance of Mark is that it is informed by a scholarly perspective. The majority of dramatic performances of Mark are by actors who are unfamiliar with the scholarship. While the major commercially available performances of Mark by Alec McCowen and Max McLean do mention Markan priority,[25] in other respects they fall short. Few instructors would be happy with the way in which these performances take for granted, in their introductions, that Mark was based on Peter's memories.[26] Moreover, both McCowen's and McLean's performances uncritically utilize the longer ending of Mark without pausing for explanation or changing the tone of voice. What for scholars is Mark's dramatic ending at 16:8 is in McCowen's and McLean's performances simply a transition in the narrative.[27] While this could provide a useful invitation to the instructor to discuss Mark's Gospel and how hearings of the text differ depending on how it begins and ends, many instructors will be delighted to recommend Tom Boomershine's performance, which ends at Mark 16:8.

"Markusevangelium Theaterabend Eric Wehrlin Soloprogram," *YouTube*, 11 October 2014, https://www.youtube.com/watch?t=3662&v=SIdBDJA0jrU. See further Eva-Maria Admiral and Eric Wehrlin, "Das Markusevangelium," *Eva-Maria Admiral and Eric Wehrlin*, http://www.admiral-wehrlin.de/cms/theater/theaterstuecke/das-markusevangelium.html.

25. This is true for both Alec McCowen (above, n. 19) and Max McLean (above, n. 23).

26. This is also true for both McCowen and McLean (see previous note).

27. See previous note. This is also true for Eric Wehrlin's performance (see n. 24 above).

The Communal Internet

One of the obvious advantages of the Internet is its ability to act as a communal resource, so teaching can become a little less isolated, less about the one teacher in the classroom and more about the sharing of resources and ideas. One of the earliest attempts to tap this potential was the Wabash initiative to share syllabi in the area of religion, a project that has survived, even thrived, for some years.[28] There are currently forty resources linked on the Gospels and Acts, several of which are specifically focused on Mark, including names like Daniel Patte.[29] This is the kind of project that is only seriously viable on the Internet. It has the potential to be hugely helpful for instructors looking to create new syllabi or to refresh old ones. Moreover, like archives of old examination papers, course syllabi can be a useful barometer for the current state of the discipline. If the Wabash initiative continues for the next twenty or thirty years, future scholars may be surprised to find out what we are encouraging our students to read and study today.

Like all Internet activities, though, there are risks. Does the public sharing of teaching materials encourage some instructors to cheat and to borrow too heavily from others' resources? Does it make the ever-increasing casualization of labor in the universities all the easier, as hard-pressed adjunct professors with expertise in different fields find themselves borrowing resources in order to survive? Should there be some kind of etiquette about the sharing of syllabi? With the proliferation of MOOCs (Massive Open Online Courses) and growing interest in learning online, these issues will become ever more pressing.

Where the communal Internet really comes into its own, though, is with the blogosphere. For over a decade there has been an ever-growing community of scholars, students, and dedicated amateurs blogging about biblical studies and the ancient world. They are informally known as "bibliobloggers," and while there are now so many of them that it is impossible to read everything they write regularly, there is still a recognized

---

28. "Resources: Syllabus Collection," *Wabash Center*, http://www.wabashcenter.wabash.edu/resources/guide_syllabi.aspx.

29. "Resources: Religion on the Web; Bible—NT—Gospels and Acts," *Wabash Center*, 2014, http://www.wabashcenter.wabash.edu/resources/result-browse.aspx?topic=629.

core of popular scholarly blogs that have proved their worth.[30] Although recent years have seen the welcome advent of the "vertical blog" from elite scholars like Larry Hurtado[31] and Bart Ehrman,[32] it is still the "horizontal blog"[33] that is the beating heart of the blogging community. The point is well illustrated by a blog post I put up about "Blogging Mark" in preparation for writing this essay. I asked the community for recommendations for good, representative blog posts that illustrated the theme of teaching Mark's Gospel, and very quickly there were twenty comments offering links to a whole range of useful blog posts that illustrate the theme,[34] including Joel Watts's discussions of blogging on Mark and how

---

30. For reflections on the history and development of blogs in this area, see James R. Davila, "Assimilated to the Blogosphere: Blogging Ancient Judaism," *SBL Forum Archive*, April 2005, http://sbl-site.org/Article.aspx?ArticleID=390; Davila, "Enter the Bibliobloggers," University of St Andrews School of Divinity, http://www.st-andrews.ac.uk/divinity/rt/otp/abstracts/enterthebibliobloggers/; Davila, "What Just Happened: The Rise of 'Biblioblogging' in the First Decade of the Twenty-First Century," paper presented at the Annual Meeting of the Society of Biblical Literature, Atlanta, GA, 22 November 2010, http://paleojudaica.blogspot.co.uk/2010_11_14_archive.html#1715486029034288246. See also Jim West, "Blogging the Bible: A Short History," *BSR* 39 (2010): 3–13; James Franklin McGrath, "Biblioblogging Our Matrix: Exploring the Potential and Perplexities of Academic Blogging," *BSR* 39 (2010): 14–25; Robert Cargill, "The Benefit of Blogging for Archaeology," *BSR* 39 (2010): 26–36. See further the papers and discussions from the inaugural meeting of the Society of Biblical Literature Blogger and Online Publication section in November 2010, helpfully gathered together in Deane Galbraith, "Biblical Studies Carnival ᛏᛃ (November 2010)," *Religion Bulletin: The Blogging Portal of the Bulletin for the Study of Religion*, 1 December 2010, http://www.equinoxpub.com/blog/2010/12/biblical-studies-carnival-nz-november-2010/ (paragraph 2). See also Mark Goodacre, "Pods, Blogs and Other Time-Wasters," *NT Blog*, 17 November 2011, http://ntweblog.blogspot.com/2011/11/pods-blogs-and-other-time-wasters.html.

31. Larry Hurtado, *Larry Hurtado's Blog*, 19 June 2015, http://larryhurtado.wordpress.com/.

32. Bart Ehrman, *Christianity in Antiquity: The Bart Ehrman Blog*, 2012–2015, http://ehrmanblog.org/. Ehrman's blog is something of a unique experiment among vertical blogs in having the majority of its posts behind a paywall.

33. For the terminology, which is my own, see Mark Goodacre, "Vertical Blogs vs. Horizontal Blogs," *NT Blog*, 8 August 2012, http://ntweblog.blogspot.com/2012/08/vertical-blogs-vs-horizontal-blogs.html.

34. Mark Goodacre, "Blogging Mark: Input Requested Please," *NT Blog*, 12 June 2013, http://ntweblog.blogspot.com/2013/06/blogging-mark-input-requested-please.html.

that contributed to work on his book,[35] Mike Kok's blog dedicated to the academic study of the Gospel of Mark,[36] Christopher Skinner's blog posts using analogies from *Columbo* and *The Godfather*,[37] Anthony LeDonne's blog post on conflict in Mark,[38] and Peter Head's comments about Internet materials he shares with students when lecturing on Mark in Greek.[39]

The range of responses to this post effectively illustrates the strengths of the blogging community and how it can forward the mutual goal of improving our teaching of Mark's Gospel. While one comment shares a group of useful links handed out to students in a course, another helpfully illustrates how the blogging of work in progress can ultimately lead to formal publication. Moreover, the colloquial, informal nature of the analogies from film and television illustrates effectively the blog post's special niche, as a means of sharing ideas and insights from teaching in a forum that is more focused than the discussion in the common room but is less formal than the peer-reviewed article.

Podcasts and the Importance of Audio Resources

After over a decade, the blogs have endured. They have survived the coming of Facebook, Twitter, and other social media and to some extent have benefited from them. Not only have the social media made it easier to communicate and publicize blog posts, but they have also helped to focus

---

35. Joel Watts, *Mimetic Criticism and the Gospel of Mark: An Introduction and Commentary* (Eugene, OR: Wipf & Stock, 2013); see Watts, *Unsettled Christianity*, blog, http://unsettledchristianity.com; the archive for posts on Mark is at http://unsettledchristianity.com/category/criticism/new-testament/mark-new-testament.

36. Mike Kok, *Euangelion Kata Markon*, http://ntmark.wordpress.com.

37. Christopher Skinner, "The Gospel of Mark and Peter Falk: 'Columbo' as Pedagogical Tool," *Peje Iesous*, 4 September 2009, http://pejeiesous.com/2009/09/04/the-gospel-of-mark-and-peter-falk-columbo-as-pedagogical-tool/; Skinner, "Dramatized Irony, Markan Intercalations, and the Godfather," *Peje Iesous*, 6 February 2012, http://pejeiesous.com/2012/02/06/dramatized-irony-markan-intercalations-and-the-godfather/.

38. The blog post is Anthony LeDonne, "Who Started the Conflict in Mark's Gospel?," *The Jesus Blog*, 12 June 2013, http://historicaljesusresearch.blogspot.com/2013/06/who-started-conflict-in-marks-gospel-le.html. This blog post is based on his essay "The Jewish Leaders," in *Jesus among Friends and Enemies: A Historical and Literary Introduction to Jesus in the Gospels*, ed. Chris Keith and Larry W. Hurtado (Grand Rapids: Baker Academic, 2011), 199–217.

39. For this and all the other comments on this blog post, see n. 34 above.

their content. In the early days of blogging, it was common to write only a few lines, simply to draw attention to something online, or to make a brief comment on an article. Since the arrival of Twitter and Facebook, bloggers can ask themselves whether something really warrants a full blog post or whether it would be better as a quick 140-character comment on Twitter or a brief link posted on Facebook.

In recent years, though, there has been another fresh development that once again provides new possibilities: the podcast. Podcasts are in several respects related to blog posts, using some of the same technology, like dissemination via RSS feeds, but they are different in offering something a little less ephemeral. While scholarly podcasts may take the opportunity to comment on emerging news stories related to the discipline, they more often focus more on materials appropriate for teaching, and, as such, they often deal with topics that are of recurrent interest.

I began the *NT Pod* in 2009 and have produced seventy-five episodes (as well as several extended episodes), several of which are specifically focused on topics in Mark's Gospel,[40] most recently on the vexed question of the ending of Mark.[41] Perhaps not surprisingly, Mark's Gospel provides a rich resource for podcasting, not least because the medium lends itself well to the asking of questions and the exploring of mysteries. I generally like to title my podcasts with a question, and there are plenty of great questions to be asked about Mark. Usually, but not always, I find myself recording materials in tandem with my teaching. If I am thinking about a given topic because of teaching it, I find it much easier to podcast about it. In one of the few other regular podcasts in the area of academic New Testament studies, Phil Harland also runs podcasts alongside his teaching,[42] although unlike me, he produces series of podcasts with discrete themes rather than podcasting on a different topic each time.

---

40. Mark Goodacre, *NT Pod*, 26 February 2015, http://podacre.blogspot.com. The podcasts focusing on Mark's Gospel are gathered under this label: http://podacre.blogspot.com/search/label/Mark.

41. Mark Goodacre, "NT Pod 71: Was the Ending of Mark's Gospel Lost?" *NT Pod*, 14 February 2014, *Podacre.blogspot.co.uk*, http://podacre.blogspot.com/2014/02/nt-pod-71-was-ending-of-marks-gospel.html.

42. Phil Harland, *Religions of the Ancient Mediterranean Podcast*, 5 January 2013, http://www.philipharland.com/Blog/category/podcasts/. His series, "Early Christian Portraits of Jesus," features two podcasts about Mark's Gospel; see http://www.philipharland.com/Blog/2009/08/31/podcast-series-2-early-christian-portraits-of-jesus/.

There are still relatively few podcasts in the area of New Testament studies and Christian origins, drastically fewer than there are blogs.[43] This is probably because of the greater time investment that producing a podcast involves, especially when scholars are producing the podcasts themselves. Planning, recording, editing, publishing, and disseminating a podcast all take far longer than the hastily typed blog post. This may change as universities become ever more attuned to the importance of producing good online content and as IT professionals take over the production work from the scholars. This will mean that the scholars only need to provide their expertise and their voice and can leave the production and publicizing of the podcast to others, and many more will participate.

One of the values of the academic podcast, in spite of its relatively light adoption so far by academics, is that it can provide a different means of introducing students to the material they are covering in class or in their readings outside class. It has a huge advantage over any other medium—the textbook, the article, the video, the blog post—in that it does not require sight. Consumers of podcasts enjoy them while driving, while walking, at the gym, while cooking, while washing the dishes,[44] while mowing the lawn. It is the perfect resource for anyone on the go.

Most academics invest far too little time in finding ways of making teaching and learning resources available to those who are blind and partially sighted. Podcasts are perfect for those who are unable to access conventional text resources. I like to imagine that if I were blind, I would prefer to listen to the voices of the scholars expressing their views than to listen to the synthesized voice of my computer program reading books, articles, or blog posts. But it is worth adding in this context that one of the great advantages of electronic texts is that they can be manipulated and greatly enlarged so that partially sighted people can read them with greater ease.[45]

---

43. I have gathered a list together at "Podcasts," *New Testament Gateway*, http://www.ntgateway.com/tools-and-resources/podcasts/. Although with a scope much broader than just the New Testament, one that is particularly worthy of mention is Tim Bulkeley, *Five Minute Bible*, http://5minutebible.com/.

44. One of my listeners told me that whenever he hears my voice he can smell dish-washing liquid, because he always listens to the *NT Pod* while washing the dishes!

45. I am grateful to Jason Brooke for some discussion of this issue as a result of one of his comments on the blog post referenced above in n. 34.

Secondary Orality and the Future

Although it is common for biblical scholars to characterize contemporary Western culture as a "literate culture" and to conceptualize activities in this world as "print determined" or "print dominated,"[46] the reality is that we are living in a digital age, and that the simple clichés about literary paradigms are no longer adequate. Already in 1982 Walter Ong was characterizing the contemporary era as an "electronic age," which, he said, "is also an age of 'secondary orality,' the orality of telephones, radio, and television, which depends on writing and print for its existence."[47] Although Ong was prescient, the explosion of electronic resources in recent decades has underlined the fact that now more than ever we live in an electronic age. Engaging with the kinds of Internet resources now available for the study of Mark's Gospel may encourage our students to think outside the literary paradigm that we were trained in. Their first encounters with Mark's Gospel are now far more likely to be electronic than they were for students a generation ago. Their first engagement with scholarship on Mark is also much more likely to be through digital resources. It is worth asking whether in this way our students are now better equipped to be able to understand the rhetorical culture of the first century.[48] For them, the printed word is not necessarily primary. Their experience of text and tradition is more dynamic, more interactive, and more varied than it was in the experience of their teachers.

Nevertheless, if there is one lesson that the development of the Internet has taught us, it is the impossibility of predicting the future. It used to be easy for scholars to ignore the Internet altogether, but the end of the "great divide" between print resources and electronic resources has

---

46. See, for example, James D. G. Dunn, "Altering the Default Setting: Re-envisaging the Early Transmission of the Jesus Tradition," *NTS* 49 (2003): 139–75, esp. 142.

47. Walter Ong, *Orality and Literacy: The Technologizing of the Word* (London: Methuen, 1982), 3. See Goodacre, *Thomas and the Gospels*, 137–40, on the problematic use of the term *secondary orality* in New Testament scholarship. The term should be reserved for the discussion of electronic communication.

48. For the term *rhetorical culture*, see Vernon K. Robbins, "Interfaces of Orality and Literature in the Gospel of Mark," in *Performing the Gospel: Orality, Memory, and Mark: Essays Dedicated to Werner Kelber*, ed. Richard Horsley, Jonathan A. Draper, and John Miles Foley (Minneapolis: Fortress, 2006), 125–46. The term is preferable to *oral culture* because of the ways that orality and literacy interacted. See further my *Thomas and the Gospels*, 140–42.

changed our teaching forever. It is not only the wealth of resources available that has revolutionized the way we think about teaching; but it is also the range of media that provides us with new possibilities, from blog posts to podcasts to online video and more. In teaching Mark's Gospel, it is a greater challenge to find ways of using the best materials inside and outside the classroom and to get the balance right among different media, but since today's students often understand the Internet better than we do, we may be well advised to make sure that we are listening to them and learning from what resources they are finding most helpful. Whatever we may think we know about teaching Mark today, it will certainly be different again in ten years' time and in ways we cannot predict.

Bibliography

Achtemeier, Paul. "*Omni Verbum Sonat*: The New Testament and the Environment of Late Western Antiquity." *JBL* 109 (1990): 3–27.

Admiral, Eva-Maria, and Eric Wehrlin. "Das Markusevangelium." *Eva-Maria Admiral and Eric Wehrlin*. http://www.admiral-wehrlin.de/cms/theater/theaterstuecke/das-markusevangelium.html.

Allison, Dale C., Jr. *Constructing Jesus: Memory, Imagination, and History*. Grand Rapids: Baker Academic, 2010.

Anderson, Janice Capel, and Stephen D. Moore. *Mark and Method: New Approaches in Biblical Studies*. 2nd ed. Minneapolis: Fortress, 2008.

Artaud, Antonin. *The Theater and Its Double*. Translated by Mary Caroline Richards. New York: Grove, 1958.

Assmann, Aleida. "Exkarnation: Gedanken zur Grenze zwischen Körper und Schrift." Pages 133–55 in *Raum und Verfahren*. Edited by Jörg Huber and Alois Martin Müller. Basel: Stroemfeld/Roter Stern, 1993.

———. "Wie wahr sind Erinnerungen?" Pages 103–22 in *Das soziale Gedächtnis: Geschichte, Erinnerung, Tradierung*. Edited by Harald Welzer. Hamburg: Hamburger Edition, 2001.

Assmann, Jan. *Das kulturelle Gedächtnis: Schrift, Erinnerung und politische Identität in frühen Hochkulturen*. Munich: Beck, 1992.

———. *Religion und kulturelles Gedächtnis: Zehn Studien*. Munich: Beck, 2000.

Aune, David E. *The New Testament in Its Literary Environment*. Cambridge: Clarke, 1988.

Barth, Karl. *Church Dogmatics*. Edited by G. W. Bromiley and T. F. Torrance. Translated by G. T. Thomson et al. 4 vols. in 13. New York: T&T Clark, 2010.

Bauckham, Richard. *Jesus and the Eyewitnesses: The Gospels as Eyewitness Testimony*. Grand Rapids: Eerdmans, 2006.

Beale, Greg. *The Book of Revelation*. NIGTC. Grand Rapids: Eerdmans, 2013.

Becker, Eve-Marie, ed. *Die antike Historiographie und die Anfänge der christlichen Geschichtsschreibung.* BZNW 129. Berlin: de Gruyter, 2005.

———. "Art. Heuristik." Pages 255–56 in *Lexikon der Bibelhermeneutik: Begriffe—Methoden—Theorien—Konzepte.* Edited by Oda Wischmeyer. Berlin: de Gruyter, 2013.

———. "Dating Mark and Matthew as Ancient Literature." Pages 123–43 in *Mark and Matthew. Vol. 1: Comparative Readings: Understanding the Earliest Gospels in Their First-Century Settings.* Edited by Eve-Marie Becker and Anders Runesson. WUNT 271. Tübingen: Mohr Siebeck, 2011.

———. "Earliest Christian Literary Activity: Investigating Authors, Genres and Audiences in Paul and Mark." Pages 87–105 in *Mark and Paul: Comparative Essays. Vol. 2: For and against Pauline Influence on Mark.* Edited by Eve-Marie Becker, Troels Engberg-Pedersen, and Mogens Mueller. BZNW 199. Berlin: de Gruyter, 2014.

———. *The Earliest Christian Shape of History-Writing: Memoria—Tempus—Historia.* New Haven: Yale University Press, forthcoming.

———. "Literarisierung und Kanonisierung im frühen Christentum: Einführende Überlegungen zur Entstehung und Bedeutung des neutestamentlichen Kanons." Pages 389–97 in *Kanon in Konstruktion und Dekonstruktion: Kanonisierungsprozesse religiöser Texte von der Antike bis zur Gegenwart; Ein Handbuch.* Edited by Eve-Marie Becker and Stefan Scholz. Berlin: de Gruyter, 2012.

———. "Die markinischen 'Streitgespräche' im Plan des Evangeliums: Eine kritische *relecture* der formgeschichtlichen Methode." Pages 433–63 in *Polemik in der frühchristlichen Literatur: Texte und Kontexte.* Edited by Oda Wischmeyer and Lorenzo Scornaienchi. BZNW 170. Berlin: de Gruyter, 2011.

———. *Das Markus-Evangelium im Rahmen antiker Historiographie.* WUNT 194. Tübingen: Mohr Siebeck, 2006.

———. "Mk 1:1 and the Debate on a 'Markan Prologue.'" *Filologia Neotestamentaria* 22 (2009): 91–106.

———, ed. *Neutestamentliche Wissenschaft: Autobiographische Essays aus der Evangelischen Theologie.* UTB 2475. Tübingen: Francke, 2003.

———. "The Place of Theology in the Contemporary Universities: Research and Resources." *STK* 88 (2012): 171–77.

———. "The Reception of 'Mark' in the 1st and 2nd Centuries C.E. and Its Significance for Genre Studies." Pages 15–36 in *Mark and Matthew.*

Vol. 2: *Comparative Readings: Reception History, Cultural Hermeneutics, and Theology*. Edited by Eve-Marie Becker and Anders Runesson. WUNT 304. Tübingen: Mohr Siebeck, 2013.

———. Review of *Transforming Graduate Biblical Eduation: Ethos and Discipline*, edited by Elisabeth Schüssler Fiorenza and Kent Harold Richards. *TLZ* 137 (2012): 917–19.

Becker, Eve-Marie, and Anders Runesson, eds. *Mark and Matthew*. Vol. 1: *Comparative Readings: Understanding the Earliest Gospels in Their First-Century Settings*. WUNT 271. Tübingen: Mohr Siebeck, 2011.

———, eds. *Mark and Matthew*. Vol. 2: *Comparative Readings: Reception History, Cultural Hermeneutics, and Theology*. WUNT 304. Tübingen: Mohr Siebeck, 2013.

Becker, Eve-Marie, Troels Engberg-Pedersen, and Mogens Mueller, eds. *Mark and Paul: Comparative Essays*. Vol. 2: *For and against Pauline Influence on Mark*. BZNW 199. Berlin: de Gruyter, 2014.

Bernstein, Richard J. *Beyond Objectivism and Relativism: Science, Hermeneutics, and Praxis*. Philadelphia: University of Pennsylvania Press, 1983.

Bibledex: A Video about Every Book in the Bible. University of Nottingham. http://www.bibledex.com/index.html.

Biblica. BSW, Biblical Studies on the Web. http://www.bsw.org/project/biblica/.

"Biblical Performances and Performers." *Biblical Performance Criticism*. Maintained by David Rhoads. Lutheran School of Theology at Chicago . http://www.biblicalperformancecriticism.org/index.php/performers-mainmenu-46.

Biggs, John. *Teaching for Quality Learning at University*. Buckingham: SHRE and Open University Press, 1999.

Bloom, Benjamin S., ed. *Taxonomy of Educational Objectives, Handbook 1: Cognitive Domain*. 2nd ed. White Plains, NY: Longman, 1984.

Bockmuehl, Marcus. "Bible versus Theology: Is 'Theological Interpretation' the Answer?" *NV* 9 (2011): 27–47.

Boomershine, Amelia Cooper. "Biblical Storytelling in Christian Ed." *GoTell Communications*. 2016, http://gotell.org/learn/education/.

Boomershine, Thomas E. "Audience Address and Purpose in the Performance of Mark." Pages 115–44 in *Mark as Story: Retrospect and Prospect*. Edited by Kelly R. Iverson and Christopher W. Skinner. RBS 65. Atlanta: Society of Biblical Literature, 2011.

———. *GoTell Communications*. 2016. http://www.gotell.org.

———. "The Medium and Message of John: Audience Address and Audience Identity in the Fourth Gospel." Pages 92–120 in *The Fourth Gospel in First-Century Media Culture*. Edited by Anthony Le Donne and Tom Thatcher. New York: T&T Clark, 2011.

———. "Memory and Story." *GoTell Communications*. 2016. http://gotell.org/learn/workshops/.

———. *The Messiah of Peace: A Performance-Criticism Commentary on Mark 14–16*. http://www.messiahofpeace.com.

———. *The Messiah of Peace: A Performance-Criticism Commentary on Mark's Passion-Resurrection Narrative*. BPC 12. Eugene, OR: Cascade, 2015.

———. *Story Journey: An Introduction to the Gospel as Storytelling*. Nashville: Abingdon, 1988.

Boring, M. Eugene. *Mark: A Commentary*. NTL. Louisville: Westminster John Knox, 2006.

Botha, Pieter J. J. *Orality and Literacy in Early Christianity*. PBC 5. Eugene, OR: Cascade, 2012.

Brabrand, Claus, and Jacob Andersen. "Teaching Teaching and Understanding Understanding." Aarhus: Aarhus University Press, 2006. *Daimi.au.dk*. http://www.daimi.au.dk/~brabrand/short-film/.

Brook, Peter. *The Empty Space*. New York: Atheneum, 1968.

Brown, Peter C., Henry L. Roediger III, and Mark A. McDaniel. *Make It Stick: The Science of Successful Learning*. Cambridge: Harvard University Press, 2014.

Brown, Raymond. *The Death of the Messiah: From Gethsemane to the Grave*. 2 vols. New York: Doubleday, 1994.

Bryan, Christopher. *A Preface to Mark: Notes on the Gospel in Its Literary and Cultural Settings*. New York: Oxford University Press, 1993.

Bulkeley, Tim. *Five Minute Bible*. http://5minutebible.com/.

Bultmann, Rudolf. *The History of the Synoptic Tradition*. Translated by John Marsh. Oxford: Blackwell, 1963.

Byrskog, Samuel. *Story as History—History as Story: The Gospel Tradition in the Context of Ancient Oral History*. WUNT 123. Tübingen: Mohr Siebeck, 2000.

"Caesarea Philippi." *Bibledex: A Video about Every Book in the Bible*. University of Nottingham. http://www.bibledex.com/israel/caesarea_philippi.html.

Cantor, Arthur, and Alec McCowen. *Alec McCowen in His Solo Performance of St. Mark's Gospel*. New York: Arthur Cantor Films, 1990.

Released on DVD as *Alec McCowen in His Solo Performance of Mark's Gospel*. Oklahoma City: Daystar Foundation and Library, 2013.
Cargill, Robert. "The Benefit of Blogging for Archaeology." *BSR* 39 (2010): 26–36.
Carr, David. M. *Writing on the Tablet of the Heart: Origins of Scripture and Literature*. New York: Oxford University Press, 2005.
Congar, Yves M. *La tradition et la vie de l'Église*. Paris: Cerf, 1984.
Conzelmann, Hans. *The Theology of St Luke*. Translated by Geoffrey Buswell. London: Faber & Faber, 1960.
Cranfield, Charles E. B. *The Gospel according to St Mark*. CGTC. Cambridge: Cambridge University Press, 1959.
Crook, Zeba A. *Parallel Gospels: A Synopsis of Early Christian Writing*. Oxford: Oxford University Press, 2011.
Culler, Jonathan. *On Deconstruction: Theory and Criticism after Structuralism*. London: Routledge, 1983.
Culley, Robert C. "Oral Tradition and Biblical Studies." *Oral Tradition* 11 (1986): 30–65.
Davies, William D., and Dale C. Allison Jr. *Matthew*. ICC. 3 vols. Edinburgh: T&T Clark, 1988–1997.
Davila, James R. "Assimilated to the Blogosphere: Blogging Ancient Judaism." *SBL Forum Archive*. April 2005. http://sbl-site.org/Article.aspx?ArticleID=390.
———. "Enter the Bibliobloggers." University of St Andrews School of Divinity. http://www.st-andrews.ac.uk/divinity/rt/otp/abstracts/enterthebibliobloggers/.
———. "What Just Happened: The Rise of 'Biblioblogging' in the First Decade of the Twenty-First Century." Paper presented at the Annual Meeting of the Society of Biblical Literature in Atlanta, GA, 22 November 2010. http://paleojudaica.blogspot.co.uk/2010_11_14_archive.html#1715486029034288246.
Dewey, Joanna. "The Gospel of Mark as an Oral-Aural Event: Implications for Interpretation." Pages 145–63 in *The New Literary Criticism and the New Testament*. Edited by Elizabeth Struthers Malbon and Edgar V. McKnight. JSNTSup 109. Sheffield: Sheffield Academic Press, 1994.
———. "Mark as Interwoven Tapestry: Forecasts and Echoes for a Listening Audience." *CBQ* 53 (1991): 221–36.
———. *The Oral Ethos of the Early Church: Speaking, Writing, and the Gospel of Mark*. BPC 8. Eugene, OR: Cascade, 2013.

———. "Oral Methods of Structuring Narrative in Mark." *Interpretation* 53 (1989): 32–44.

Donahue, John R., and Daniel J. Harrington. *The Gospel of Mark*. SP 2. Collegeville, MN: Liturgical Press, 2002.

Doole, J. Andrew. *What Was Mark for Matthew? An Examination of Matthew's Relationship and Attitude to His Primary Source*. WUNT 2/344. Tübingen: Mohr Siebeck, 2013.

Dormeyer, Detlev. *Das Neue Testament im Rahmen der antiken Literaturgeschichte: Eine Einführung*. Darmstadt: Wissenschaftliche Buchgesellschaft, 1993.

Dowd, Sharyn E. *Reading Mark: A Literary and Theological Commentary on the Second Gospel*. Reading the New Testament 2. Macon, GA: Smith & Helwys, 2000.

Drummond, Di. "Research That Matters: Expanding Definitions of 'Research-Led Teaching' in History." Pages 66–73 in *What Is Research-Led Teaching? Multi-disciplinary Perspectives*. Edited by Alisa Miller, John Sharp, and Jeremy Strong. London: Crest, 2012. http://www.crest.ac.uk.

Dubs, Rolf. "Besser schriftlich prüfen: Prüfungen valide und zuverlässig durchführen." Griffmarke H 5.1 in *Neues Handbuch Hochschullehre*. Edited by Brigitte Berendt, Hans-Peter Voss, and Johannes Wildt. Berlin: Raabe, 2006.

Dulles, Avery. *Models of Revelation*. Maryknoll, NY: Orbis, 1992.

Dunn, James D. G. "Altering the Default Setting: Re-envisaging the Early Transmission of the Jesus Tradition." *NTS* 49 (2003): 139–75.

———. *Christianity in the Making*. Vol. 1 of *Jesus Remembered*. Grand Rapids: Eerdmans, 2003.

Ehrman, Bart. *Christianity in Antiquity: The Bart Ehrman Blog*. 2012–2015. http://ehrmanblog.org/.

Entwistle, Noel J. *Styles of Learning and Teaching*. London: David Fulton, 1988.

Evans, Craig A. *Mark 8:27–16:20*. WBC 34B. Nashville: Nelson, 2001.

Eve, Eric. *Behind the Gospels: Understanding the Oral Tradition*. Minneapolis: Fortress, 2014.

Fackenheim, Emil L. *The Jewish Bible after the Holocaust: A Re-reading*. Bloomington: Indiana University Press, 1990.

Fascher, Eric. *Die formgeschichtliche Methode: Eine Darstellung und Kritik; Zugleich ein Beitrag zur Geschichte des synoptischen Problems*. BZNW 2. Giessen: Töpelmann, 1924.

Fish, Stanley. *Is There a Text in This Class? The Authority of Interpretive Communities.* Cambridge: Harvard University Press, 1980.
Foley, John Miles. *How to Read an Oral Poem.* Urbana: University of Illinois Press, 2002.
Fowler, Robert M. "How the Secondary Orality of the Electronic Age Can Awaken Us to the Primary Orality of Antiquity, or What Hypertext Can Teach Us about the Bible, with Reflections on the Ethical and Political Issues of the Electronic Frontier." Paper presented at the Annual Meeting of the Society of Biblical Literature, Chicago, 19 November 1994. Reproduced at *Homepages.bw.edu.* http://homepages.bw.edu/~rfowler/pubs/secondoral/index.html.
———. "In the Boat with Jesus: Imagining Ourselves in Mark's Story." Pages 233–58 in *Mark as Story: Retrospect and Prospect.* Edited by Kelly R. Iverson and Christopher W. Skinner. RBS 65. Atlanta: Society of Biblical Literature, 2011.
———. "Why Everything We Know about the Bible Is Wrong: Lessons from the Media History of the Bible." Pages 3–18 in *The Bible in Ancient and Modern Media: Story and Performance.* Edited by Holly E. Hearon and Philip Ruge-Jones. BPC 1. Eugene, OR: Cascade, 2009.
Frei, Hans. *The Eclipse of Biblical Narrative: A Study in Eighteenth and Nineteenth Century Hermeneutics.* New Haven: Yale University Press, 1974.
Frey, Jörg, Clare Rothschild, and Jens Schröter, eds. *Die Apostelgeschichte im Kontext antiker und frühchristlicher Historiographie.* BZNW 162. Berlin: de Gruyter, 2009.
Frost, Robert. "Mending Wall." Page 33 in *The Poetry of Robert Frost: The Collected Poems, Complete and Unabridged.* New York: Holt, 1969.
Galbraith, Deane. "Biblical Studies Carnival מ (November 2010)." *Religion Bulletin: The Blogging Portal of the Bulletin for the Study of Religion.* 1 December 2010. http://www.equinoxpub.com/blog/2010/12/biblical-studies-carnival-nz-november-2010/.
Gergen, Kenneth. "Erzählung, moralische Identität und historisches Bewusstsein." Pages 170–202 in *Erzählung, Identität, und historisches Bewusstsein: Die psychologische Konstruktion von Zeit und Geschichte.* Edited by Jürgen Straub. Erinnerung, Geschichte, Identität 1. Frankfurt: Suhrkamp, 1998.
Gerhardsson, Birger. *Memory and Manuscript: Oral Tradition and Written Transmission in Rabbinic Judaism and Early Christianity.* 2nd ed. ASNU 20. Lund: Gleerup; Copenhagen: Munksgaard, 1964.

———. *The Reliability of the Gospel Tradition*. Peabody, MA: Hendrickson, 2001.

———. "The Secret of the Transmission of the Unwritten Jesus Tradition." *NTS* 52 (2006): 319–36.

Gieseler, Johann Karl Ludwig. *Historisch-kritischer Versuch über die Entstehung und die frühesten Schicksale der schriftlichen Evangelien*. Leipzig: Engelmann, 1818.

Giesen, Bernhard. *Kollektive Identität*. Die Intellektuellen und die Nation 2. Frankfurt: Suhrkamp, 1999.

Gnilka, Joachim. *Das Evangelium nach Markus*. 5th ed. 2 vols. EKKNT 2. Zurich: Benziger; Neukirchen-Vluyn: Neurkirchener Verlag, 1999.

Goguel, Maurice. "Une nouvelle école de critique évangélique, la *Form- und traditionsgeschichtliche Schule*." *RHR* 94 (1926): 114–60.

Goodacre, Mark. "Blogging Mark: Input Requested Please." *NT Blog*. 12 June 2013. http://ntweblog.blogspot.com/2013/06/blogging-mark-input-requested-please.html.

———. "'Drawing from the Treasure Both New and Old': Current Trends in New Testament Studies." *ScrB* 27 (1997): 66–77.

———. "Gospel of Mark: Audio and Video." *New Testament Gateway*. http://www.ntgateway.com/gospel-and-acts/gospel-of-mark/audio-and-video.

———. "How and Why the NT Gateway Was Rebooted, Revitalized and Relaunched." *NT Blog*. 16–19 November 2009. http://ntweblog.blogspot.com/search/label/How%20and%20why.

———. *The New Testament Gateway*. http://NTGateway.com.

———. "NT Gateway Future." http://ntweblog.blogspot.com/search/label/NT%20Gateway%20future.

———. *NT Pod*. 26 February 2015. http://podacre.blogspot.com.

———. "NT Pod 71: Was the Ending of Mark's Gospel Lost?" *NT Pod*. 14 February 2014. http://podacre.blogspot.com/2014/02/nt-pod-71-was-ending-of-marks-gospel.html.

———. "Podcasts." *New Testament Gateway*. http://www.ntgateway.com/tools-and-resources/podcasts/.

———. "Pods, Blogs and Other Time-Wasters." *NT Blog*. 17 November 2011. http://ntweblog.blogspot.com/2011/11/pods-blogs-and-other-time-wasters.html.

———. *Thomas and the Gospels: The Case for Thomas's Familiarity with the Synoptics*. Grand Rapids: Eerdmans, 2012.

———. "Tom Boomershine Performs Mark." *NT Blog*. 25 June 2013. http://ntweblog.blogspot.com/2013/06/tom-boomershine-performs-mark.html.

———. "Tom Boomershine Performs Mark's Gospel." *YouTube*, 16 April 2009, 21 July 2001, 2 November 2011, 16 December 2011, 25–26 April 2014, https://www.youtube.com/watch?v=Aytp-1OpMVE&list=PL7DR0ecPG8I1WonZetQ6-Fj7gC4g4ED-L.

———. "Vertical Blogs vs. Horizontal Blogs." *NT Blog*. 8 August 2012. http://ntweblog.blogspot.com/2012/08/vertical-blogs-vs-horizontal-blogs.html.

Gooder, Paula. "The Gospel of Mark." *YouTube.com*. 20 July 2012. http://www.youtube.com/watch?v=XyV2tuE84FA.

———. "The Gospel of Mark, Part 2." *YouTube.com*. 4 September 2012. http://www.youtube.com/watch?v=P1tvW7t0WZY.

Guttenberger, Gudrun. "Das Markusevangelium in religionspädagogischer Perspektive." Pages 433–51 in *Religionspädagogischer Kommentar zur Bibel*. Edited by Bernhard Dressler and Harald Schroeter-Wittke. Leipzig: Evangelische Verlagsanstalt, 2012.

Hadas, Moses. *Ancilla to Classical Reading*. New York: Columbia University Press, 1954.

Halbwachs, Maurice. *Les cadres sociaux de la mémoire*. 2nd ed. BEH 8. Paris: Michel, 1994.

———. *La mémoire collective*. 2nd ed. BEH 28. Paris: Michel, 1997.

Haley, Cortney, director and ed. "The Messiah of Peace: Mark 14–16 told in English by Dr. Tom Boomershine." *YouTube.com*. 25 April 2014. https://www.youtube.com/watch?v=fnPtuXiYcBw.

———. "The Messiah of Peace: Mark 14–16 told in Greek by Dr. Tom Boomershine." 26 April 2015. *Youtube.com*. https://www.youtube.com/watch?t=43&v=3dwo3z9T7HY.

Haran, Brady, producer. "Mark." *Bibledex: A Video about Every Book in the Bible*. University of Nottingham. http://www.bibledex.com/videos/mark.html.

Harland, Phil. "Early Christian Portraits of Jesus." *Religions of the Ancient Mediterranean Podcast*. 31 August 2009. http://www.philipharland.com/Blog/2009/08/31/podcast-series-2-early-christian-portraits-of-jesus/.

———. *Religions of the Ancient Mediterranean Podcast*. 5 January 2013. http://www.philipharland.com/Blog/category/podcasts/.

Harris, William. *Ancient Literacy*. Cambridge: Harvard University Press, 1989.
Havelock, Eric A. *Preface to Plato*. Cambridge: Harvard University Press, 1963.
Hays, Richard. "Reading the Bible with Eyes of Faith: The Practice of Theological Exegesis." *JTI* 1 (2007): 5–21.
Healey, Mick. "Linking Research and Teaching: Exploring Disciplinary Spaces and the Role of Inquiry-Based Learning." Pages 67–78 in *Reshaping the University: New Relationships between Research, Scholarship and Teaching*. Edited by Ronald Barnett. Society for Research into Higher Education. Berkshire, UK: Open University Press, 2005.
Hearon, Holly E. *The Mary Magdalene Tradition: Witness and Counter-Witness in Early Christian Communities*. Collegeville, MN: Liturgical Press, 2004.
Hearon, Holly E., and Philip Ruge-Jones, eds. *The Bible in Ancient and Modern Media: Story and Performance*. BPC 1. Eugene, OR: Cascade, 2009.
Herder, Johann Gottfried. *Vom Erlöser der Menschen: Nach unsern drei Evangelien*. Vol. 2 of *Christliche Schriften*. Riga: Hartknoch, 1796.
———. *Von Gottes Sohn, der Welt Heiland: Nach Johannes Evanglium; Nebst einer Regel der Zusammenstimmung unserer Evangelien aus ihrer Entstehung und Ordnung*. Vol. 3 of *Christliche Schriften*. Riga: Hartknoch, 1797.
Hezser, Catherine. *Jewish Literacy in Roman Palestine*. TSAJ 81. Tübingen: Mohr Siebeck, 2001.
Holladay, Carl R. *A Critical Introduction to the New Testament: Interpreting the Message and Meaning of Jesus Christ*. Nashville: Abingdon, 2005.
Hooker, Morna D. *The Gospel according to Saint Mark*. BNTC. London: Black; Peabody, MA: Hendrickson, 1991.
Horsley, Richard A., Jonathan A. Draper, and John Miles Foley, eds. *Performing the Gospel: Orality, Memory, and Mark: Essays Dedicated to Werner Kelber*. Minneapolis: Fortress, 2006.
Hübenthal, Sandra. "Erfahrung, die sich lesbar macht. Kol und 2 Thess als fiktionale Texte." Pages 295–336 in *Wie Geschichten Geschichte schreiben: Frühchristliche Literatur zwischen Faktualität und Fiktionalität*. Edited by Susanne Luther, Jörg Röder, and Eckart D. Schmidt. WUNT 2/395. Tübingen: Mohr Siebeck, 2015.
———. *Das Markusevangelium als kollektives Gedächtnis*. FRLANT 253. Göttingen: Vandenhoeck und Ruprecht 2014.

———. "Pseudepigraphie als Strategie in frühchristlichen Identitätsdiskursen? Überlegungen am Beispiel des Kolosserbriefs." SNTSU.A 36 (2011): 63–94.

———. "Reading Mark as Collective Memory." In *Social Memory and Social Identity in the Study of Early Judaism and Early Christianity*. Edited by Samuel Byrskog, Raimo Hakola, and Jutta Jokiranta. NTOA/SUNT. Göttingen: Vandenhoeck & Ruprecht, forthcoming.

———. "Social and Cultural Memory in Biblical Exegesis." Pages 175–99 in *Cultural Memory in Biblical Exegesis*. Edited by Pernille Carstens, Trine Bjørnung Hasselbalch, and Niels Peter Lemche. Piscataway NJ: Gorgias, 2012.

Hurtado, Larry W. *Larry Hurtado's Blog*. 19 June 2015. http://larryhurtado.wordpress.com/.

———. "Oral Fixation and New Testament Studies? 'Orality,' 'Performance' and Reading Texts in Early Christianity." *NTS* 60 (2014): 321–40.

Iverson, Kelly R., ed. *From Text to Performance: Narrative and Performance Criticisms in Dialogue and Debate*. BPC 10. Eugene, OR: Cascade, 2014.

———. "Performance Criticism." Pages 97–105 in vol. 2 of *The Oxford Encyclopedia of Biblical Interpretation*. Edited by Steven McKenzie. New York: Oxford University Press, 2013.

———. "The Present Tense of Performance: Immediacy and Transformative Power in Luke's Passion." Pages 131–57 in *From Text to Performance: Narrative and Performance Criticisms in Dialogue and Debate*. Edited by Kelly R. Iverson. BPC 10. Eugene, OR: Cascade, 2014.

Iverson, Kelly R., and Christopher W. Skinner, eds. *Mark as Story: Retrospect and Prospect*. RBS 65. Atlanta: Society of Biblical Literature, 2011.

Johnson, Todd E., and Dale Savidge. *Performing the Sacred: Theology and Theatre in Dialogue*. Grand Rapids: Baker Academic, 2009.

Juel, Donald H. *A Master of Surprise: Mark Interpreted*. Minneapolis: Fortress, 1994.

Kamiuouchi, Alberto de Mingo. *"But It Is Not So among You": Echoes of Power in Mark 10.32–45*. JSNTSup 249. London: T&T Clark, 2003.

Kee, Howard C. *Community of the New Age: Studies in Mark's Gospel*. Philadelphia: Westminster, 1977.

Kelber, Werner H. *The Oral and the Written Gospel: The Hermeneutics of Speaking and Writing in the Synoptic Tradition, Mark, Paul, and Q*. Bloomington: Indiana University Press, 1997.

———. "The Work of Walter J. Ong and Biblical Scholarship." Pages 441–64 in *Imprints, Voiceprints, and Footprints of Memory: Collected Essays of Werner H. Kelber*. RBS 74. Atlanta: Society of Biblical Literature, 2013.

Kennedy, Declan, Áine Hyland, and Norma Ryan. "Writing and Using Learning Outcomes: A Practical Guide." Griffmarke C 3.4-1 in *Neues Handbuch Hochschullehre*. Edited by Brigitte Berendt, Birgit Szczyrba, Hans-Peter Voss, and Johannes Wildt. Berlin: Raabe, 2009.

Kirk, Alan, and Tom Thatcher, eds. *Memory, Tradition, and Text: Uses of the Past in Early Christianity*. SemeiaSt 52. Atlanta: Society of Biblical Literature, 2005.

Klatzky, Roberta. *Human Memory: Structures and Processes*. San Francisco: Freeman, 1980.

Kok, Mike. *Euangelion Kata Markon*. http://ntmark.wordpress.com.

Krathwohl, David R., Benjamin S. Bloom, and Bertram B. Masia, eds. *Taxonomy of Eductional Objectives, Handbook 2: Affective Domain*. 2nd ed. White Plains, NY: Longman, 1999.

Lagrange, Marie-Joseph. *Évangile selon Saint Marc*. EBib. Paris: Gabalda, 1920.

Lane, William L. *Commentary on the Gospel of Mark*. NICNT. Grand Rapids: Eerdmans, 1974.

LeCoq, Jacques. *The Moving Body: Teaching Creative Theatre*. Translated by David Bradby. New York: Routledge, 2001.

LeDonne, Anthony. "The Jewish Leaders." Pages 199–217 in *Jesus among Friends and Enemies: A Historical and Literary Introduction to Jesus in the Gospels*. Edited by Chris Keith and Larry W. Hurtado. Grand Rapids: Baker Academic, 2011.

———. "Who Started the Conflict in Mark's Gospel?" *The Jesus Blog*. 12 June 2013. http://historicaljesusresearch.blogspot.com/2013/06/who-started-conflict-in-marks-gospel-le.html.

Levinas, Emmanuel. *Totality and Infinity: An Essay on Exteriority*. Translated by Alphonso Lingis. Pittsburgh: Duquesne University Press, 1998.

Lewis, C. S. *The Abolition of Man, or Reflections on Education with Special Reference to the Teaching of English in the Upper Forms of Schools*. New York: Macmillan, 1947.

Lipman, Doug. *Improving Your Storytelling: Beyond the Basics for All Who Tell Stories in Work or Play*. Atlanta: August House, 1999.

Lohmeyer, Ernst. *Das Evangelium des Markus*. 17th ed. Meyers Kommentar. Göttingen: Vandenhoeck & Ruprecht, 1967.

Lord, Albert B. *The Singer of Tales*. Cambridge: Harvard University Press, 1960.

Ludlow, Morwena. "'Criteria of Canonicity' in the Early Church." Pages 69–93 in *Die Einheit der Schrift und die Vielfalt des Kanons/The Unity of Scripture and the Diversity of the Canon*. Edited by John Barton and Michael Wolter. BZNW 118. Berlin: de Gruyter, 2003.

Malbon, Elizabeth Struthers. "Disciples/Crowds/Whoever: Markan Characters and Readers." *NovT* 28 (1986): 104–30.

———. "Echoes and Foreshadowings in Mark 4–8: Reading and Rereading." *JBL* 112 (1993): 213–32.

———. *Hearing Mark: A Listener's Guide*. Harrisburg, PA: Trinity Press International, 2002.

———. *In the Company of Jesus: Characters in Mark's Gospel*. Louisville: Westminster John Knox, 2000.

———. *Mark's Jesus: Characterization as Narrative Christology*. Waco, TX: Baylor University Press, 2009.

———. "Narrative Criticism: How Does the Story Mean?" Pages 29–57 in *Mark and Method: New Approaches in Biblical Studies*. Edited by Janice Capel Anderson and Stephen D. Moore. 2nd ed. Minneapolis: Fortress, 2008.

———. *Narrative Space and Mythic Meaning in Mark*. San Francisco: Harper & Row, 1986.

———. Review of Eric C. Stewart, *Gathered around Jesus: An Alternative Spatial Practice in the Gospel of Mark*, *RBL* (March 2011). http://www.bookreviews.org/bookdetail.asp?TitleId=7638.

———. "The SBL in the Classroom: Pedagogical Reflections." Pages 169–88 in *Foster Biblical Scholarship: Essays in Honor of Kent Harold Richards*. Edited by Frank Ames and Charles William Miller. BSNA 24. Atlanta: Society of Biblical Literature, 2010.

———. "The Year of Mark." Pages 13–14 in *Sundays and Seasons 2009*. Minneapolis: Augsburg Fortress, 2008.

Marcus, Joel. *Mark 1–8*. AYB 27. New York: Doubleday; New Haven: Yale University Press, 2002.

———. *Mark 9–16*. AYB 27A. New York: Doubleday; New Haven: Yale University Press, 2009.

Martin, Dale. *Introduction to New Testament History and Literature*. iTunes U. Yale University. 2009. https://itunes.apple.com/us/itunes-u/introduction-to-new-testament/id341652026; *YouTube.com*. http://www.youtube.com/course?list=EC279CFA55C51E75E0.

McGrath, Alister E. *Christian Theology: An Introduction*. Oxford: Blackwell, 2001.
McGrath, James Franklin. "Biblioblogging Our Matrix: Exploring the Potential and Perplexities of Academic Blogging." *BSR* 39 (2010): 14–25.
McKenzie, Stephen L., ed. *Oxford Encyclopedia of Biblical Interpretation*. 2 vols. New York: Oxford University Press, 2013.
McLean, Max, narrator. *The Listener's Bible*. Fellowship for Performing Arts. 2006–2015. http://www.listenersbible.com/.
———. *Mark's Gospel on Stage with Max McLean*. http://www.markonstage.com/.
Metzger, Bruce. *A Textual Commentary on the Greek New Testament*. Stuttgart: United Bible Societies, 1975.
Millard, Alan. *Reading and Writing in the Time of Jesus*. New York: New York University Press, 2000.
Miller, Alisa, John Sharp, and Jeremy Strong, eds. *What Is Research-Led Teaching? Multi-disciplinary Perspectives*. London: Crest, 2012. http://www.crest.ac.uk.
Moberly, Walter. "'Interpret the Bible Like Any Other Book'? Requiem for an Axiom." *JTI* 4 (2010): 91–110.
Moloney, Francis J. *The Gospel of Mark: A Commentary*. Peabody, MA: Hendrickson, 2002. Repr., Grand Rapids: Backer Academic, 2012.
———. *Reading the New Testament in the Church: A Primer for Pastors, Religious Educators, and Believers*. Grand Rapids: Baker Academic, 2015.
Moltmann-Wendel, Elisabeth. *The Women around Jesus*. Translated by John Bowden. New York: Crossroad, 1982.
Moore, Stephen D. *Mark and Luke in Poststructuralist Perspectives: Jesus Begins to Write*. New Haven: Yale University Press, 1992.
Müller, Peter. *Mit Markus erzählen: Das Markusevangelium im Religionsunterricht*. Stuttgart: Calwer, 1999.
Myers, Ched. *Binding the Strong Man: A Political Reading of Mark's Story of Jesus*. 2nd ed. Maryknoll, NY: Orbis, 2008.
Neirynck, Frans. *Duality in Mark: Contributions to the Study of the Markan Redaction*. 2nd ed. BETL 31. Leuven: Leuven University Press; Peeters, 1988.
Network of Biblical Storytellers International. 2010. http://www.nbsint.org/.
Niles, John D. *Homo Narrans: The Poetics and Anthropology of Oral Literature*. Philadelphia: University of Pennsylvania Press, 1999.

Nineham, Dennis E. *The Gospel of Mark*. Pelican Gospel Commentaries. Harmondsworth: Penguin Books, 1963.
Nipperdey, Thomas. "Kann Geschichte objektiv sein?" Pages 62–83 in *Kann Geschichte objektiv sein? Historische Essays*. Edited by Paul Nolte. Munich: Beck, 2013.
Nowak, Paul. "Improving Your Memory." *Lynda.com*. http://www.lynda.com/Business-Skills-tutorials/Improving-Your-Memory/172858-2.html.
O'Malley, John W. *What Happened at Vatican II*. Cambridge: Harvard University Press, 2008.
Ong, Walter J., S.J. *Interfaces of the Word: Studies in the Evolution of Consciousness and Culture*. Ithaca, NY: Cornell University Press, 1977.
———. *Orality and Literacy: The Technologizing of the Word*. London: Methuen, 1982.
———. *The Presence of the Word*. New Haven: Yale University Press, 1967.
Parry, Milman. *The Making of Homeric Verse: The Collected Papers of Milman Parry*. Oxford: Clarendon, 1971.
Pelias, Ronald. *Performance Studies: The Interpretation of Aesthetic Texts*. New York: St. Martin's, 1992.
Polkinghorne, Donald E. "Narrative Psychologie und Geschichtsbewusstsein: Beziehungen und Perspektiven." Pages 12–45 in *Erzählung, Identität, und historisches Bewusstsein: Die psychologische Konstruktion von Zeit und Geschichte*. Edited by Jürgen Straub. Erinnerung, Geschichte, Identität 1. Frankfurt: Suhrkamp, 1998.
Pontifical Biblical Commission. *The Interpretation of the Bible in the Church*. Rome: Libreria Editrice Vaticana, 1993.
Postman, Neil, and Charles Weingartner. *Teaching as a Subversive Activity*. New York: Delacorte, 1969.
Prensky, Marc. "Digital Natives, Digital Immigrants." *On the Horizon* 9.5 (2001): 1–6. Reproduced at Marc Prensky: Home Page. http://www.marcprensky.com/.
———. "Digital Natives, Digital Immigrants, Part 2: Do They Really *Think* Differently?" *On the Horizon* 9. 6 (2001): 1–6. Reproduced at http://www.marcprensky.com/.
Rad, Gerhard von. *Old Testament Theology*. Translated by D. M. G. Stalker. 2 vols. Louisville: Westminster John Knox, 2001.
Ramsden, Paul. *Learning to Teach in Higher Education*. London: Routledge, 1992.

Ratzinger, Joseph. "Revelation Itself." Pages 170–80 in vol. 3 of *Commentary on the Documents of Vatican II*. Edited by Herbert Vorgrimler. Translated by Lalit Adolphus, Kevin Smyth, and Richard Strachan. 5 vols. London: Burns & Oates; New York: Herder & Herder, 1967–1969.

Reis, Oliver. "Kompetenzorientierung als hochschuldidaktische Chance für die Theologie." Pages 19–38 in *Vom Lehren zum Lernen: Didaktische Wende in der Theologie?* Edited by Monika Scheidler and Oliver Reis. Theologie und Hochschuldidaktik 1. Münster: LIT, 2008.

Reis, Oliver, and Sylvia Ruschin. "Kompetenzorientiert Prüfen: Bausteine eines gelungenen Paradigmenwechsels." Pages 45–57 in *Prüfungen auf die Agenda! Hochschuldidaktische Perspektiven auf Reformen im Prüfungswesen*. Edited by Sigrid Dany, Birgit Szczyrba, and Johannes Wildt. Blickpunkt Hochschuldidaktik 118. Bielefeld: Bertelsmann, 2008.

Repschinski, Boris. "Die literarische Form der Streitgespräche." Pages 415–32 in *Polemik in der frühchristlichen Literatur: Texte und Kontexte*. Edited by Oda Wischmeyer and Lorenzo Scornaienchi. BZNW 170. Berlin: de Gruyter, 2011.

Reymond, Bernard. *Théâtre et Christianisme*. Geneva: Labor et Fides, 2002.

Rhoads, David. "Biblical Performance Criticism: Performance as Research." *Oral Tradition* 25 (2010): 157–98.

———. *A Dramatic Presentation of the Gospel of Mark*. 1992. DVD available from *Select Learning*. http://www.selectlearning.org/.

———. "Performance Criticism: An Emerging Methodology in Second Temple Studies." *BTB* 36 (2006): 118–33, 164–84.

———. "What Is Performance Criticism?" Pages 83–100 in *The Bible in Ancient and Modern Media: Story and Performance*. Edited by Holly E. Hearon and Philip Ruge-Jones. BPC 1. Eugene, OR: Cascade, 2009.

Riesenfeld, Harald. *The Gospel Tradition and Its Beginnings: A Study in the Limits of "Formgeschichte."* 2nd ed. London: Mowbray, 1961.

Robbins, Vernon. "Interfaces of Orality and Literature in the Gospel of Mark." Pages 125–46 in *Performing the Gospel: Orality, Memory, and Mark: Essays Dedicated to Werner Kelber*. Edited by Richard Horsley, Jonathan A. Draper, and John Miles Foley. Minneapolis: Fortress, 2006.

Rodi, Frithjof, ed., *Urteilskraft und Heuristik in den Wissenschaften: Beiträge zur Entstehung des Neuen*. Weilerswist: Velbrück Wissenschaft, 2003.

Ruge-Jones, Philip L. *The Beginning of the Good News*. 2009. DVD available from *Select Learning*. http://www.selectlearning.org/.

———. "Orality Studies and Oral Tradition: *New Testament*." Pages 63–72 in vol. 2 of *The Oxford Encyclopedia of Biblical Interpretation*. Edited by Steven McKenzie. 2 vols. New York: Oxford University Press, 2013.

———. "The Word Heard: How Hearing a Text Differs from Reading One." Pages 101–13 in *The Bible in Ancient and Modern Media: Story and Performance*. Edited by Holly E. Hearon and Philip Ruge-Jones. BPC 1. Eugene, OR: Cascade, 2009.

Schermutzky, Margret. "Learning Outcomes—Lernergebnisse; Begriffe, Zusammenhänge, Umsetzung und Erfolgsermittlung Lernergebnisse und Kompetenzvermittlung als elementare Orientierungen des Bologna-Prozesses." Griffmarke E 3.3 in *Neues Handbuch Hochschullehre*. Edited by Brigitte Berendt, Hans-Peter Voss, and Johannes Wildt. Berlin: Raabe, 2008.

Schmithals,Walter. *Einleitung in die drei ersten Evangelien*. Berlin: de Gruyter, 1985.

Schmitz, Thomas A., and Nicolas Wiater. "Introduction: Approaching Greek Identity." Pages 15–45 in *The Struggle for Identity: Greeks and Their Past in the First Century BCE*. Edited by Thomas A. Schmitz and Nicolas Wiater. Stuttgart: Steiner, 2011.

Schottroff, Luise. "Maria Magdalena und die Frauen am Grabe Jesu." *EvT* 42 (1982): 3–25.

Schulte, Dagmar. "Veranstaltungsplanung: Probleme und Methoden." Griffmarke B 1.2 in *Neues Handbuch Hochschullehre*. Edited by Brigitte Berendt, Hans-Peter Voss, and Johannes Wildt. Berlin: Raabe, 2002.

Schüssler Fiorenza, Elisabeth, and Kent Harold Richards, eds. *Transforming Graduate Biblical Education: Ethos and Discipline*. GPBS 10. Atlanta: Society of Biblical Literature, 2010.

Schutz, Roger, and Max Thurian. *Revelation, a Protestant View: The Dogmatic Constitution on Divine Revelation; A Commentary*. Westminster, MD: Newman, 1968.

Schweizer, Eduard. *The Good News according to Mark*. Translated by Donald H. Madvig. London: SPCK, 1971.

Scornaienchi, Lorenzo "Jesus als Polemiker oder: Wie polemisch darf Jesus sein? Historische und normative Aspekte." Pages 381–413 in *Polemik in der frühchristlichen Literatur: Texte und Kontexte*. Edited by Oda Wischmeyer and Lorenzo Scornaienchi. BZNW 170. Berlin: de Gruyter, 2011.

Scott, Bernard Brandon, and Margaret Ellen Lee. *Sound Mapping the New Testament*. Salem, OR: Polebridge, 2009.

Segovia, Fernando, and Mary Ann Tolbert, eds. *Teaching the Bible: The Discourses and Politics of Biblical Pedagogy*. Maryknoll, NY: Orbis, 1998.

Seland, Torrey. "Resource Pages for Biblical Studies." *Torreys.org*. http://torreys.org/bible/.

———. "Resource Pages for Biblical Studies Resurrected!" *Philonica et Neotestamentica* blog. 13 October 2012. http://biblicalresources.wordpress.com/2012/10/13/resource-pages-for-biblical-studies-resurrected/.

Shiner, Whitney T. *Proclaiming the Gospel: First-Century Performance of Mark*. Harrisburg, PA: Trinity Press International, 2003.

Skinner, Christopher. "Dramatized Irony, Markan Intercalations, and the Godfather." *Peje Iesous*, 6 February 2012. http://pejeiesous.com/2012/02/06/dramatized-irony-markan-intercalations-and-the-godfather/.

———. "The Gospel of Mark and Peter Falk: 'Columbo' as Pedagogical Tool." *Peje Iesous*. 4 September 2009. http://pejeiesous.com/2009/09/04/the-gospel-of-mark-and-peter-falk-columbo-as-pedagogical-tool/.

Slusser, Michael. "Reading Silently in Antiquity." *JBL* 111 (1992): 499.

Sohns, Ricarda. *Das Markusevangelium: Das biblische Buch als Ganzschrift*. Religion betrifft uns 2013.1. Aachen: Bergmoser & Höller, 2013.

Stendahl, Krister. *Paul among Jews and Gentiles and Other Essays*. Philadelphia: Fortress, 1976.

Stewart, Eric C. *Gathered around Jesus: An Alternative Spatial Practice in the Gospel of Mark*. Cambridge: James Clarke, 2009.

Stoakes, Geoff, and Pauline Couper. "Visualizing the Research-Teaching Nexus." Pages 11–16 in *What Is Research-Led Teaching? Multi-disciplinary Perspectives*. Edited by Alisa Miller, John Sharp, and Jeremy Strong. London: Crest, 2012. http://www.crest.ac.uk.

Straub, Jürgen. "Geschichten erzählen, Geschichte bilden: Grundzüge einer narrativen Psychologie historischer Sinnbildung." Pages 81–169 in *Erzählung, Identität, und historisches Bewusstsein: Die psychologische Konstruktion von Zeit und Geschichte*. Edited by Jürgen Straub. Erinnerung, Geschichte, Identität 1. Frankfurt: Suhrkamp, 1998.

———. "Psychology, Narrative, and Cultural Memory: Past and Present." Pages 215–28 in *Cultural Memory Studies: An International and Interdisciplinary Handbook*. Edited by Astrid Erll and Ansgar Nünning. Berlin: de Gruyter, 2008.

Swanson, Richard W. *Provoking the Gospel: Methods to Embody Biblical Storytelling through Drama*. Cleveland: Pilgrim, 2004.

———. *Provoking the Gospel of John: A Storyteller's Commentary, Years A, B, and C*. Cleveland: Pilgrim, 2010.

———. *Provoking the Gospel of Luke: A Storyteller's Commentary, Year C*. Cleveland: Pilgrim, 2006.

———. *Provoking the Gospel of Mark: A Storyteller's Commentary, Year B*. Cleveland: Pilgrim, 2005.

———. *Provoking the Gospel of Matthew: A Storyteller's Commentary, Year A*. Cleveland: Pilgrim, 2007.

———. *The Provoking the Gospel Project*. http://www.provokingthegospel.com.

———. "Taking Place/Taking up Space." Pages 129–41 in *The Bible in Ancient and Modern Media: Story and Performance*. Edited by Holly E. Hearon and Philip Ruge-Jones. BPC 1. Eugene, OR: Cascade, 2009.

Szczyrba, Birgit, and Matthias Wiemer. "Lehrinnovation durch doppelten Perspektivenwechsel. Fachkulturell tradierte Lehrpraktiken und Hochschuldidaktik im Kontakt." Pages 101–10 in *Fachbezogene und fächerübergreifende Hochschuldidaktik*. Edited by Isa Jahnke and Johannes Wildt. Bielefeld: Bertelsmann, 2011.

Tannehill, Robert C. "The Disciples in Mark: The Function of a Narrative Role." *JR* 57 (1977): 386–405.

"The Theologians." *Bibledex: A Video about Every book in the Bible*. University of Nottingham. http://www.bibledex.com/team/theologians.html.

Taylor, Vincent. *The Gospel according to St. Mark*. 2nd ed. London: Macmillan, 1966.

Tolbert, Mary Ann. *Sowing the Gospel: Mark's World in Literary-Historical Perspective*. Philadelphia: Fortress, 1989.

Tyson, Joseph B. "The Blindness of the Disciples in Mark." *JBL* 80 (1961): 261–68.

Van Oyen, Geert, and Patty Van Cappellen. "Mark 15,34 and the *Sitz im Leben* of the Real Reader." *ETL* 91 (2015): 269–99.

Ward, Richard F. "The End Is Performance: Performance Criticism and the Gospel of Mark." Pages 88–101 in *Preaching Mark's Unsettling Messiah*. Edited by David Fleer and Dave Bland. St. Louis: Chalice, 2006.

Watts, Joel. *Mimetic Criticism and the Gospel of Mark: An Introduction and Commentary*. Eugene, OR: Wipf & Stock, 2013.

———. *Unsettled Christianity*. blog. http://unsettledchristianity.com.

Wehrlin, Eric. "Markusevangelium Theaterabend Eric Wehrlin Soloprogram." *YouTube.com*. 11 October 2014. https://www.youtube.com/watch?t=3662&v=SIdBDJA0jrU.

Weiss, Johannes. *Die drei älteren Evangelien*. 3rd ed. SNT 1. Göttingen: Vandenhoeck & Ruprecht, 1917.

———. "Literaturgeschichte des NT." *RGG* 3:2175–2215.

Wellhausen, Julius. *Einleitung in die drei ersten Evangelien*. Berlin: Reimer, 1905. 2nd ed. 1911.

Welzer, Harald. "Das gemeinsame Verfertigen von Vergangenheit im Gespräch." Pages 160–78 in *Das soziale Gedächtnis: Geschichte, Erinnerung, Tradierung*. Edited by Harald Welzer. Hamburg: Hamburger Edition, 2001.

———. *Grandpa Wasn't a Nazi: National Socialism and the Holocaust in German Memory Culture*. New York: American Jewish Committee, 2005.

———. *Das kommunikative Gedächtnis: Eine Theorie der Erinnerung*. Munich: Beck, 2002.

Wendland, Paul. *Die urchristlichen Literaturformen*. Pages 257–405 in HNT 1.3. 2nd and 3rd eds. Tübingen: Mohr Siebeck, 1912.

West, Jim. "Blogging the Bible: A Short History." *BSR* 39 (2010): 3–13.

Wild, Elke, and Klaus-Peter Wild. "Jeder lernt auf seine Weise…. Individuelle Lernstrategien und Hochschullehre." Griffmarke A 2.1 in *Neues Handbuch Hochschullehre*. Edited by Brigitte Berendt, Hans-Peter Voss, and Johannes Wildt. Berlin: Raabe, 2001.

Wildt, Johannes. "Vom Lehren zum Lernen." Griffmarke A 3.1 in *Neues Handbuch Hochschullehre*. Edited by Brigitte Berendt, Hans-Peter Voss, and Johannes Wildt. Berlin: Raabe, 2006.

Wildt, Johannes, and Beatrix Wildt. "Lernprozessorientiertes Prüfen im 'Constructive Alignment.'" Griffmarke H 6.1 in *Neues Handbuch Hochschullehre*. Edited by Brigitte Berendt, Hans-Peter Voss, and Johannes Wildt. Berlin: Raabe, 2011.

Wilson, Paul Scott. "Preaching, Performance, and the Life and Death of 'Now.'" Pages 37–52 in *Performance in Preaching: Bringing the Sermon*

to Life. Edited by Jana Childers and Clayton J. Schmit. Grand Rapids: Baker Academic, 2008.
Wimbush, Vincent L. "Signifying the Fetish II: Outlines for a New Critical Orientation." *TLZ* 138 (2013): 909–22.
Winko, Simone. "Kanon/Kanonizität VII: Literaturwissenschaftlich." Pages 316–17 in *Lexikon der Bibelhermeneutik: Begriffe—Methoden—Theorien—Konzepte.* Edited by Oda Wischmeyer. Berlin: de Gruyter, 2013.
Wire, Antoinette C. *The Case for Mark Composed in Performance.* BPC 3. Eugene, OR: Cascade, 2011.
Wischmeyer, Oda, David C. Sim, and Ian J. Elmer, eds. *Mark and Paul: Comparative* Essays. Vol. 1: *Two Authors at the Beginnings of Christianity.* BZNW 198. Berlin: de Gruyter, 2014.
World Council of Churches Commission on Faith and Order. *Faith and Order Findings: The Final Report of the Theological Commissions to the Fourth World Conference on Faith and Order.* London: SCM, 1963.
Yarbro Collins, Adele. *Mark: A Commentary.* Hermeneia. Minneapolis: Fortress, 2007.
Zamorski, Barbara. "Research-Led Teaching and Learning in Higher Education: A Case." *Teaching in Higher Education* 7 (2002): 411–27.

CONTRIBUTORS

Eve-Marie Becker is Professor of New Testament Exegesis at Aarhus University, Denmark. Her research interests include Pauline exegesis, Markan studies, early Christian literary history, and New Testament hermeneutics. Recent publications include *Der Begriff der Demut bei Paulus* (2015); *Trauma and Traumatization in Individual and Collective Dimensions: Insights from Biblical Studies and Beyond* (2014); and *Mark and Paul: Comparative Essays*. Vol. 2: *For and Against Pauline Influence on Mark* (2014).

Thomas E. Boomershine served as the G. Ernest Thomas Distinguished Professor of Christianity and Communication at United Theological Seminary in Dayton, Ohio from 2004–2006 where he also served as Professor of New Testament from 1979–2000. He now writes and produces multimedia resources for the interpretation of the Bible in digital culture. Boomershine founded the Network of Biblical Storytellers in 1977 and has lectured and led biblical storytelling workshops around the world. A leader in the rediscovery of the Gospel as story, his dissertation at Union Theological Seminary, *Mark the Storyteller*, was the first systematic study of the Gospel narratives as story. A recent book is *The Messiah of Peace: A Performance Criticism Commentary on Mark's Passion and Resurrection Narrative* (2015).

Mark Goodacre is Professor of New Testament and Christian Origins at Duke University in Durham, North Carolina. His research interests include the Synoptic Gospels, the Historical Jesus, and the Gospel of Thomas. Goodacre is the author of four books including *The Case Against Q: Studies in Markan Priority and the Synoptic Problem* (2002) and *Thomas and the Gospels: The Case for Thomas's Familiarity with the Synoptics* (2012). He is well known for The New Testament Gateway, the web directory of academic New Testament resources, and has his own regular podcast on the New Testament, the NT Pod.

Sandra Huebenthal is Professor for Exegesis and Biblical Theology at the Universität Passau, Germany. Her research interests include the Gospel of Mark, Social Memory Theory, Biblical Traditions and Economic Thought, and University Didactics. Her most recent publications are *Das Markusevangelium als kollektives Gedächtnis* (2014) and "Reading Mark as Collective Memory," in *Social Memory and Social Identity in the Study of Early Judaism and Early Christianity* (forthcoming in 2015).

Alberto de Mingo Kaminouchi is Associate Professor at the Alphonsian Academy, Rome, and Professor at Saint Louis University, Madrid. His main research interest is New Testament Ethics, while other academic interests include Theological Interpretation of the Bible and Oral Tradition behind the Synoptic Gospels. His most recent books are *Introducción a la Ética Cristiana en el Horizonte del Nuevo Testamento* (2015); *Símbolos de Salvación. Redención, victoria, sacrificio* (2007); and *But It Is Not So among You: Echoes of Power in Mark 10.32–45* (2003).

Elizabeth Struthers Malbon is a Professor in the Department of Religion and Culture at Virginia Tech (Virginia Polytechnic Institute and State University). Her research is focused on narrative criticism of the Gospel of Mark, especially narrative space and characterization. She also has an interest in the Bible and art, especially early Christian art, and has served the Society of Biblical Literature in both areas. Her most recent books are *Mark's Jesus: Characterization as Narrative Christology* (2009) and, as editor, *Between Author and Audience in Mark: Narration, Characterization, Interpretation* (2009).

Francis J. Moloney, SDB, is a Senior Professorial Fellow at Australian Catholic University, Melbourne, and the Director of the Centre for Biblical and Early Christian Literature in the Institute for Religion and Critical Inquiry. He has had a lifelong interest in the Gospels and more recently in narrative theory. His most recent publications are *Love in the Gospel of John. An Exegetical, Theological, and Literary Study* (2013); *The Resurrection of the Messiah: A Narrative Commentary on the Resurrection Accounts in the Four Gospels* (2013); and *A Body Broken for a Broken People: Divorce, Remarriage, and the Eucharist* (2015).

Elizabeth E. Shively is Lecturer of New Testament Studies at the University of St Andrews, Scotland. Her current research interests are the Gospel of Mark, Jewish apocalyptic thought, narrative criticism, and the intersection of narratology and the cognitive sciences. Her publications include *Apocalyptic Imagination in the Gospel of Mark: The Literary and Theological Role of Mark 3:22–30* (2012), "Characterizing the Non-human: Satan in the Gospel of Mark," in *Character Studies and the Gospel of Mark* (2014), and "The Story Matters: Solving the Problem of the Parables in Mark 3:22–30," in *Between Author and Audience in Mark: Narration, Characterization, Interpretation* (2009).

Richard W. Swanson is Professor of Religion/Philosophy/Classics at Augustana College in Sioux Falls, South Dakota and is the Director of the *Provoking the Gospel Storytelling Project*, a group of actors and interpreters who create performances of biblical narratives. He has collaborated to create performances with composer Christopher Stanichar and poet Patrick Hicks on the *St. Mark Passion* and with composer John Pennington on *The Book of Job: A Man, A Simple Man*. He has written a commentary series on the four canonical Gospels using the performance-critical approach he developed with the *Provoking the Gospel Storytelling Project*.

Geert Van Oyen is professor New Testament at the Université catholique de Leuven, Belgium. Since his doctoral thesis on the narrative doublet of the multiplication of the loaves in Mark, this Gospel carries his interest. He also does research on the question of the Historical Jesus and the Book of Revelation. He is the president of the RRENAB (the French speaking network on Narratology and Bible). He is the coeditor of *Resurrection of the Dead* (2012) and *Le lecteur* (2015) and author of *Reading Mark as a Novel* (2013).

Index of Ancient Sources

Old Testament

Judges
- 9:45 — 138

1 Kings
- 23:10 — 137

2 Kings
- 2:19–22 — 138

Psalms
- 22 — 124
- 121 — 162

Isaiah
- 40:3 — 24
- 66:24 — 137

Ezekiel
- 16:4 — 138
- 43:24 — 138

Zephaniah
- 2:9 — 138

Josephus, *Antiquitates Judaicae*
- 18.116–119 — 59

New Testament

Matthew
- 5:13 — 131, 149
- 18:6–9 — 130–31, 149

Mark
- 1:1 — 24, 92, 101
- 1:1–13 — 133
- 1:1–15 — 62
- 1:1–16:8 — 34
- 1:2–3 — 24
- 1:4 — 123
- 1:5 — 62
- 1:8 — 62
- 1:9 — 62
- 1:14–15 — 24
- 1:14–8:30 — 133
- 1:14–15:42 — 133
- 1:15 — 61, 123
- 1:16–18 — 62
- 1:16–8:26 — 61
- 1:19–20 — 62
- 2:1 — 145
- 2:1–3:6 — 37
- 2:11 — 145
- 2:14 — 62
- 2:18 — 15
- 2:24 — 15
- 3:4 — 15
- 3:13–14 — 145
- 3:13–19 — 62, 145
- 3:14 — 145
- 3:14–19 — 145
- 3:20 — 145
- 3:20–21 — 145
- 3:21 — 145
- 3:21–35 — 145
- 3:23–29 — 92
- 3:31–35 — 145
- 3:35 — 63

INDEX OF ANCIENT SOURCES

Mark (continued)
3:35–37   145
4–8   37
4:3–9   92
4:11–32   92
5:19   145
5:38   145
6:17–29   59
6:52   92
7:3–4   92
7:17   145
7:30   145
8:3   145
8:17   118
8:22–26   133, 142
8:22–30   133
8:22–9:30   142
8:22–10:42   142
8:22–10:52   104, 142
8:26–11:10   61
8:26   145
8:27   15
8:27–10:45   106
8:29   125
8:31   130, 133
8:31–9:29   133
8:31–10:44   134
8:31–10:52   133
8:31–15:47   133
8:32   104
8:32–33   133
8:34–38   104
8:34–9:1   92, 137
8:34–9:29   133
9:28   145
9:30–31   133
9:30–10:31   133
9:31   130–31, 133–34, 142, 147
9:31–41   143
9:31–10:30   135
9:31–10:31   142–43, 145
9:32   134
9:32–34   133, 139
9:32–50   143
9:33   145
9:33–34   104, 131–32, 134, 137, 144, 147
9:33–35   131
9:33–50   129, 135–36, 138, 145
9:34   134–35, 137
9:34–35   148
9:35   134, 144
9:35–36   143
9:35–37   139, 143
9:35–10:31   133
9:36   144
9:36–37   134–35, 143–44, 148
9:37   131, 135, 144, 146
9:38   134–35, 139
9:38–41   135–36, 139, 144–45, 148
9:39   135
9:41   131, 135
9:42   129, 131, 135–37, 139, 143–44, 146–47
9:42–47   144, 148
9:42–50   8, 129–36, 138–39, 141–143, 148–50
9:43   130–31, 136–38, 146
9:43–47   129, 137, 144, 146–47
9:43–50   148
9:44   130
9:45   131, 136, 138, 146
9:46   130
9:47   131, 136, 138, 146
9:48   130, 137
9:48–49   147
9:48–50   129
9:49   130, 137–38, 148
9:49–50   131–32, 137, 147
9:50   129, 136–139, 144, 147, 148
10:1   129
10:1–9   144
10:1–12   143
10:1–31   143
10:10–12   144
10:13–16   143
10:13–31   143
10:14   144
10:14–15   144
10:14–16   144

10:16	144	15:40	168
10:17–22	144	15:40–42	9
10:23–31	144	16:1–8	133
10:29–31	145	16:8	125–26, 133, 184
10:30	63	16:9–20	34
10:32–34	130, 133, 142		
10:32–45	133	Luke	
10:32–52	142	14:34–35	131, 149
10:35–37	133	17:1–2	131, 149
10:37	104		
10:38–40	133	Romans	
10:41	133	9–11	43
10:42–44	133	12–16	43
10:42–45	7, 92, 95, 102, 105–6		
10:45	134	1 Corinthians	
10:46–52	79–81, 85–86, 133, 142	12	42
11:1	142	13	42
11:11–15:37	61	14	42
11:28	15	15:1–5	24
13:4	15		
13:4–36	92	2 Corinthians	
15	164, 166–71	4:7	41
15:22–41	164		
15:34	124	Philippians	
15:39	125	2:5	97

Index of Modern Authors

Achtemeier, Paul	75	Conzelmann, Hans	132
Admiral, Eva-Maria	184	Couper, Pauline	3–4
Allison, Dale C., Jr.	131, 136–37	Cranfield, Charles E. B.	137
Andersen, Jacob	53	Crook, Zeba A.	34–35
Anderson, Janice C.	46	Culler, Jonathan	134
Artaud, Antonin	156, 170	Culley, Robert C.	111
Assmann, Aleida	48–49	Davies, W. D.	131
Assmann, Jan	49	Davila, James R.	186
Aune, David E.	13	Dewey, Joanna	36, 96, 159, 165
Barth, Karl	162	Dibelius, Martin	109
Bauckham, Richard	97, 182	Donahue, John R.	35
Becker, Eve-Marie	14–16, 18, 20–24, 26	Doole, J. Andrew	24
Beale, Greg	4	Dormeyer, Detlev	13
Bernstein, Richard	158	Dowd, Sharyn	35
Biggs, John	53	Draper, Jonathan A.	22
Bloom, Benjamin S.	53, 65	Drummond, Di	4
Bockmuehl, Marcus	46	Dubs, Rolf	54
Boomershine, Amelia Cooper	81	Dulles, Avery	100
Boomershine, Thomas E.	36, 76, 79, 82, 89–92, 183–84	Dunn, James D. G.	97, 182, 190
		Ehrman, Bart	182, 186
Boring, M. Eugene	35	Elmer, Ian J.	23
Botha, Pieter J. J.	75	Engberg-Pedersen, Troels	23
Brabrand, Claus	53	Entwistle, Noel J.	53
Brook, Peter	155	Eve, Eric	111
Brown, Peter C.	82	Evens, Craig A.	130, 135
Brown, Raymond	165	Fackenheim, Emil L.	162
Bryan, Christopher	96	Fascher, Erich	109
Bulkeley, Tim	189	Finnegan, Ruth	110
Bultmann, Rudolf	96–97, 109, 131, 143, 145, 165	Fish, Stanley	160
		Foley, John Miles	22, 159–60
Byrskog, Samuel	97, 110	Fowler, Robert M.	160, 176, 183
Cantor, Arthur	183	Frei, Hans	74–75
Cargill, Robert	186	Frey, Jörg	13
Carr, David M.	75	Frost, Robert	157, 162
Congar, Yves M.	101	Galbraith, Deane	186

-222-

INDEX OF MODERN AUTHORS

Gerhardsson, Birger	97, 110	Lane, William L.	130
Gergen, Kenneth	50	LeCoq, Jacques	154, 159
Giesen, Bernhard	49	LeDonne, Anthony	187
Gieseler, Johann Karl Ludwig	108	Lee, Margaret Ellen	76, 79
Gnilka, Joachim	131, 139	Levinas, Emmanuel	157–58
Goodacre, Mark	176–77, 179–81, 183, 186–90	Lewis, C.S.	152
		Lipman, Doug	93
Gooder, Paula	182	Lohmeyer, Ernst	138
Goody, Jack	110	Lord, Albert B.	103, 110
Goguel, Maurice	109	Ludlow, Morwenna	149
Guttenberger, Gudrun	46	Malbon, Elizabeth Struthers	29–32, 51, 96, 101, 104, 178
Hadas, Moses	75, 84		
Halbwachs, Maurice	49–50	Marcus, Joel	101, 129–30, 135–36, 138
Haley, Cortney	183	Martin, Dale	182
Haran, Brady	181	Masia, Bertram B.	53, 65
Harland, Phil	188	McCowen, Alec	183–84
Harrington, Daniel J.	35	McDaniel, Mark A.	82
Harris, William	75	McGrath, Alister E.	100
Havelock, Eric A.	103, 110	McGrath, James Frankline	186
Hays, Richard	46	McKenzie, Stephen L.	31
Healey, Mick	3–4	McLean, Max	104, 183–84
Hearon, Holly E.	36–37, 159	Metzger, Bruce	101
Herder, Johann Gottfried	108	Millard, Alan	140
Hezser, Catherine	140	Miller, Alisa	3
Holladay, Carl R.	21	Moberly, Walter	46
Hooker, Morna D.	35, 136, 138	Moloney, Francis J.	35, 132–35, 145
Horsley, Richard A.	22	Moltmann-Wendel, Elisabeth	167
Hübenthal, Sandra	47, 49–50, 61, 66–67	Moore, Stephen D.	46, 160–61
Hurtado, Larry W.	95–96, 112–13, 114, 140, 149, 186	Mueller, Mogens	23
		Müller, Peter	46
Hyland, Áine	52	Myers, Ched	35
Iverson, Kelly R.	90, 139, 141–42, 144, 183	Neirynck, Frans	113
		Niles, John D.	162
Juel, Donald	169	Nineham, Dennis E.	129
Johnson, Todd E.	162	Nipperdey, Thomas	25
Kaminouchi, Alberto de Mingo	96, 103, 146	Nowak, Paul	81
		O'Malley, John W.	100
Kee, Howard C.	103	Ong, Walter	73, 75, 98, 103, 110, 190
Kelber, Werner H.	22, 73, 110–12, 177	Parry, Milman	103, 110
Kennedy, Declan	52	Peabody, Berkley	110
Kirk, Alan	22	Pelias, Ronald	120
Klatzky, Roberta	82	Polkinghorne, Donald E.	50
Kok, Mike	187	Pontifical Biblical Commission	46
Krathwohl, David R.	53, 65	Postman, Neil	152
Lagrange, Marie-Joseph	135	Prensky, Marc	175

Rad, Gerhard von	162	Strong, Jeremy	3
Ramsden, Paul	53	Swanson, Richard W.	37, 88, 143, 151–52, 161
Ratzinger, Joseph	100		
Reis, Oliver	54	Szczyrba, Birgit	65
Repschinski, Boris	15	Tannehill, Robert	177–78
Reymond, Bernard	154–56	Taylor, Vincent	134, 138, 165
Rhoads, David	34, 36, 84, 90, 95, 108, 112, 115–20, 139–40, 156	Thatcher, Tom	22
		Thurian, Max	99
Richards, Kent Harold	2, 18	Tolbert, Mary Ann	1–2, 91
Riesenfeld, Harald	110	Tyson, Joseph	177–78
Robbins, Vernon K.	190	Van Cappellen, Patty	124
Rodi, Frithjof	14	Van Oyen, Geert	124
Roediger, Henry L., III	82	Ward, Richard F.	115, 117
Rothschild, Clare	13	Watts, Joel	186–87
Ruge-Jones, Philip	34, 36–37, 77–78, 140, 159	Wehrlin, Eric	183–84
		Weingartner, Charles	152
Runesson, Anders	23	Weiss, Johannes	109
Ruschin, Sylvia	54	Wellhausen, Julius	109
Ryan, Norma	52	Welzer, Harald	49
Savidge, Dale	162	Wendland, Paul	109
Schermutzky, Margret	52	West, Jim	186
Schmithals, Walter	109	Wiater, Nicolas	22
Schmitz, Thomas A.	22	Wiemer, Matthias	65
Schottroff, Luise	165	Wild, Elke	65
Schröter, Jens	13	Wild, Klaus-Peter	65
Schulte, Dagmar	53, 65	Wildt, Beatrix	53
Schüssler Fiorenza, Elisabeth	2, 18	Wildt, Johannes	53–54, 65
Schutz, Roger	99	Wilson, Paul Scott	153
Schweizer, Eduard	136	Wimbush, Vincent L.	20
Scornaienchi, Lorenzo	15	Winko, Simone	22
Scott, Bernard Brandon	76, 79	Wire, Antoinette C.	112, 139, 144, 149, 160, 165, 167
Segovia, Fernando	1–2		
Seland, Torrey	179–80	Wischmeyer, Oda	23
Sharp, John	3	Wright, N.T.	182
Shiner, Whitney	37, 75, 84, 139, 154, 159	Yarbro Collins, Adela	35, 130
		Zamorski, Barbara	4
Sim, David C.	23		
Skinner, Christopher W.	183, 187		
Slusser, Michael	76		
Sohns, Ricarda	46		
Stanton, Graham	182		
Stendahl, Krister	43		
Stewart, Eric C.	38		
Stoakes, Geoff	3–4		
Straub, Jürgen	49–50		

Subject Index

assessment in teaching, 53–55, 68
audience involvement, 31, 39, 43, 107, 127–28, 143, 146, 154–55, 158–60, 162–64
autobiography, 20, 32–33. *See also* autobiographical reflection
autobiographical reflection, 6, 19–21, 25–26
Bibledex, 181–82
biblical theology, 46
blog, 8, 176, 180, 185–89, 191
canonical approach, 46
canonization, 22
chiasm, 30, 37
choral reading in teaching, 42
chunking, 82
collective memory. *See* memory, collective
Colossians, 67
commentaries, 74, 130, 151
   use in teaching, 35–39, 122–23
comparative exegesis, 19, 23, 25. *See also* contextualization: literary-historical
composition criticism, 31
composition history of Mark, 24, 27
constructive alignment, 53–54, 65
contextualization
   literary-historical, 13–14, 19–20, 23–26, 41
   pedagogic, 13
Council of Trent, 100
cultural criticism, 2
cultural studies, 14, 36, 60
deconstruction, 31, 36
diachronic analysis, 25, 67

diachronic programmatic analysis, 14
diakonia, 167–68
digital learning environment, 121
disciple(s), 15, 62–63, 80, 105, 110, 118, 120, 122, 127, 129, 131, 133, 135, 137, 139–40, 142–45, 147–48, 165–67, 170, 177
   asking questions, 15
   failure of in Mark, 104–5, 133–34, 139
   lack of comprehension in Mark, 51, 63, 66, 134, 170
document culture, 74
echo, 95, 102–6
Enlightenment, 74–75, 140
ensemble performance, 8
epistles
   Catholic, 66
   Pauline, 40, 43, 66, 94, 119
epistolography, Pauline, 23
Eucharist, 106
Eusebius, 25
exam, 42, 52–55, 74
Facebook, 187–88
Farrer hypothesis, 40
feminist criticism, 31, 36
form criticism, 23, 75, 102, 109–10, 113, 131, 140
Formgeschichte. *See* form criticism
four levels of meaning, 74
Fourth World Conference on Faith and Order, 99
framing, as rhetorical device, 31
Ganzschriftlektüre, 45–46
Gattung. *See* genre
gender mainstreaming, 18

genre, 67
  in literary study of the Bible, 41
  of narrative texts, 58
genre criticism, 23
globalization, 18–20
Gospel of Thomas, 42
Gospels, 31, 33–34, 39–42, 48, 90, 94, 98, 102, 106–8, 112–14, 116, 119, 151, 168, 185. *See also* Synoptic Gospels
Gutenberg, Johannes, 150
hermeneutics, 3, 5–6, 18–19, 25, 46–47, 50, 52, 54–56, 58–59, 66, 68, 74, 86, 92–93, 110, 112, 130, 156–57, 160–61, 163–64, 166, 168–69
  of digital culture, 77
Herodotus, 84
heuristics, 5–6, 13–20, 26–27
historical criticism, 1, 20, 30, 32, 45–46, 48, 56, 67, 74, 76, 84, 131, 145, 147, 149–50
historical Jesus research, 48
historical psychology, 49
historiography, 13, 19, 23–26, 48
historiographical literature. *See* historiography
identity construction, 49–50, 66
ideological studies, 31
implied audience, 30, 37, 112
implied author, 30, 37, 115
implied reader. *See* implied audience
intended learning outcome. *See* learning outcome
intercalation, 30
intergenerational recollection, 49. *See also* memory: collective; social memory theory
Internet, 5, 8, 175–82, 185, 187, 190–91
interreligious communication, 18
irony, 31, 120, 125
iTunes U, 182
James,
  character in Mark, 62
  Epistle of, 66
Jeremiah, book of, 94
Jesus, 21, 25, 33–34, 48, 50, 63–64, 66, 73, 86–87, 90, 96–98, 100–102, 105–6, 109–12, 114–15, 134–35, 140–41, 144, 149, 161
  in Mark, 6, 15, 25, 37–39, 50–51, 59–64, 66, 69, 80–81, 85–87, 92, 96, 101–2, 104–6, 110, 115, 118, 121–27, 129–31, 133–39, 141–49, 158, 164–67, 169–71
Jewish-Roman War, 21, 42
Job, book of, 151, 172
John, Gospel of, 34, 79, 132
John the Apostle, 62, 135, 139, 145
John the Baptist, 59, 115
Josephus, 23, 26, 59
Jude, Epistle of, 66
juxtaposition, rhetorical/literary device, 30–31, 37, 39, 41, 43
kerygma, 24, 99. *See also* oral tradition, of gospel proclamation
learning outcome, 52–55, 65, 68, 121
  affective, 65
Levi, 62
linguistic disorientation, 111
literacy, 22, 75–76, 113, 140, 177, 190
literary criticism, 2, 7, 31–32, 41, 46, 117, 131, 143, 161
literarization, 21–22
Latin Vulgate. *See* Vulgate
Lucian, 84
Luke, 13, 21, 23, 34, 39–40, 79, 105, 131–32, 149, 161
Luke-Acts, 13, 23–26
LXX. *See* Septuagint
maieutics. *See* Socratic method
manuscript culture, 73–74, 98
map, use in teaching, 37
Mary, 63
Matthew, 21, 23, 34, 39–40, 79, 105, 130, 132
meaning as reference, 74
memory, 22, 25, 48–50, 60–61, 64, 76, 81–83, 85, 90, 97, 101, 103, 106
  collective, 6, 47–52, 54–56, 60, 64, 66–69
  cultural, 50

long-term, 82–83
short-term, 82–83
social, 49–50. *See also* social memory theory
memorization, 25, 73–74, 76, 81–82, 98–99, 101, 103, 106, 110, 112, 182
messianic secret, 51, 66, 181
metaphor
  in literary study of the Bible, 41–42
  in Mark, 120, 138, 147
  in teaching Pauline Epistles, 43
MOOC (Massive Open Online Course), 185
music video, 92
narrative criticism, 6–7, 20, 30–32, 36, 38, 46, 56–57, 67, 91, 107–8, 112, 117–24, 126–28, 132, 140, 143, 145, 149–50
narrative theology, 45
opponent, of Jesus asking questions, 15
oral culture, 73–74, 98, 103, 114
oral literature, 7, 96, 103
orality, 6–7, 21, 31, 34, 49, 107–12, 141, 177, 190
  second, 97–98, 176, 190
oral performance. *See* performance
oral tradition, 5, 24, 46, 73, 96–98, 101–2, 106, 108–9, 111, 113, 140, 149
oratorio, 88
pantomime
  in teaching, 42
parallelism, 79–80
  as rhetorical device, 31
pedagogics. *See* pedagogy
pedagogy, 1–3, 5–7, 14–15, 18–19, 29, 31–32, 37–39, 43, 73–77, 89–90, 121, 151–53, 163–64, 171
performance, 7, 8, 76–81, 83–85, 88–89, 93–96, 107–8, 110, 112–21, 123–28, 134, 139–43, 164, 166–72, 182–184
  difference between ancient and modern, 84, 116, 154
performance criticism, 5–8, 31, 34, 79, 84–85, 88–92, 95–97, 107–10, 112–18, 127–28, 131, 139–40, 143, 153, 156, 163, 169, 172

performance literature, 77, 94, 159
  Mark as, 6–7, 77, 89, 92–94
performance text. *See* performance literature
Pentateuch, 94
Peter, 62, 104, 108, 122, 125, 165, 167, 184
Philemon, Epistle to, 66
plot, 30–31, 41, 58, 91, 103, 111, 118–19
  in Mark, 34, 37, 43, 127, 133
podcast, 187–89, 191
point of view, 91, 122
  in literary study of the Bible, 41
postcolonial criticism, 18, 36
poststructuralism, 157
print culture, 74, 98
Psalms, 94
Q, 21, 40
Quellenkritik. *See* source criticism
questions, 7–8, 13, 20, 22, 24, 46–47, 56, 66, 114, 125, 129, 131–32, 140, 150, 188
  for an eclectic approach to a biblical text, 148–49
  for curriculum design, 54–55
  for studying New Testament books, 66
  for studying narrative texts, 57–59, 66, 69
  for studying Mark, 56–57, 59–60, 69
  from students, 38, 60, 121–23, 127
  in Mark, 15, 38, 133
  in teaching, 7, 13–15, 40–42, 56–57, 79, 86, 106, 121–23, 128, 148–49
  on exam, 53
  programmatically answered in Mark, 61
  rhetorical, 15, 38
questioning, 14–15, 26
reader response, 31, 36, 128
real addressee. *See* real audience
real audience, 30, 112
real author, 30
reception history, 8, 24, 38
redaction criticism, 23, 31, 41, 45, 75, 113, 131–32, 143, 145, 150
Redaktionskritik. *See* redaction criticism

Reformation, 150
reorientation, in the process of textualization, 111
repetition, 113, 143
  in oral literature, 7, 95–96, 103
  in Mark, 7, 30, 85, 95–96, 104–5, 113, 121, 127, 146–47
  in memorization, 83, 103
research-led teaching, 3–6, 17, 52
Revelation of John, 94
rhetoric, 79, 117, 119, 154
  in narrative, 30–31, 41
  Markan, 37–39, 43, 95, 120
rhetorical criticism, 2
rhetorical culture, 190
rhetorical questions. *See* questions: rhetorical
role-play, 41–42
Romans, Epistle to the, 66
RSS feed, 188
Second Vatican Council, 99, 100
Septuagint, 23
sensory registers, 82
setting
  canonical setting of Mark, 27
  contemporary setting of Mark, 27. *See also*, contextualization: literary-historical
  in narrative, 29–31, 41, 43
  literary setting of Mark, 24. *See also*, contextualization: literary-historical
Shakespeare, 155
silent reading, 6, 8, 34, 74–77, 79, 113, 118, 153, 166
Sitz im Leben, 96, 109, 116
  of academic questioning, 15
skit, 42
social criticism, 36
social memory theory, 6, 47–50, 56, 60–61, 64, 67–68
sociology, 49
Socratic method, 15
sola scriptura, 99
sound map, 79–81, 90–91
source criticism, 23–24, 75, 131
storytelling workshop, 79–88
structuralism, 31
subtext, 7, 107, 118–26, 128
Suetonius, 23
Synoptic Gospels, 13–14, 31, 39–40, 42
Synoptic problem, 108, 130
Synoptic studies, 13–14
Tacitus, 23, 26
textual criticism, 130
textualization, 111
theological interpretation, 46
Titus, 66
tradition criticism, 162
tradition history, 84
transmutation, 111
Twelve, 62, 104, 135, 139
Twitter, 187–188
two-source theory, 21
Vulgate, 150
YouTube, 181–184

www.ingramcontent.com/pod-product-compliance
Lightning Source LLC
Chambersburg PA
CBHW021808220426
43662CB00006B/224